FASHIONBOX

FASHIONBOX

With text by Antonio Mancinelli

Abrams, New York

On the front cover: Audrey Hepburn, 1954 (Everett Collection); Sarah Jessica Parker, 2008 (New Line Cinema/Everett Collection)

Top flap: Ursula Andress, 1962 (Everett Collection); Marilyn Monroe, 1961 (Eve Arnold/Magnum Photos); Jackie Onassis, 1975 (Philippe Achache/Gamma/Eyedea); Madonna, 1990 (Eligio Paoni/Contrasto); Grace Kelly, 1960s (Swann/Gamma/Eyedea)

Bottom flap: Gwen Stefani, 2007 (Carlos Duran/Reuters); Marlene Dietrich, 1930 (Everett Collection); Ursula Andress, 1962 (Everett Collection); Brigitte Bardot, 1960s (Album); Beyonce Knowles, 2007 (Kristin Callahan/Everett Collection)

On the back cover: Jacqueline Kennedy, 1960 (Eve Arnold/Magnum Photos); Coco Chanel, 1960s (Kammerman/Rapho/Eyedea); Patti Smith, 1980s (Everett Collection); Natalie Wood, 1950s (Everett Collection); Joan Crawford, 1934 (Everett Collection); Angelina Jolie, 2005 (20th Century Fox/Everett Collection); Brigitte Bardot, 1960 (Nicolas Tikhomiroff/Magnum Photos); Grace Kelly, 1954 (Everett Collection); Jane Fonda, 1967 (Keystone/Eyedea Presse); Scarlett Johansson, 2006 (Fotoblitz/Gamma/Eyedea); Sofia Loren, 1958 (Everett Collection); Twiggy, 1967 (Keystone-France/Keystone); Charlize Theron, 2006 (Europapress/Gamma/Eyedea); Audrey Hepburn, 1967 (20th Century Fox/Album); Catherine Bach, 1980s (Warner Bros./Everett Collection); Jane Birkin, 1970 (Botti/Gamma/Eyedea); Jennifer Beals, 1983 (Paramount Pictures/Album); Marilyn Monroe, 1953 (20th Century Fox/Everett Collection); Meryl Streep, 2006 (20th Century Fox/Everett Collection); Katharine Hepburn, 1961 (Bob Henriques/Magnum Photos)

Cover design by Kara Strubel

Cataloging-in-Publication Data has been applied for and may be obtained from the Library of Congress.
ISBN 978-0-8109-9754-7

First published in 2010 by Contrasto due srl, Rome
Photographs copyright © 2010 the photographers

See pages 470–475 for photography credits

Printed and bound in China
10 9 8 7 6 5 4 3 2 1

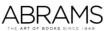

THE ART OF BOOKS SINCE 1949
115 West 18th Street
New York, NY 10011
www.abramsbooks.com

Contents

Fashion is one of the ways in which human beings sacrifice the external to the public domain, in order to safeguard their inner freedom more completely.
GEORG SIMMEL, *FASHION*

Fashion fades; only style remains the same.
COCO CHANEL

Introduction

Icons of Style:
Our Desires Made Real

In *The Empire of Fashion: Dressing Modern Democracy*, Gilles Lipovetsky writes that 'dress, hairstyles and makeup are the most obvious signs of self-affirmation. If fashion governs personal appearance to such an extent, it is because fashion is a privileged way of expressing the uniqueness of individuals.'[1]

We become individuals only when we have internalized, firstly, the basic methods of human expression – speaking, writing, literature – and, secondly, our relationship with ourselves and with the reality that surrounds us. What results is a complex configuration of forces: our personalities are in constant interchange between the internal and the external, between the drives within us and the desires evoked by the world. The construction of what we call our 'self' is a patchwork of many fragmentary, and sometimes contradictory, impulses. Fashion represents the most visible aspect of this contradiction, which sociologist Georg Simmel saw as the coming together of two opposing tendencies that coexist in every individual: on the one hand, we feel a need to conform; on the other hand, we also want to differentiate ourselves. When someone adopts a particular fashion, it strengthens their sense of identification with others who do the same, and this imitation elevates

the individual, at least symbolically, to a higher level. But this division between the individual and the collective also has another dimension: the tension between the desire for continuous change and the emotional drive to cling to certain fixed points that are fundamental and unchanging. This is the paradoxical basis of fashion, and it has been brought into particularly sharp focus in the 21st century, a time in which it seems we can have anything we want, except certainty. Our infatuation with a generic and generalized past has gradually been subsumed, as we slowly move towards a period of reawakening our own memories. As our personal histories, national cultures and the demands of the modern world converge, they prompt us to re-create and rediscover traditional images that can sustain the new dynamics of everyday life.

Although designers dictate new trends and satisfy our desire to stay in fashion, we still want more. Put simply, we need fashion to give us icons: key pieces that are accessible and attainable, but never lose their appeal because they are such perfect examples of their type. A T-shirt, blue jeans, a white shirt, a black turtleneck or a tailored suit: all of these are embodiments of style, which is different from fashion because it lasts over time. When Coco Chanel said 'Fashion fades;

only style remains the same,' she was speaking of a cultural continuity: the letters in an aesthetic alphabet that we all use to define our own images; the basic building blocks of our fashion dreams. Of course, we can still wear a pair of jeans in our own way, personalize a T-shirt and own a variant of the little black dress, but without the presence of those key pieces, we would gaze into our wardrobes in confusion every morning. The great fashion basics give us a sense of security that stops us from losing our heads, yet at the same time they can be adapted to fit our personal style. In *The Language of Clothes*[2] Alison Lurie compares clothes to a spoken language that has its own grammar, syntax and vocabulary (even swear words!); within this framework, every outfit, piece of jewelry and accessory corresponds to a word, which in turn can be cross-referenced with the image of a thing, a passion, a person or a personality.

'We are shaped and fashioned by what we love,' wrote Johann Wolfgang von Goethe. Indeed, the image of an iconic garment often overlaps with the image of the star who made it famous, to the point where the two become inextricably linked. Audrey Hepburn 'is' the little black dress, Diane Keaton 'is' the androgynous look, Grace Kelly 'is' the twinset and Madonna 'is' the corset.

We could think of these stars as variations on the concept of 'augmented reality', a kind of computer-generated image in which artificial elements are superimposed on a view of the real world. The difference is that in this case the 'augmentation' is not created by technology, but is superimposed by our collective memory, popular culture and enduring fantasies, and allows these female icons to transcend their origins and cross the boundaries of time and space, elevating them to an aspirational, almost dream-like realm. When this extraordinary charisma is reflected onto quite ordinary items of clothing, it transforms them into 'cult' items to be imitated and venerated, endowing them with great longevity, if not actual immortality. The bringing together of fashion icons with female icons of glamour also creates a reframing of the dialogue between a particular personality and a particular item of clothing. Suddenly it seems as if one cannot exist without the other, be it in our memories, our hearts, or in our wardrobes.

The spread of the cinema, television and the internet can be credited with creating this phenomenon. It is the culmination of a process that began in the 1950s, when the post-war industrialized world said goodbye to the worship of the idealized and inaccessible, and ushered in a more diverse era of pop culture. Our new icons of style are much more human, and their attraction lies in the fact that they wear and do exactly what the rest of us wear and do, only *better*.

'We know,' Georg Simmel said, 'that it is often a state of mind or a particular demand from a certain individual that gives rise to a fashion.' And so it is that certain celebrities are indelibly linked with a commonplace piece of clothing in a unique way. Why do millions of people today still view Marilyn Monroe as the ultimate sex symbol, and why does Audrey Hepburn's photograph hang in the bedrooms of teenagers who have never even seen *Breakfast at Tiffany's?* These actresses' images have been created by cinematic storytelling, but are also powerfully bound up with their physical appearances. Their bodies are clothed in outfits that reflect their constructed personalities and, at the same time, send out signals that we do not always perceive consciously. In the Hollywood of the 1950s, actresses wore the same styles off-screen in their day-to-day lives as their on-screen characters, thereby taking them beyond the realm of fiction and giving rise to a real 'politics of dress' that affected their relationship with the world. Cinema is

constantly in search of meanings, and uses various methods to imbue clothes with certain ideas, often holding on to the most successful patterns of the past and repeating them over and over again. Perhaps, however, this is exactly what we want films to do.

Fashion has always been a means of escape from the boredom of the everyday world. Nonetheless, we also want our fashion and movie icons to be fixed stars in the stormy firmament of our lives, maybe because they make us feel a little less lonely.

[1] Gilles Lipovetsky, *The Empire of Fashion: Dressing Modern Democracy*, Princeton: Princeton University Press, 1994.

[2] Alison Lurie, *The Language of Clothes*, New York: Random House, 1983.

Audrey Hepburn,
Breakfast at Tiffany's, 1961

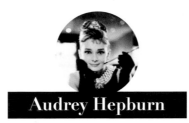

Audrey Hepburn

The Little Black Dress

Scheherazade is easy, a little black dress is difficult.
COCO CHANEL

Icon **Audrey Hepburn**
Designer **Coco Chanel, Hubert de Givenchy**
Film *Breakfast at Tiffany's*, 1961

Audrey Hepburn, *Breakfast at Tiffany's*, 1961

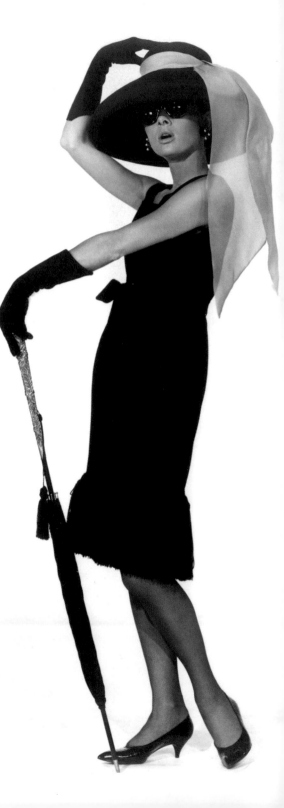

When Hubert de Givenchy was told that 'Miss Hepburn' wanted to meet him, he was expecting to see Katharine Hepburn come in. Instead, he found Audrey Hepburn standing before him, but he was not disappointed. 'I told her, "Mademoiselle, I would love to help you, but I have very few seamstresses, I am in the middle of doing a collection, I can't make you clothes." So she said, "Show me what you have already made for the collection." She tried on the dresses – "It's exactly what I need!" – and they fit her, too.'

This was in 1954, for the film *Sabrina*, directed by Billy Wilder. A few years later, in Blake Edwards's 1961 adaptation of *Breakfast at Tiffany's*, the 'little black dress', often known simply by its initials LBD, became a key chapter in fashion history. The little black dress was born from an idea of Coco Chanel's in 1926, and rechristened the 'Ford dress' by US *Vogue*. And just like Henry Ford's Model T car, the LBD instantly became the epitome of sophisticated chic, and of an elegant and modern simplicity. Chanel was well aware of its poise: when rival couturier Paul Poiret, who had designed costumes for the ballet *Scheherazade*, teased her by asking 'Madame, for whom are you in mourning?', she replied smartly: 'For you, monsieur!'

Stars are still closely associated with the legendary LBD today, as is demonstrated by the cover of the first DVD collection of *Sex and the City*, the television series that has influenced contemporary fashion more than any other, which shows the four heroines all wearing little black dresses. Another example is the 2005 short film entitled *The Little Black Dress*, starring Rosario Dawson, in which a young woman exploits the power of an LBD to advance her professional career. Today, the little black dress signifies the ultimate combination of desire and

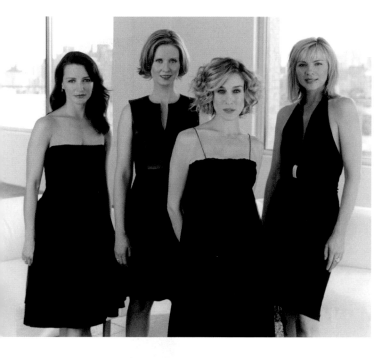

Kristin Davis, Cynthia Nixon, Sarah Jessica Parker, Kim Cattrall, *Sex and the City*, 2002

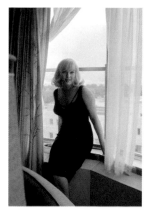

Marilyn Monroe, backstage during filming of *The Misfits*, 1960

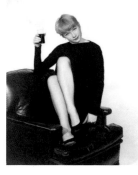

Shirley MacLaine, *Career*, 1959

comfort, elegance and restraint, naturalness and fantasy. Its extraordinary versatility has made it a must for every woman. Its feel and style can easily be altered by switching accessories (proving that the vital accessory is, of course, the dress itself), and the LBD can change its shape and adapt itself to the person wearing it. It hugs Marilyn Monroe's curves in Howard Hawks's *Gentlemen Prefer Blondes* (1953) and Billy Wilder's *Some Like it Hot* (1959); it enhances Jayne Mansfield's shape in Frank Tashlin's *The Girl Can't Help It* (1956); it moulds itself to Jeanne Moreau's silhouette in Louis Malle's *Les amants* (1958) and to Shirley MacLaine's in Joseph Anthony's *Career* (1959). The power of black can evoke a wide range of feelings and emotional nuances, as demonstrated in *Little Black*

Dress: An Anthology of Short Stories by Women Writers (ed. Susie Maguire, 2006), a collection of stories written by authors as diverse as Stella Duffy and Candia McWilliam, Muriel Gray and Yvonne Adhiambo Owuor, relating tales of love, individuality, solitude and sex. But perhaps the most timeless account is Truman Capote's description of Holly Golightly in his novel *Breakfast at Tiffany's*: 'It was a warm evening, nearly summer, and she wore a slim cool black dress, black sandals, a pearl choker.' Style and sensitivity, united in an enduring partnership.

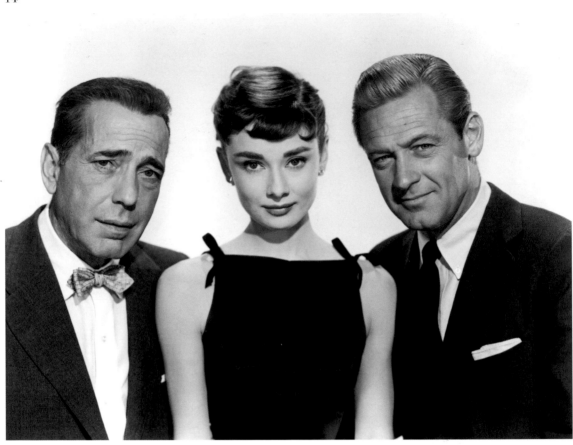

Humphrey Bogart, Audrey Hepburn, William Holden, *Sabrina*, 1954

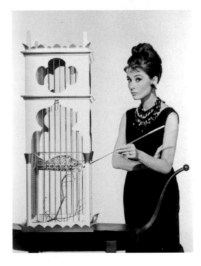

Audrey Hepburn, *Breakfast at Tiffany's*, 1961

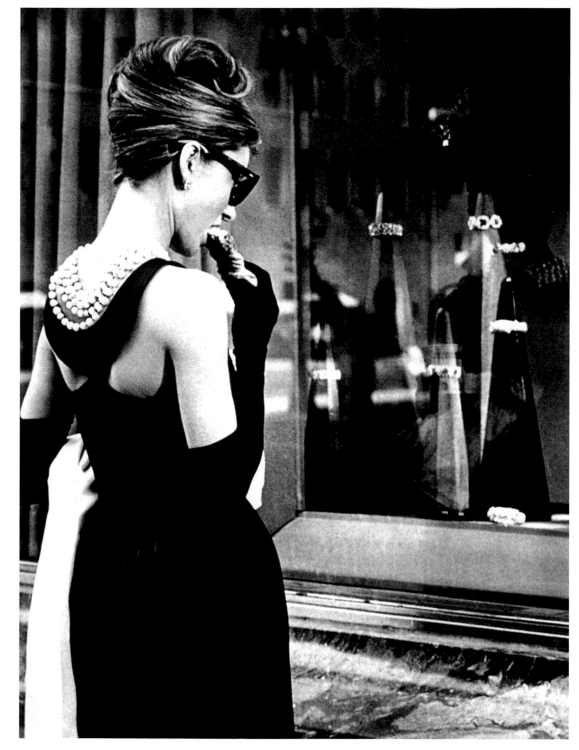

Audrey Hepburn, *Breakfast at Tiffany's*, 1961

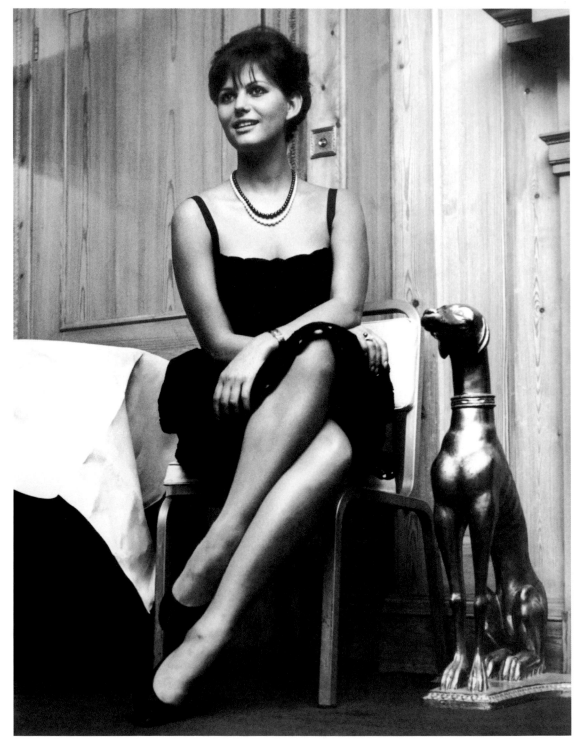

Claudia Cardinale, London, 1962

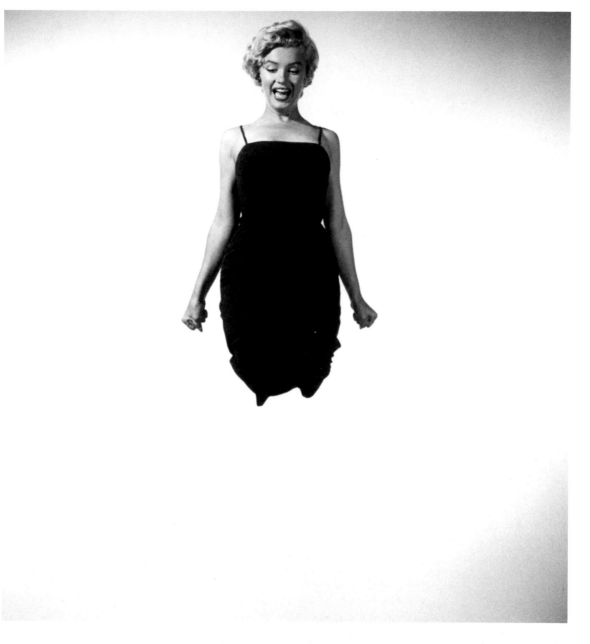

Marilyn Monroe, New York, 1959

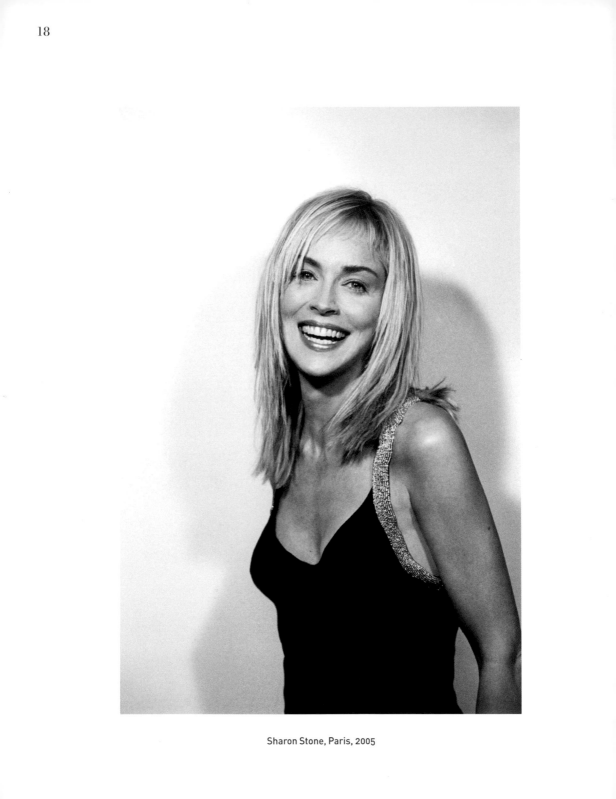

Sharon Stone, Paris, 2005

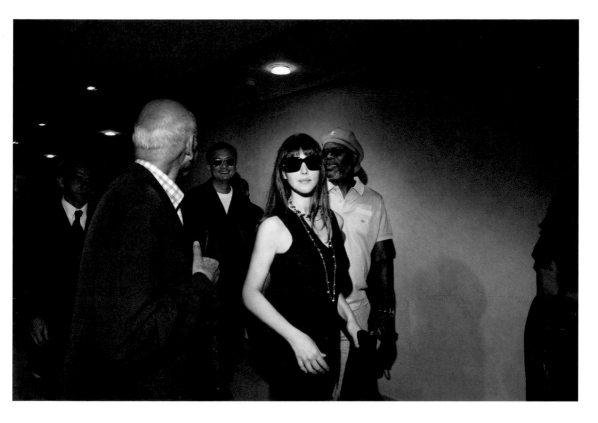

Gilles Jacob, Monica Bellucci, Samuel L. Jackson and Wong Kar-Wai, Cannes, 2006

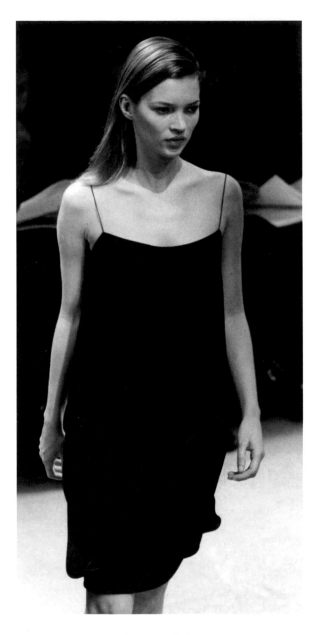

Kate Moss, New York, 1997

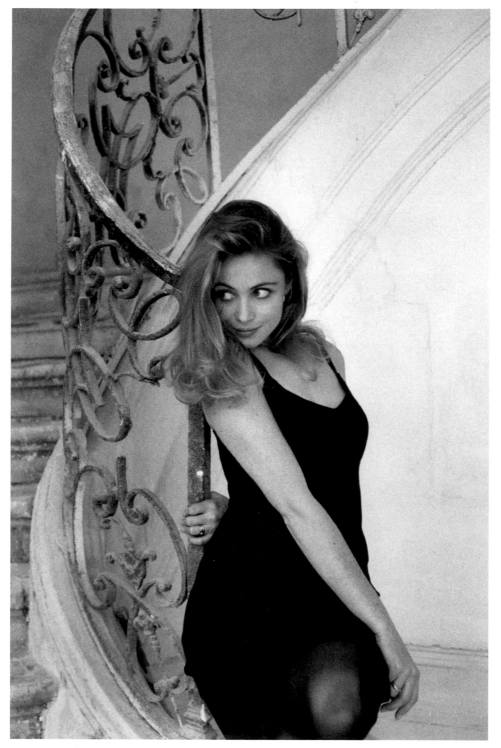

Emmanuelle Beart, Paris, 1989

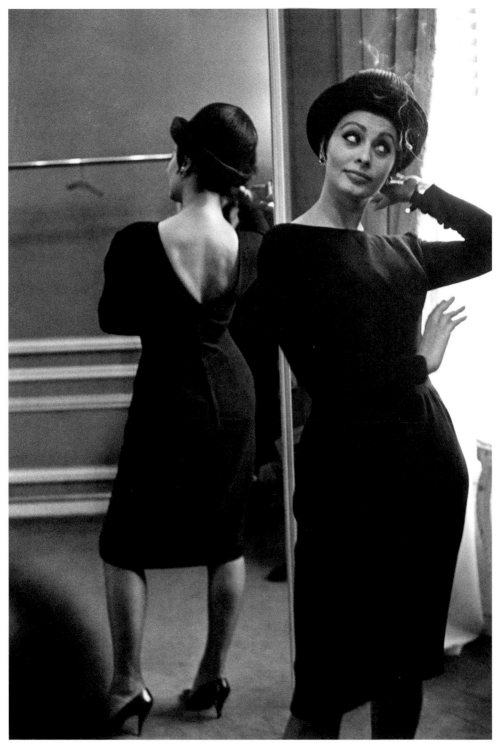

Sophia Loren, Paris, 1960s

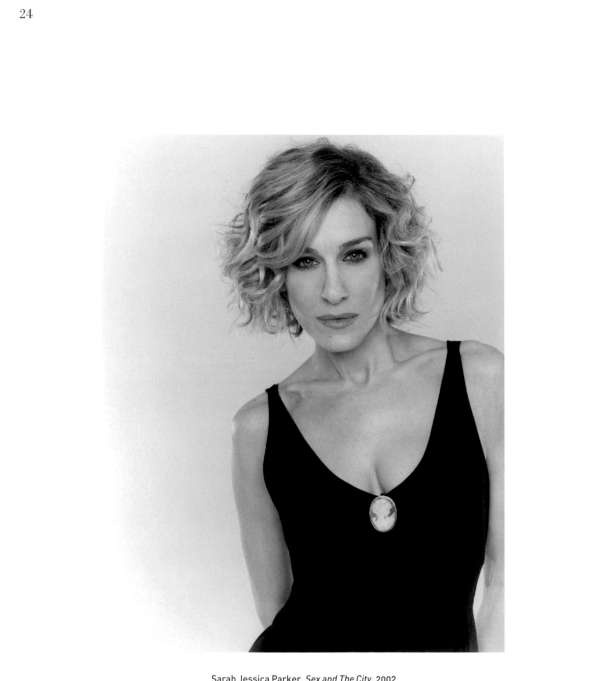

Sarah Jessica Parker, *Sex and The City*, 2002

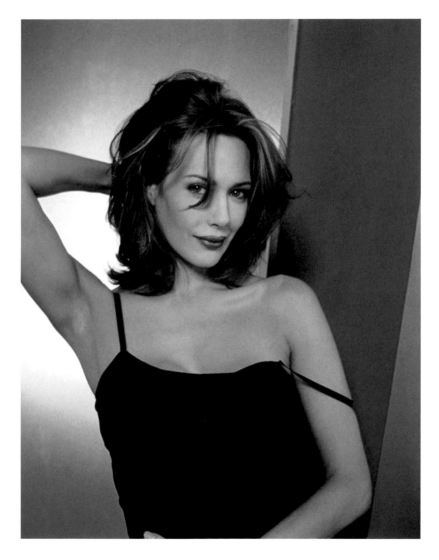

Hunter Tylo, *The Bold and the Beautiful*, 2000

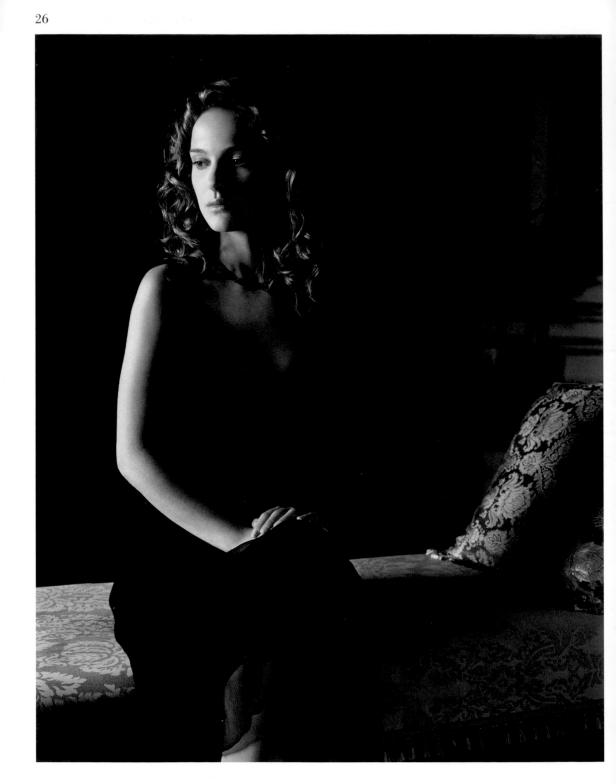

Natalie Portman, *V for Vendetta*, 2005

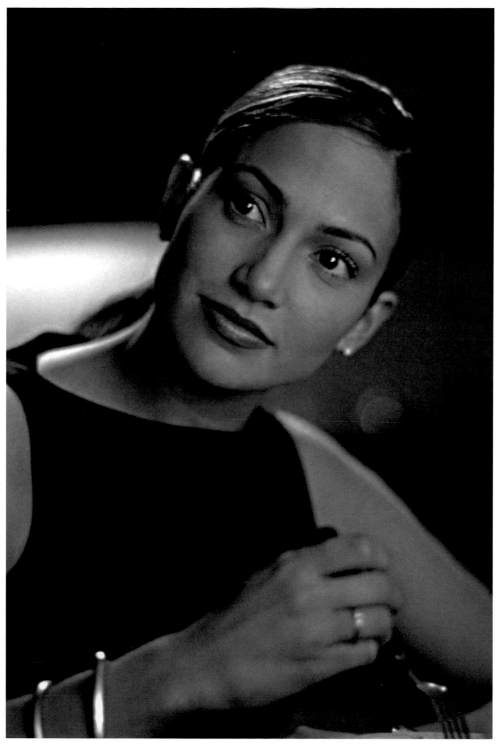

Jennifer Lopez, *The Wedding Planner*, 2001

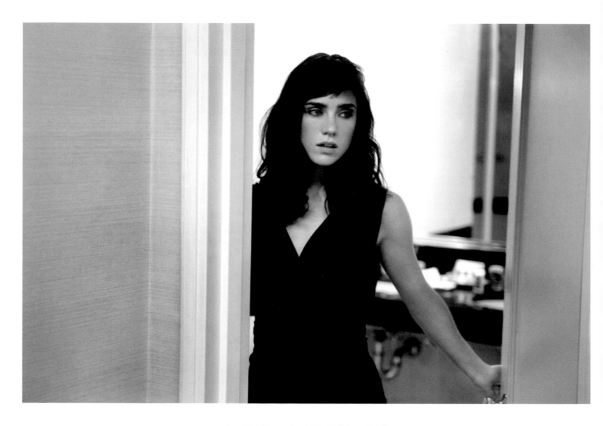

Jennifer Connelly, *Little Children*, 2006

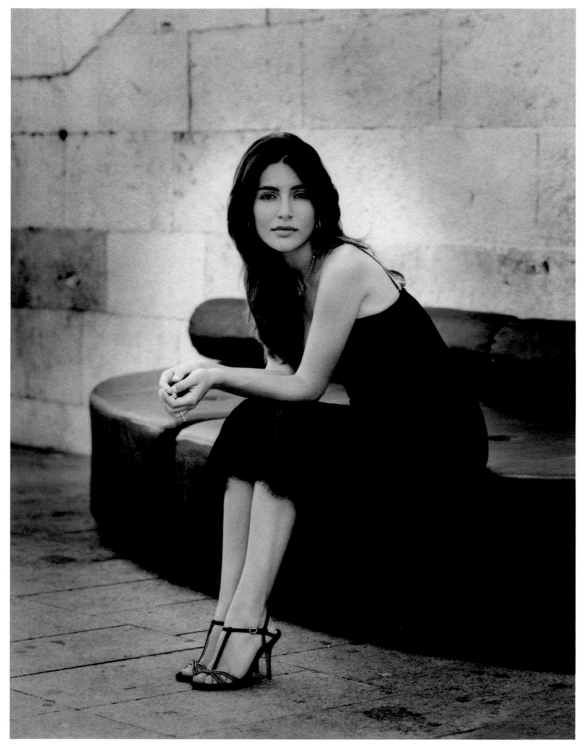

Caterina Murino, Cagliari, Italy, 2006

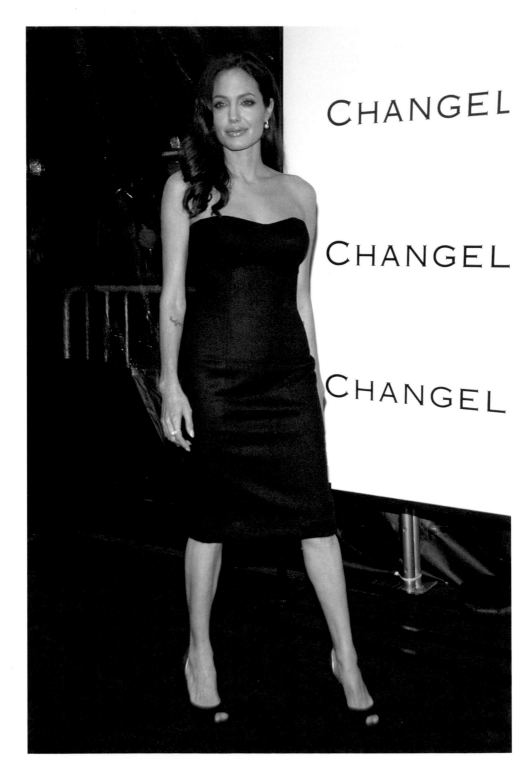

Angelina Jolie, New York, 2008

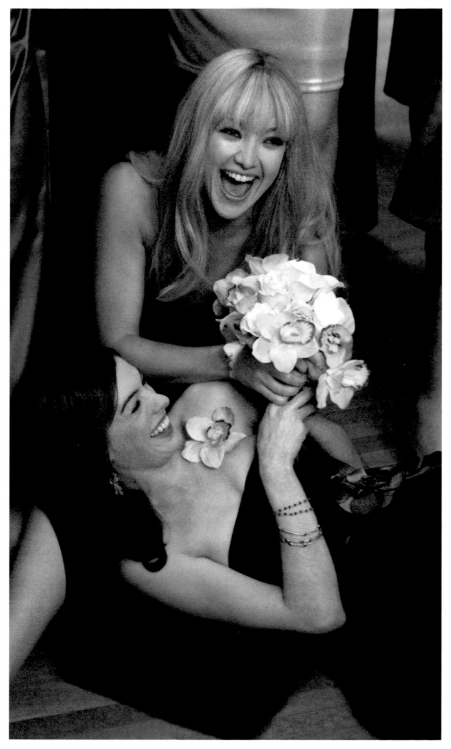

Kate Hudson and Anne Hathaway, *Bride Wars*, 2009

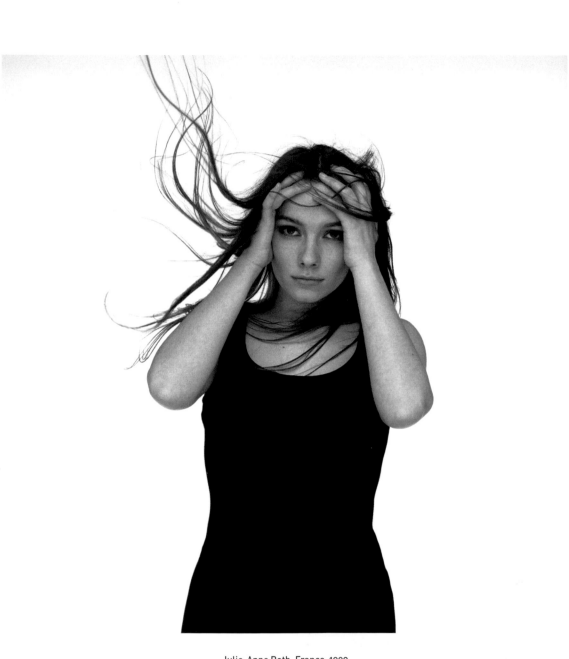

Julie-Anne Roth, France, 1999

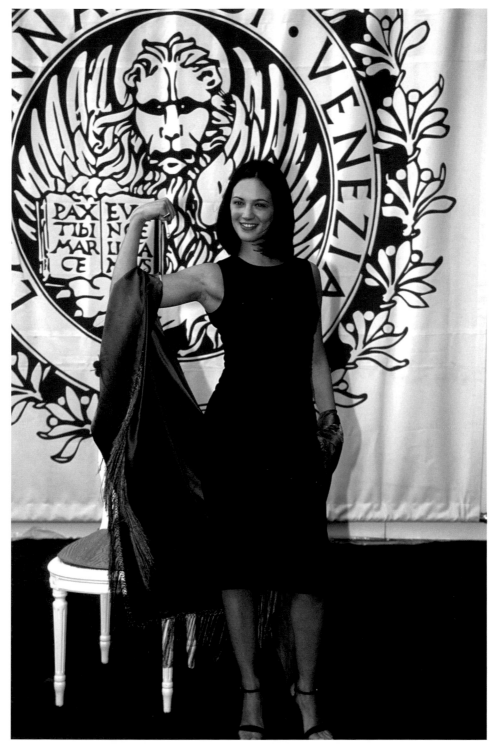

Asia Argento, Venice, 1998

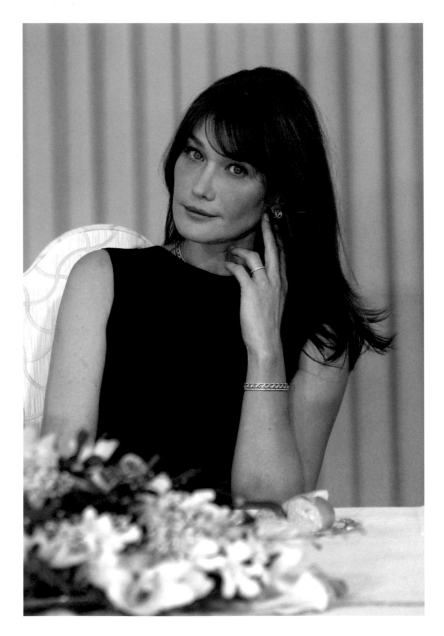

Carla Bruni, Tunisia, 2008

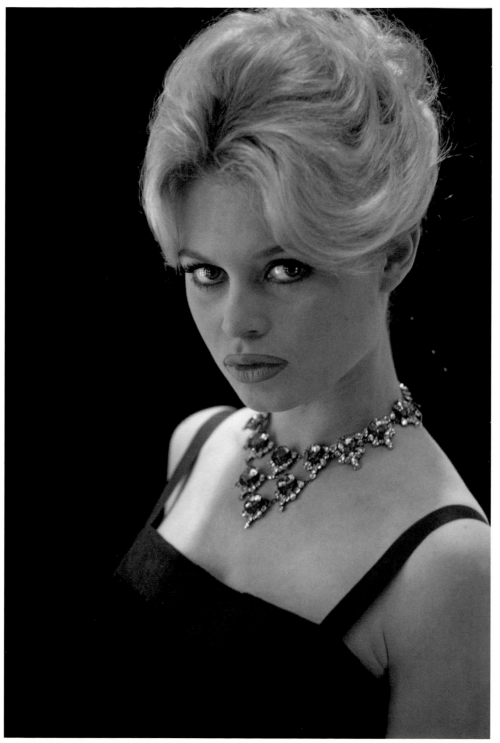

Brigitte Bardot, Paris, 1958

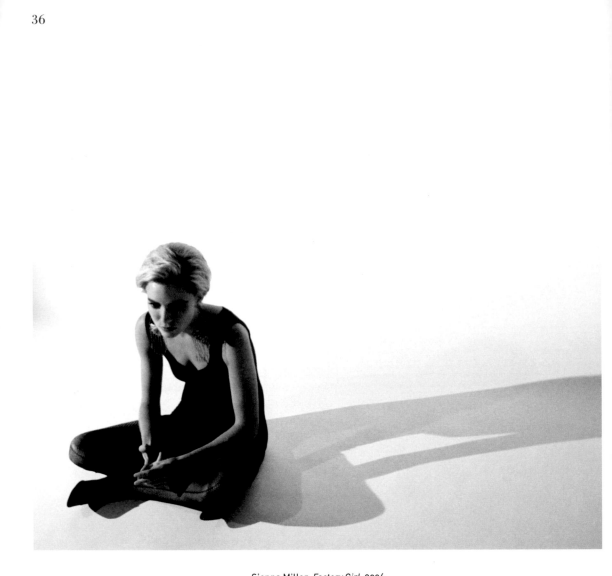

Sienna Miller, *Factory Girl*, 2006

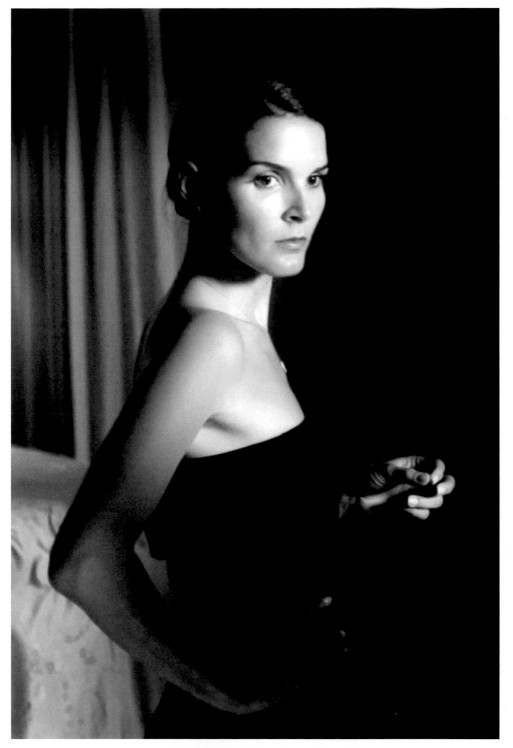

Angie Harmon, *Glass House: The Good Mother*, 2006

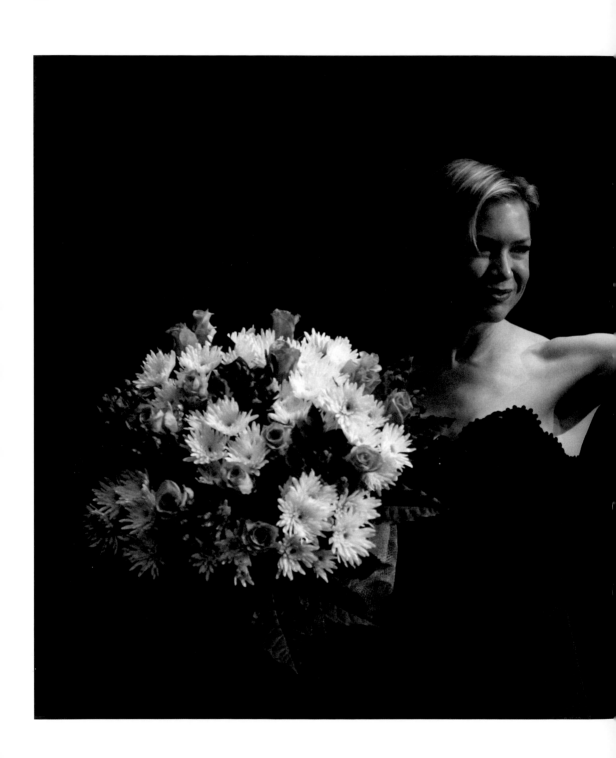

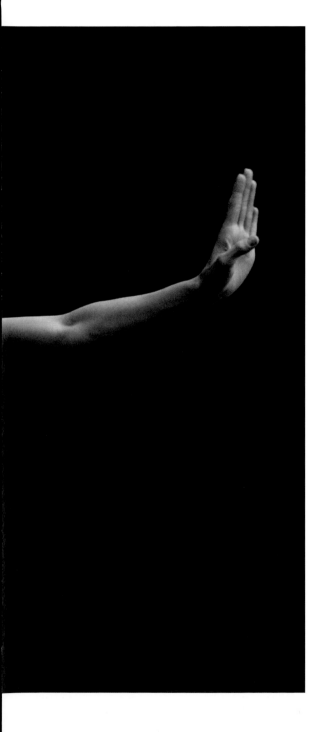

Renee Zellweger, Karlovy Vary, 2007

Katharine Hepburn,
backstage during filming of
Long Day's Journey Into Night, 1961

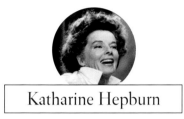

Katharine Hepburn

The White Shirt

The white blouse can be light and floating, impeccable and austere, sumptuous and all-enveloping, tight and close-fitting. It rises up to frame the face. It sculpts the body by transforming itself into a second skin. Imbued with glamour and poetry, freedom and impetuousness, the prim white shirt turns out to have a thousand identities…

GIANFRANCO FERRÉ

Icon **Katharine Hepburn**
Designer **Gianfranco Ferré**
Film ***Holiday**, George Cukor, 1938*

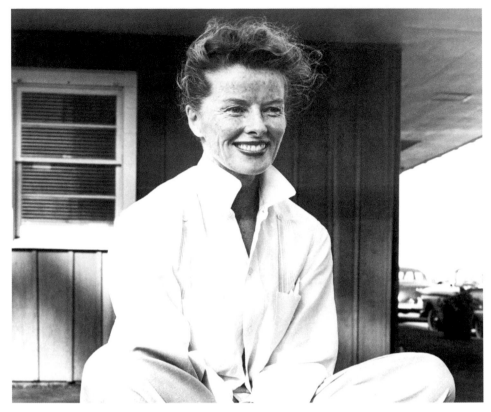

Katharine Hepburn,
1950s

Katharine Hepburn was a true independent, a non-conformist with a relaxed style and a fondness for menswear basics: jackets with squared-off shoulders and men's trousers. Above all, however, she is associated with masculine white shirts, worn as a public declaration of a femininity that was well aware of its innate power. As she once said: 'If you want to give up the admiration of thousands of men for the disdain of one, go ahead, get married.' Hepburn was quite capable of poking fun at herself and other people, and at human weaknesses in general. She was also far too lively to stay in love with the same man for her entire life – a man such as Spencer Tracy, who would never marry her, although the two of them appeared together in many films.

George Cukor's delicious 1938 comedy *Holiday* is a story for all those who believe in the subversive power of love. It is candid but not naive, just like a white shirt.

White is both powerful and mysterious. It evokes the expression of an idea, just as the whiteness of a blank page represents a moment of quiet meditation in today's hectic, multicoloured world. It conveys innocence, purity, and, by extension, consciousness, knowledge, grace, faith and goodness. White also signifies cleanliness, austerity and rationality. No other garment in our wardrobe has the capacity to translate our feelings and emotions like a white shirt. Its apparent neutrality is, in reality, the meeting place between our desire to be ourselves and our need to be part of the external world without appearing incongruous, affected or out of place. Iconic, but unencumbered by stereotypes; multifaceted, but still part of the uniform, the joy of the white shirt that it is so completely universal that it can be redesigned and reinterpreted from a thousand different points of view, all of which are equally valid.

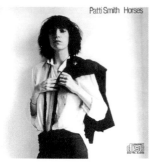

Patti Smith,
Horses, 1975

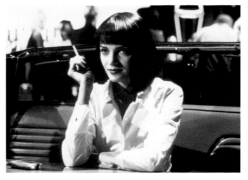

Uma Thurman,
Pulp Fiction, 1994

Grace Kelly,
Rear Window, 1954

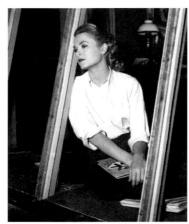

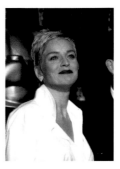

Sharon Stone,
Los Angeles,
1999

Kim Basinger,
9½ Weeks, 1986

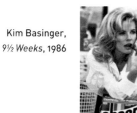

It is polyvalent without being ambiguous, and one of the many aspects of its fascination is its democratic potential: it always retains its innate perfection.

Although it is the ultimate in formalwear (it is no coincidence that the men and women of the powerful American trade union, the United Automobile Workers, celebrate White Shirt Day on 11 February as a way of emphasizing the equality of blue-collar workers with their white-collar employers), the white shirt can also communicate the idea of freedom, purity and aesthetic autonomy. White shirts can be as classic as the ones worn by Grace Kelly in *Rear Window* (1954); as anarchic as the one Robert Mapplethorpe photographed Patti Smith wearing for the album cover of *Horses* (1975); as sexy as Kim Basinger's shirt in *9½ Weeks* (1986); or as androgynous as Uma Thurman's in *Pulp Fiction* (1994). Even away from the silver screen, film divas have made it a declaration of bold but personal chic. Sharon Stone wore a white shirt over a sumptuous evening dress by Vera Wang at the 1999 Oscars, as did Ali McGraw for the same occasion in 2001. According to the sociologist Wendy Griswold, the white shirt is a 'cultural object' in that its significance is embodied by a particular form. However, because its meanings and variations are now virtually infinite, they reflect the identity of the person wearing the shirt, and not the other way around.

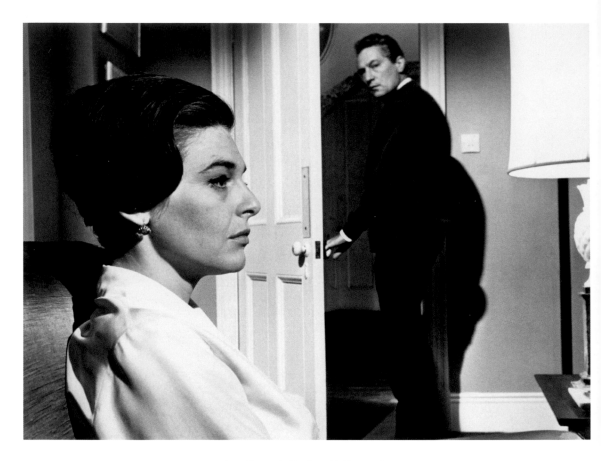

Anne Bancroft, *The Pumpkin Eater*, 1964

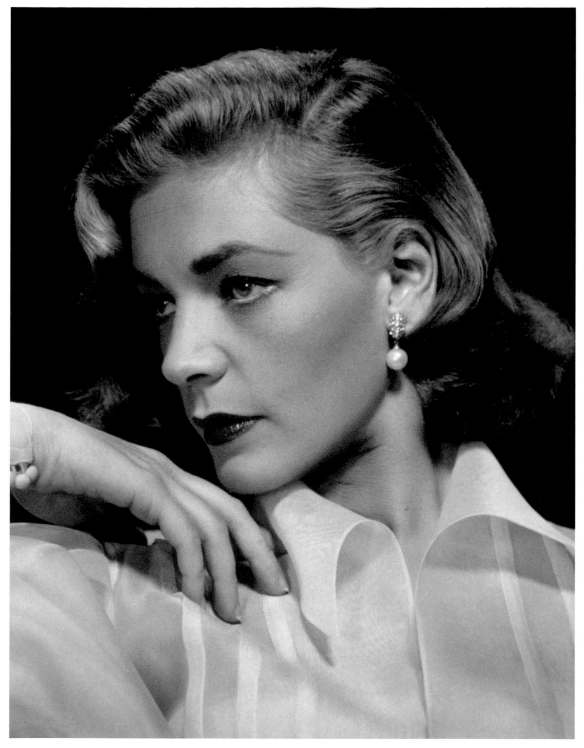

Lauren Bacall, USA, 1944

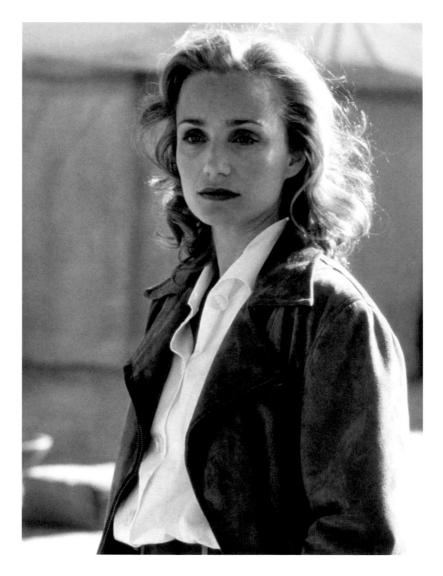

Kristin Scott Thomas, *The English Patient*, 1996

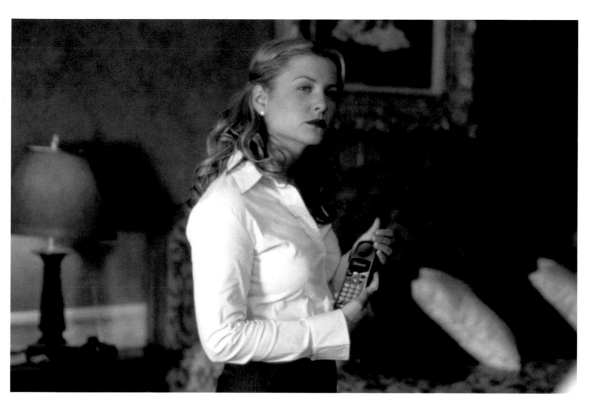

Jessica Capshaw, *Valentine*, 2001

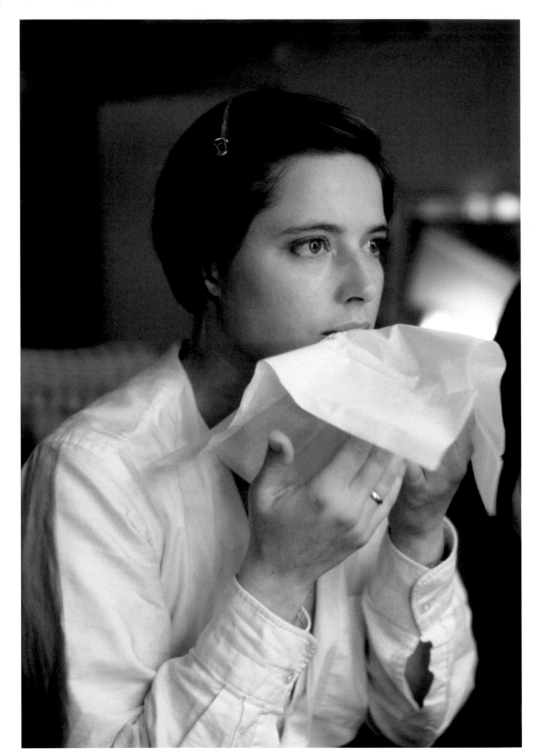

Isabella Rossellini, *White Nights*, 1984

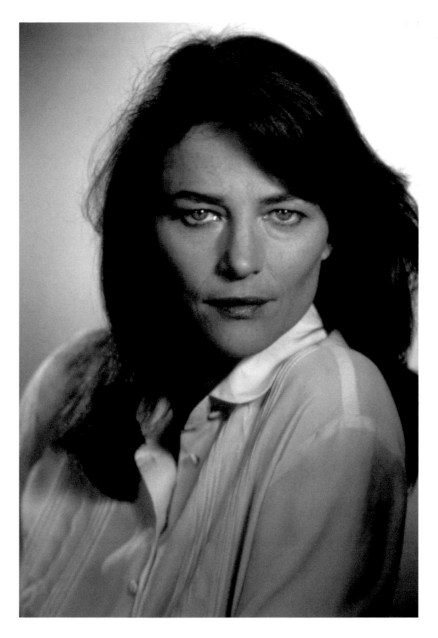

Charlotte Rampling, 1970s

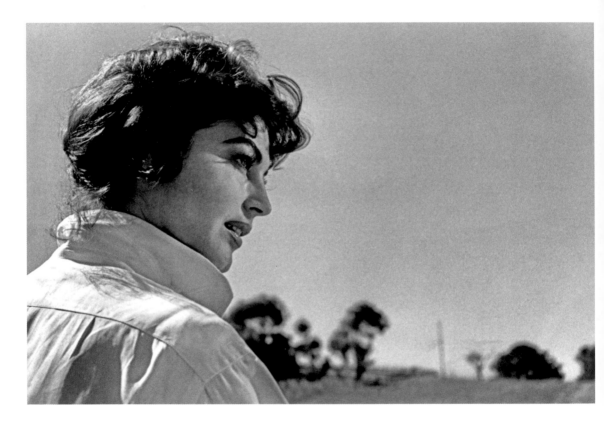

Ava Gardner, *On the Beach*, 1959

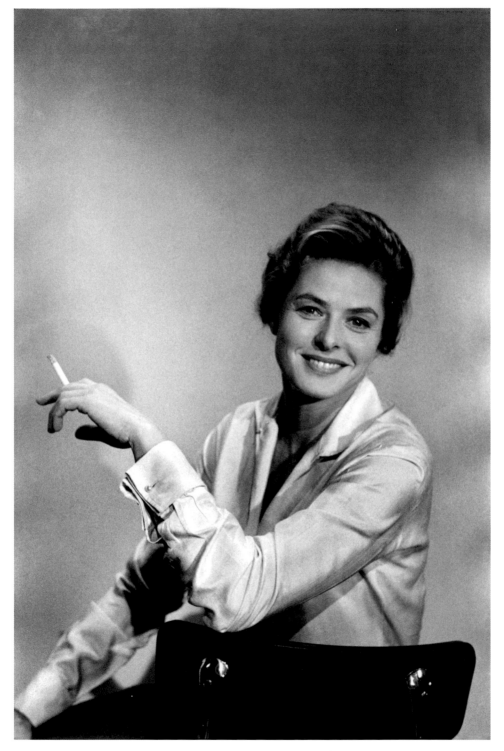

Ingrid Bergman, USA, 1950

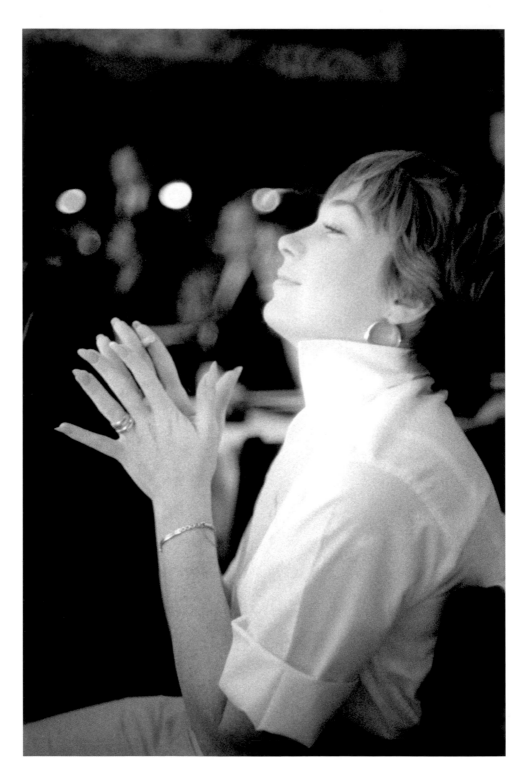

Shirley MacLaine, New York, 1960

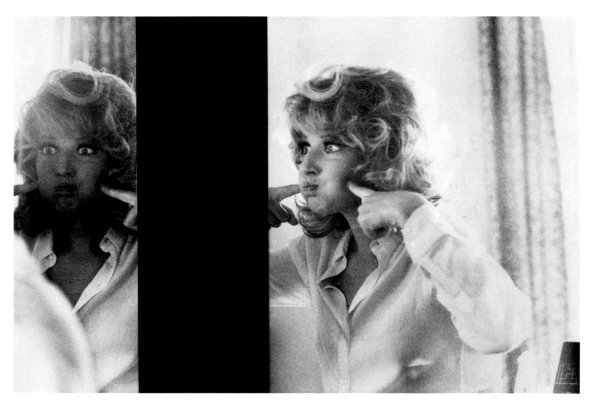

Monica Vitti, backstage during filming of *Modesty Blaise*, 1965

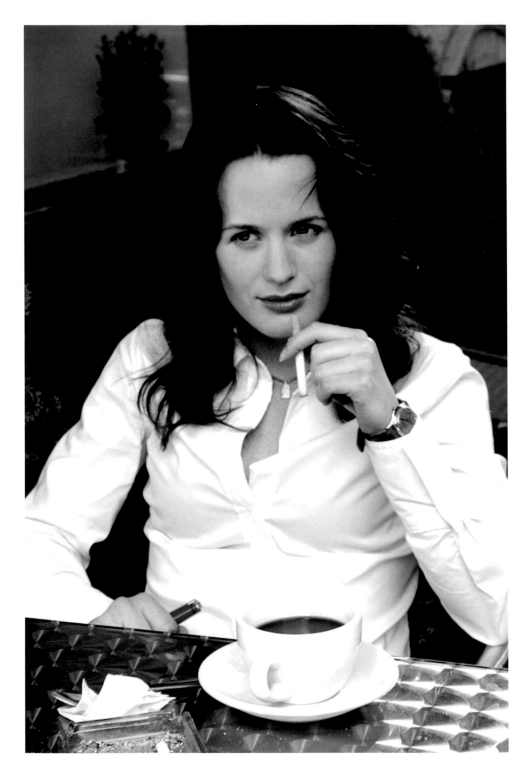

Elizabeth Reaser, *Puccini for Beginners*, 2006

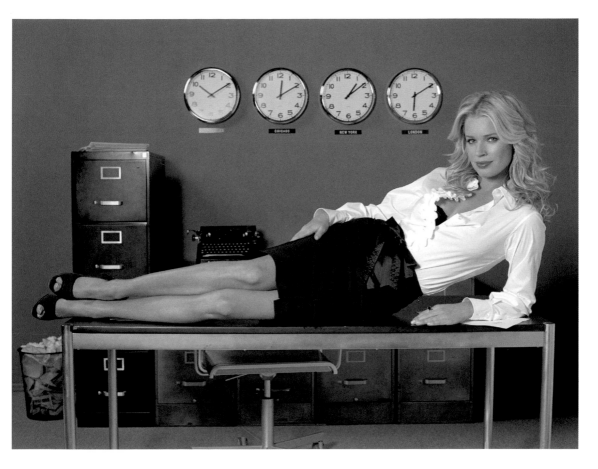

Rebecca Romijn, *Pepper Dennis*, 2006

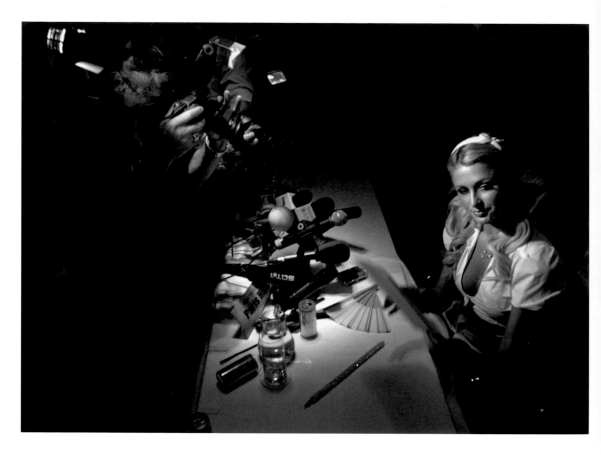

Paris Hilton, Palma, Spain, 2006

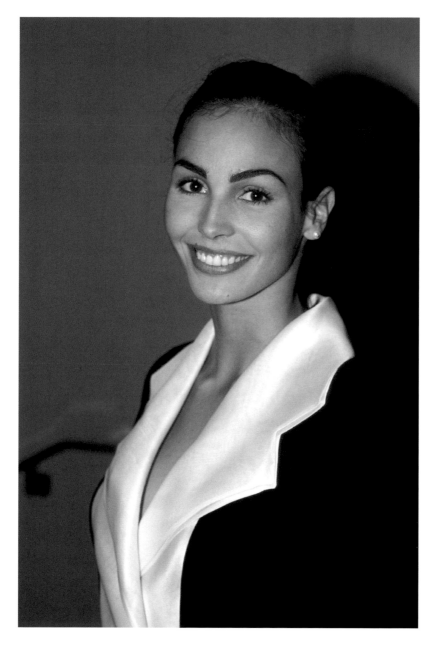

Ines Sastre, Paris, 1996

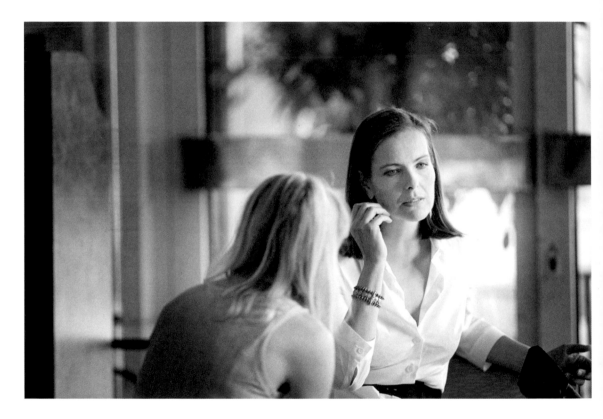

Carole Bouquet, Cannes, 2005

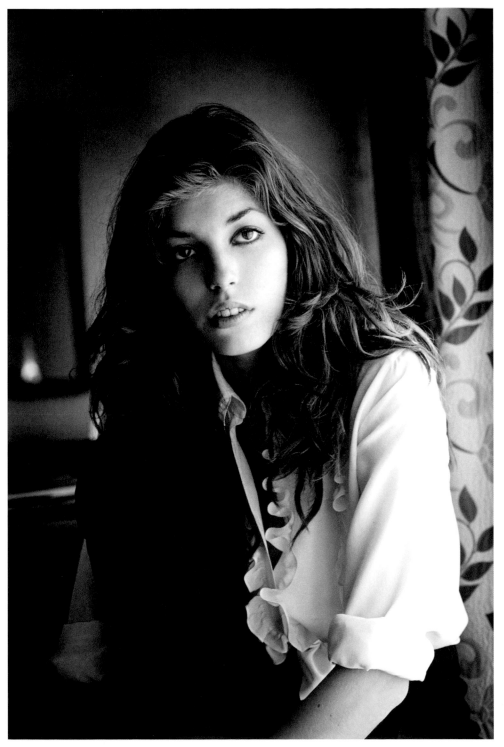

Lou Doillon, 2006

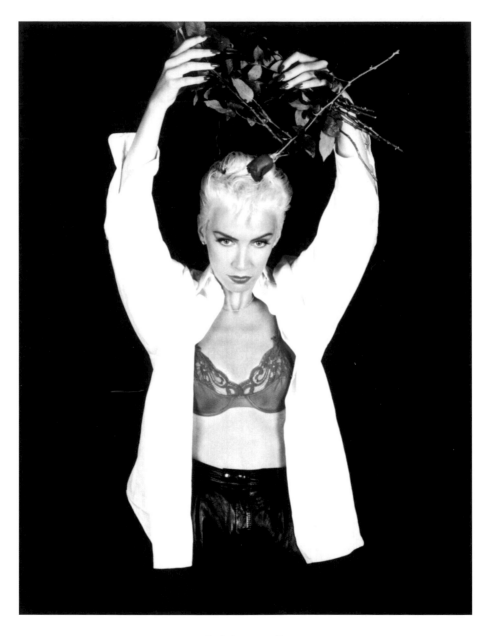

Annie Lennox, 1980

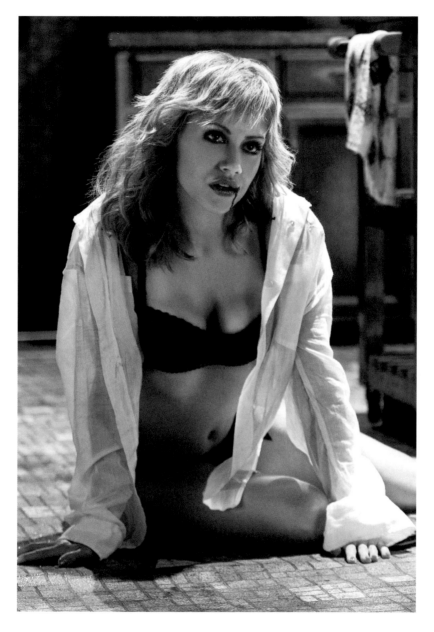

Brittany Murphy, *Sin City*, 2005

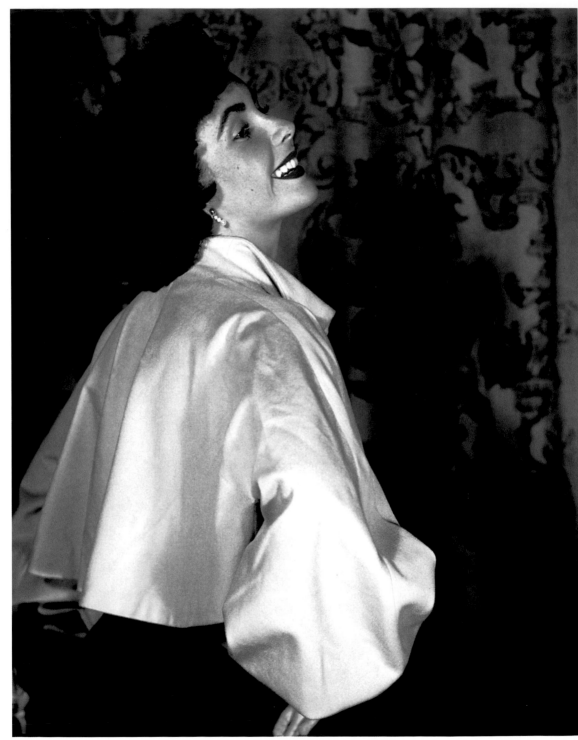

Elizabeth Taylor, 1950

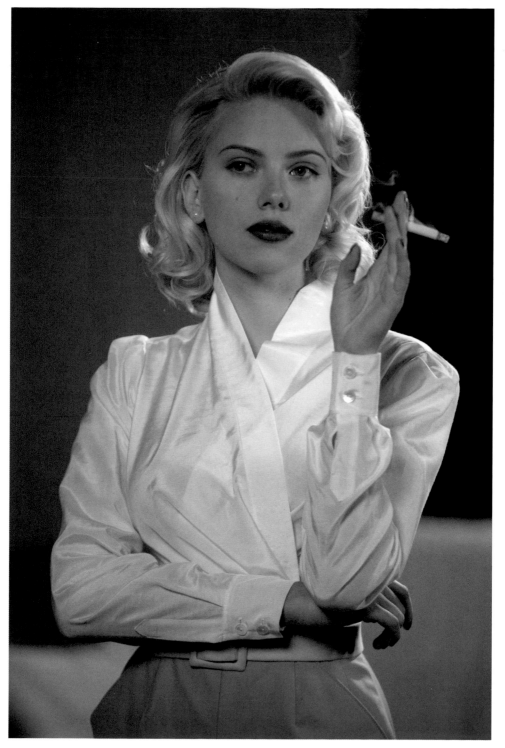

Scarlett Johansson, *Black Dahlia*, 2006

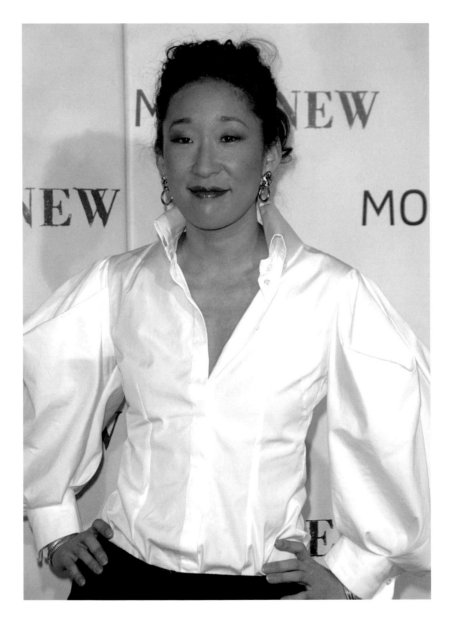

Sandra Oh, Los Angeles, 2009

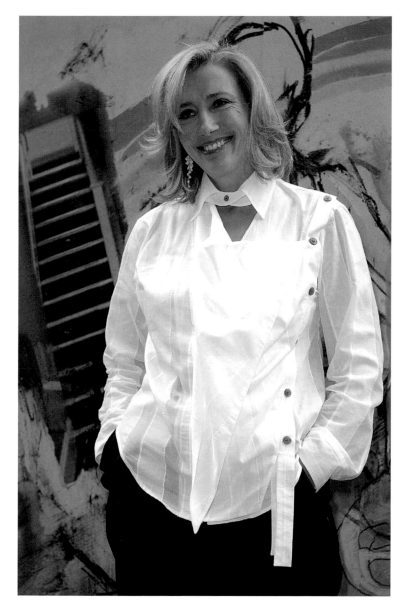

Emma Thompson, New York, 2009

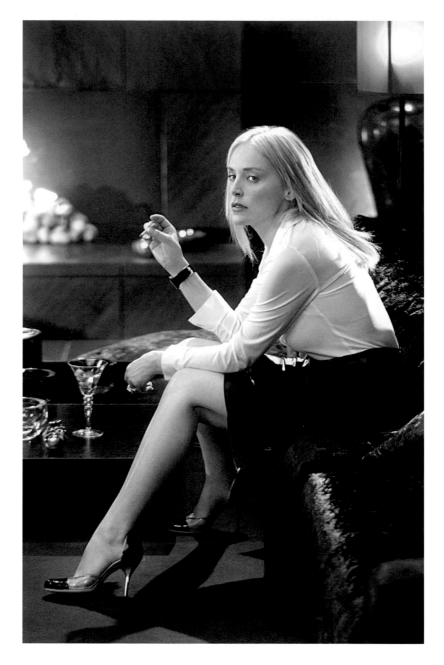

Sharon Stone, *Basic Instinct 2*, 2006

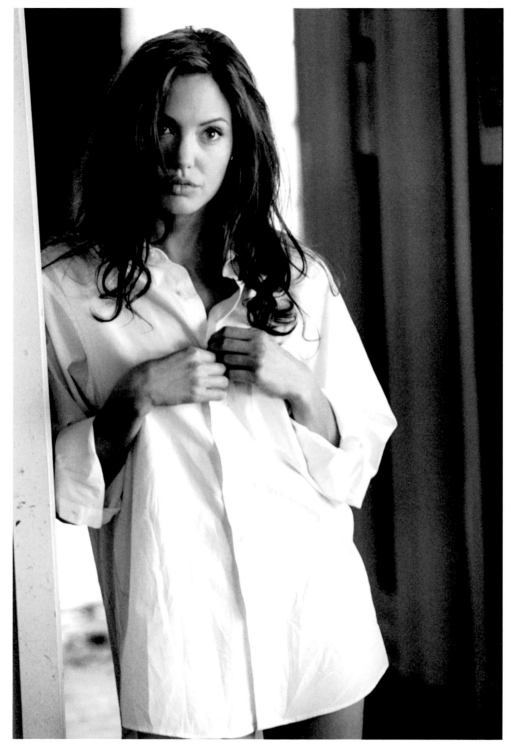

Angelina Jolie, *Mr & Mrs Smith*, 2005

Jean Simmons, *Guys and Dolls*, 1954

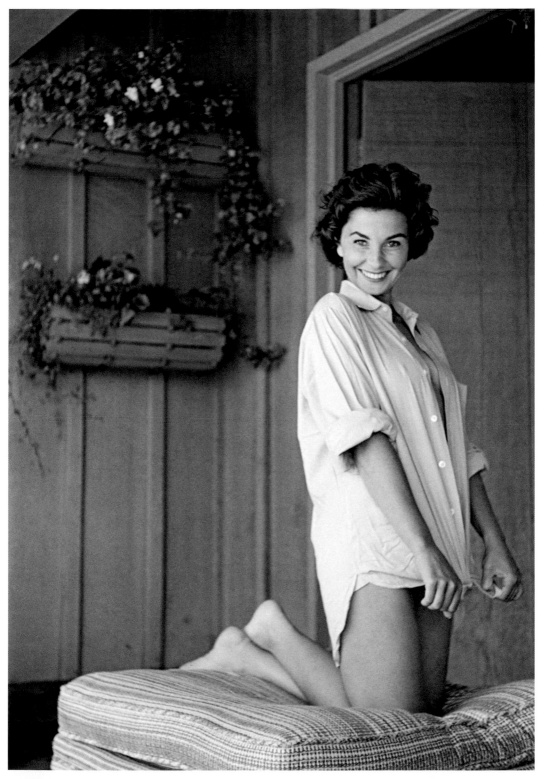

Marilyn Monroe, *The Misfits*, 1960

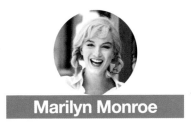

Marilyn Monroe

Jeans

I wish I had invented blue jeans. They have expression,
modesty, sex appeal, simplicity – all I hope for in my clothes.
YVES SAINT LAURENT

Icon Marilyn Monroe
Designer Levi Strauss
Film *The Misfits*, John Huston, 1961

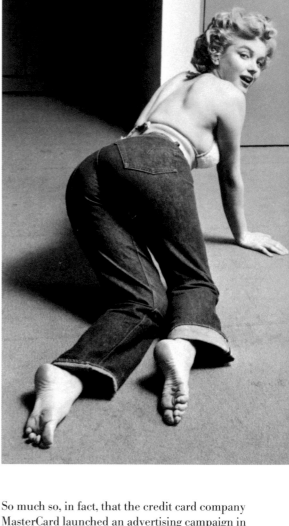

Marilyn Monroe
posing for the cover of *Life* magazine, 1952

Although she did not enjoy the experience, when Marilyn Monroe played the role of Kay, a saloon bar singer in *River of No Return*, it was the first time in her career that she portrayed a character that took her beyond the cliché of the blonde airhead and allowed her to express a sexy but fragile femininity, a character that revealed something of herself to the public without showing them everything. 'They kind of like to take a piece of you. It stirs up envy, fame does,' she said in an interview at the time. Something similar happened when she played the character of the beautiful and naive Roslyn in *The Misfits* (John Huston, 1961). It might have been only a coincidence, but in both movies she wore jeans and denim jackets that skimmed over her curves and took her far away from the blonde bombshell of *Gentlemen Prefer Blondes* (Howard Hawks, 1953).

Sincerity, authenticity, and body consciousness: jeans, especially in blue denim, epitomize these values. Even with designer labels and ornate details, they still retain the robust poetry that they have always possessed. They even have an official birthday: 20 May 1873 was the day on which the United States Patent Office granted drygoods merchant Levi Strauss and tailor Jacob W. Davis the exclusive authorization to produce trousers made from strong cotton reinforced with metal rivets. Their name, however, comes from a corruption of 'Gênes', the French name for the Italian port of Genoa, where they were cut and sewn for sailors who had to endure long voyages and hard physical work, which meant that their clothes had to be made from strong fabric. They used dark blue cloth from the French city of Nimes; and the phrase 'de Nimes' is the root of the word 'denim'.

Everyone seems to own at least one pair of jeans. Some see them as a way of life; others regard them as a cult object; and still others simply view them as a fashion that never goes out of style.

So much so, in fact, that the credit card company MasterCard launched an advertising campaign in the USA featuring images of three iconic figures – Marlon Brando, James Dean and Marilyn Monroe – wearing jeans and accompanied by the slogan: 'The perfect pair of jeans: priceless'. Denim also has a darker side, as it can be an aid to seduction or an expression of desire, whether it is the teenage Brooke Shields whispering in an ad for Calvin Klein: 'You want to know what comes between me and my Calvins? Nothing,' or the denim-clad army of the counterculture in the 1970s and 80s. Andy Warhol designed the cover for the Rolling Stones's album *Sticky Fingers* in 1971, featuring a close-up of a man's crotch in jeans with a real zip;

James Dean, *Giant*, 1956

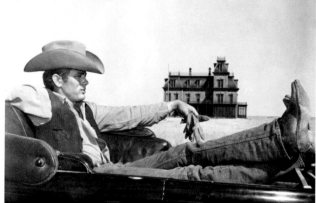

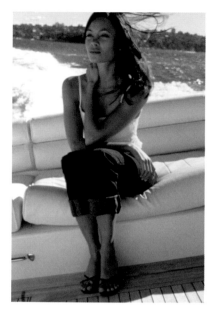

Thandie Newton,
Mission: Impossible 2, 2000

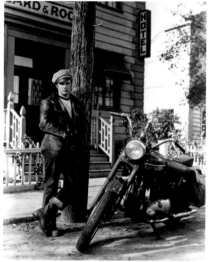

Marlon Brando,
The Wild One, 1954

a few years earlier, the band's lead singer, Mick Jagger, was best man at the wedding of Catherine Deneuve and David Bailey, dressed entirely in denim. Later, the female leads in the television series *Charlie's Angels* made jeans their uniform. After a brief period of oblivion, denim made a comeback: it enclosed Kelly McGillis's agile legs in *Top Gun* (Tony Scott, 1986), hugged Thandie Newton's figure in *Mission: Impossible 2* (John Woo, 2000), had a country-style twist in Dsquared²'s designs for Madonna's pop video *Don't Tell Me* in 2000, and gave Anne Hathaway supermodel glamour when she wore Chanel jeans in *The Devil Wears Prada* (David Frankel, 2006).

Less successfully, Barack Obama wore baggy 'mom jeans' at a baseball game in St Louis that provoked ironic comments in the American media and even became the subject of a parody on the satirical television show *Saturday Night Live*. Obama bashfully excused himself: 'I'm a little frumpy. Basically, up until a few years ago, I only had four suits. [Michelle] used to tease me cause they'd get really shiny. I hate to shop. Those jeans are comfortable, and for those of you who want your president to look great in his tight jeans, I'm sorry – I'm not the guy.' Mr President, don't undervalue your jeans: just make use of your MasterCard.

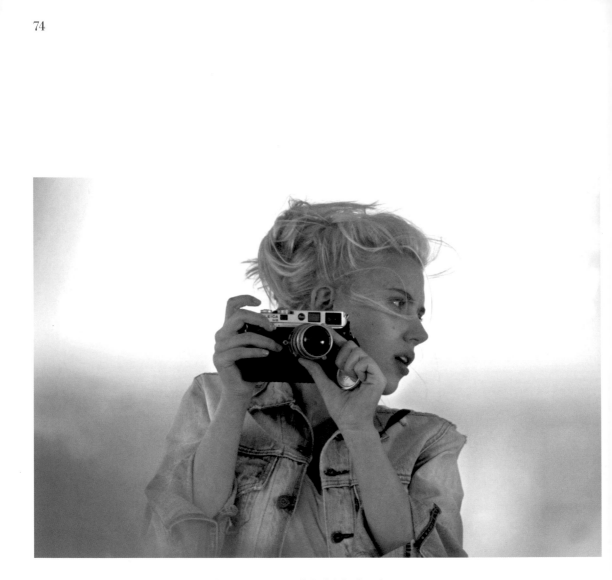

Scarlett Johansson, *Vicky Cristina Barcelona*, 2007

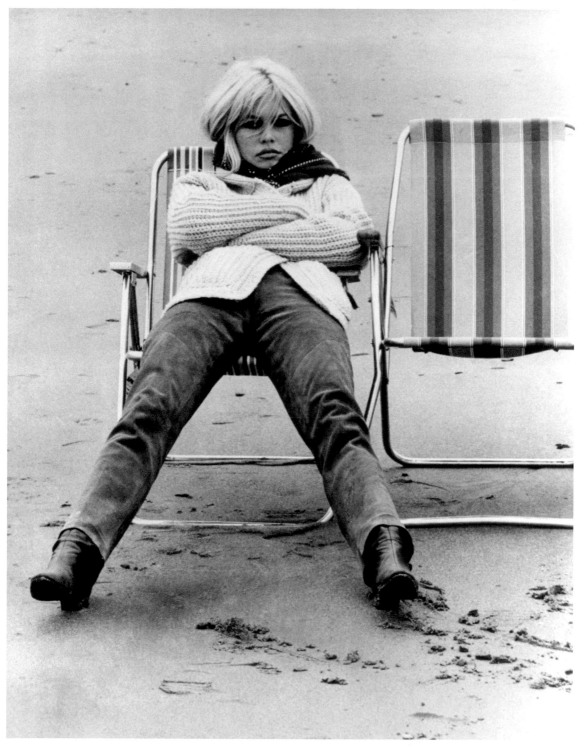

Brigitte Bardot, France, 1960

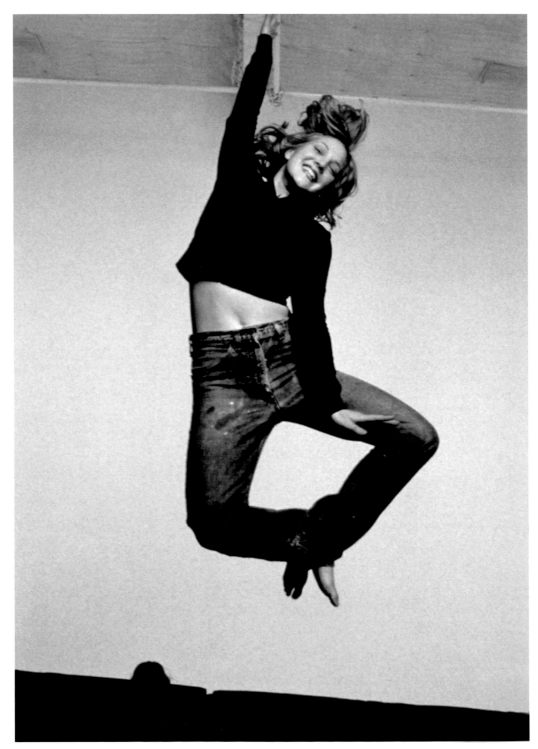

Drew Barrymore, *Never Been Kissed*, 1999

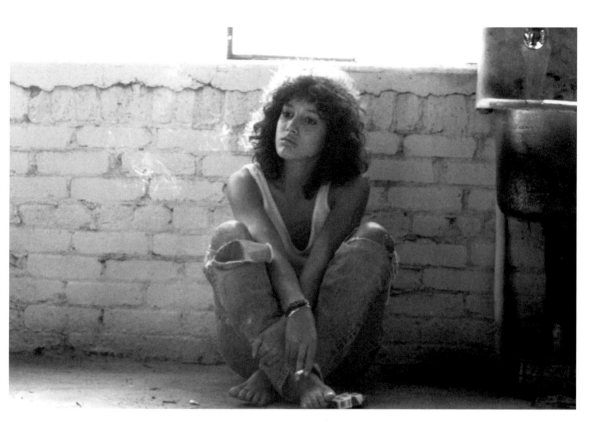

Jennifer Beals, *Flashdance*, 1983

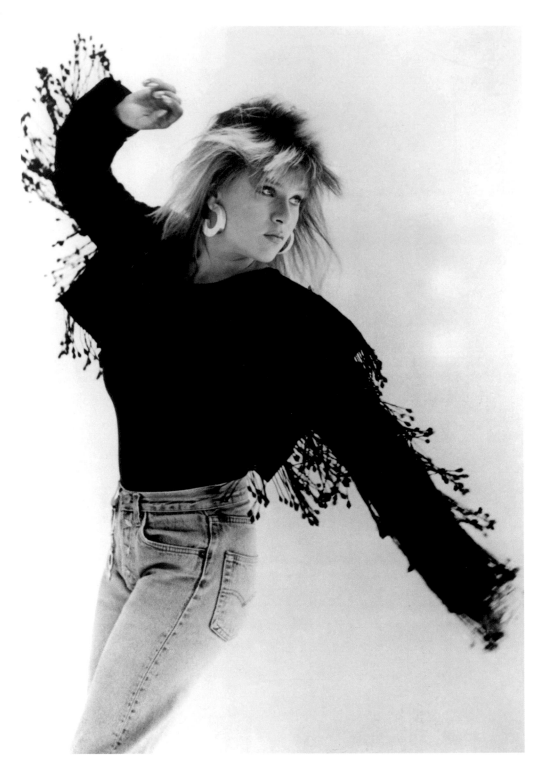

Samantha Fox, 1980

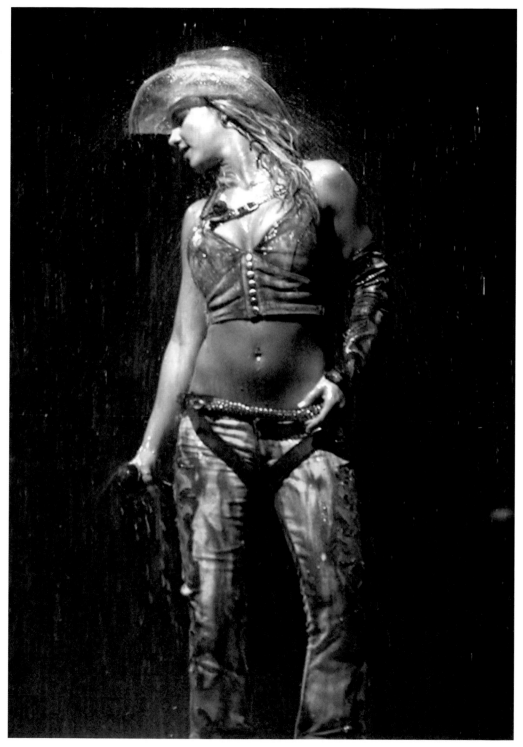

Britney Spears, Florida, USA, 2002

Amy Winehouse, London, 2008

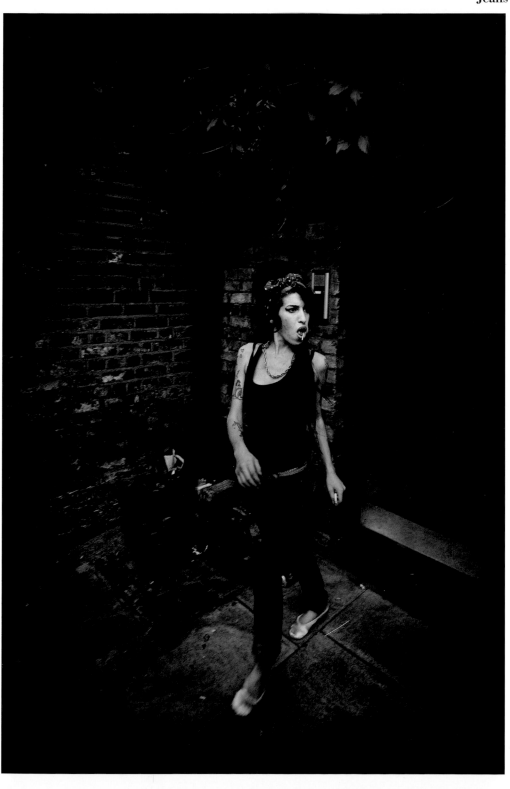

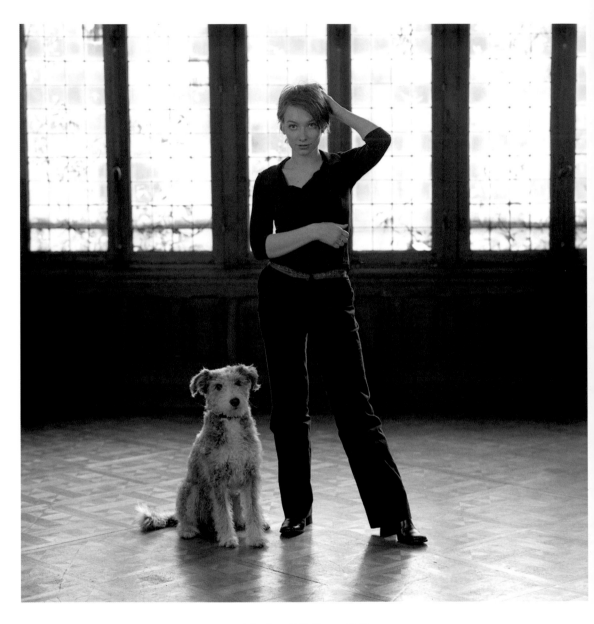

Julie-Anne Roth, France, 2002

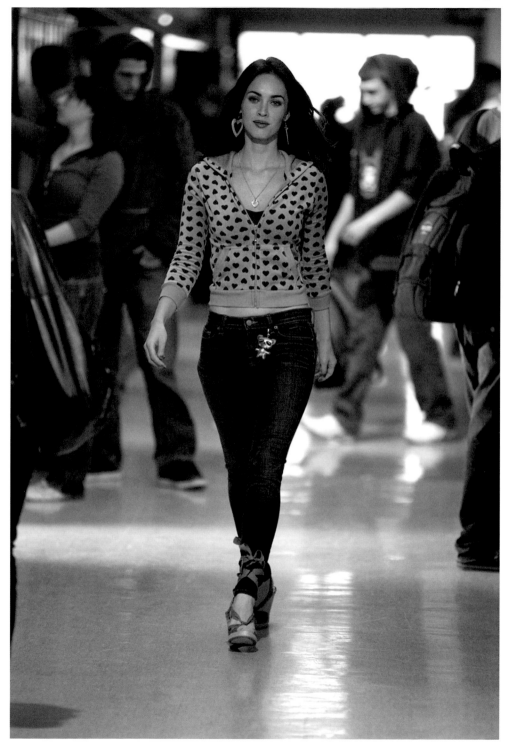

Megan Fox, *Jennifer's Body*, 2009

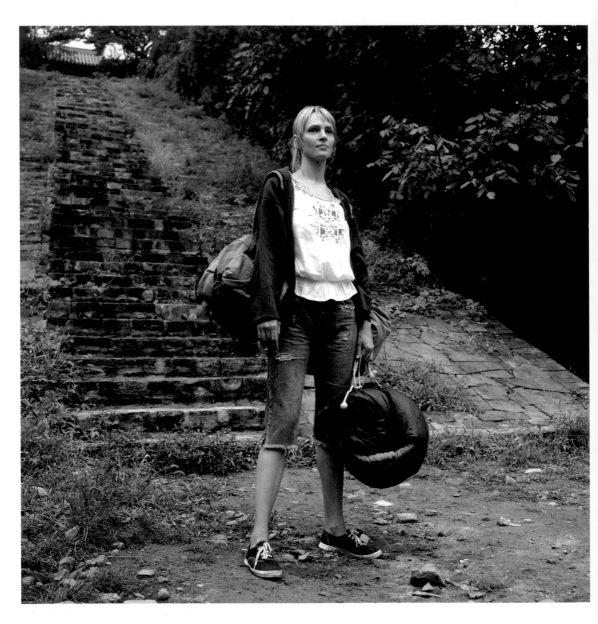

Uma Thurman, *Kill Bill: Vol. 2*, 2004

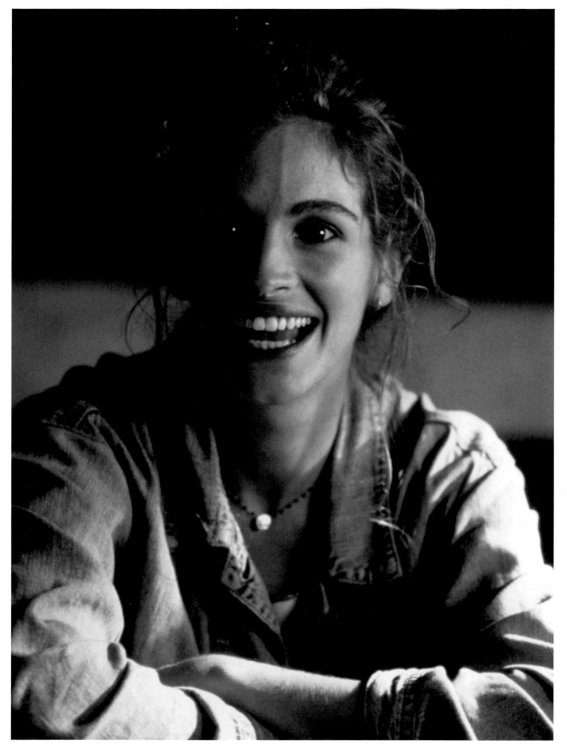

Julia Roberts, *The Pelican Brief*, 1993

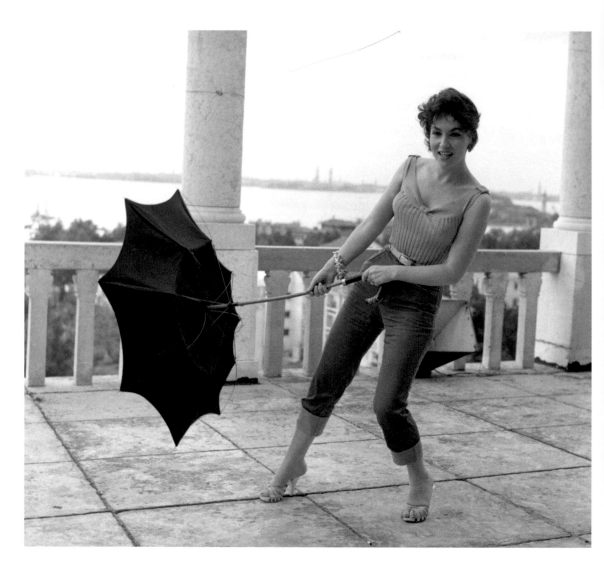

Gina Lollobrigida, Venice, 1956

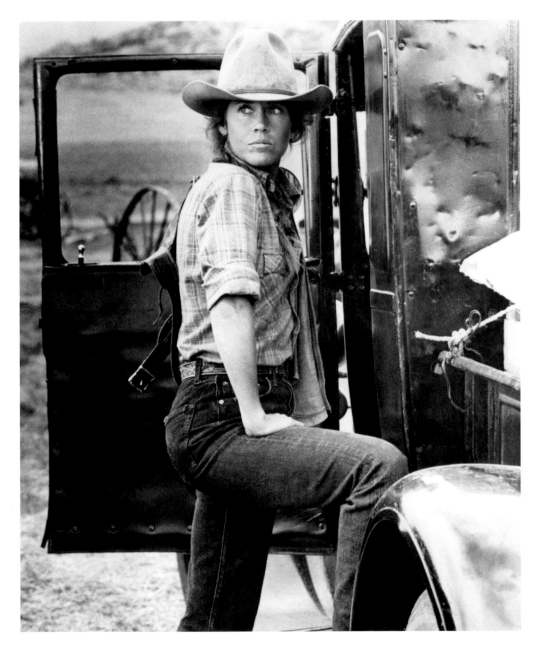

Jane Fonda, *Comes a Horseman*, 1978

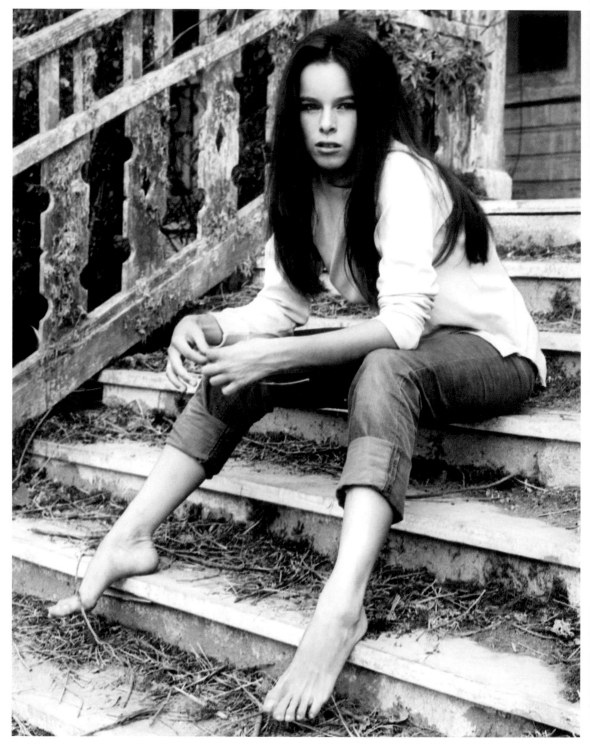

Geraldine Chaplin, backstage during the filming of *Doctor Zhivago*, 1965

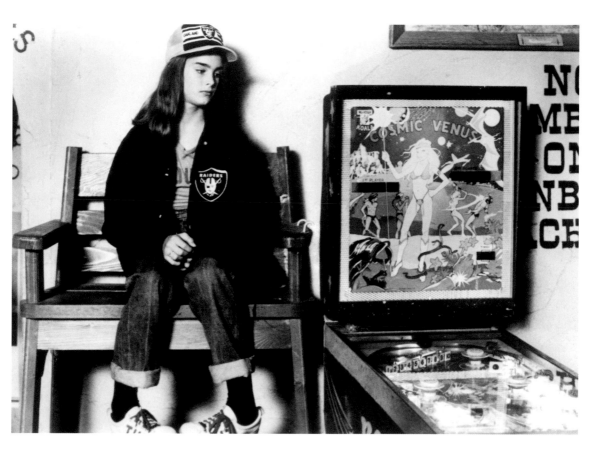

Brooke Shields, *Tilt*, 1979

Rosanna Arquette,
Paris, 2002

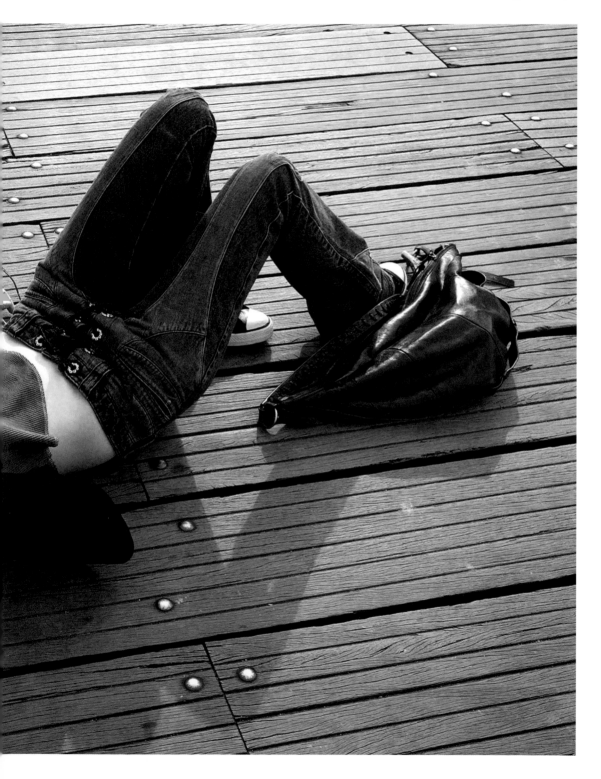

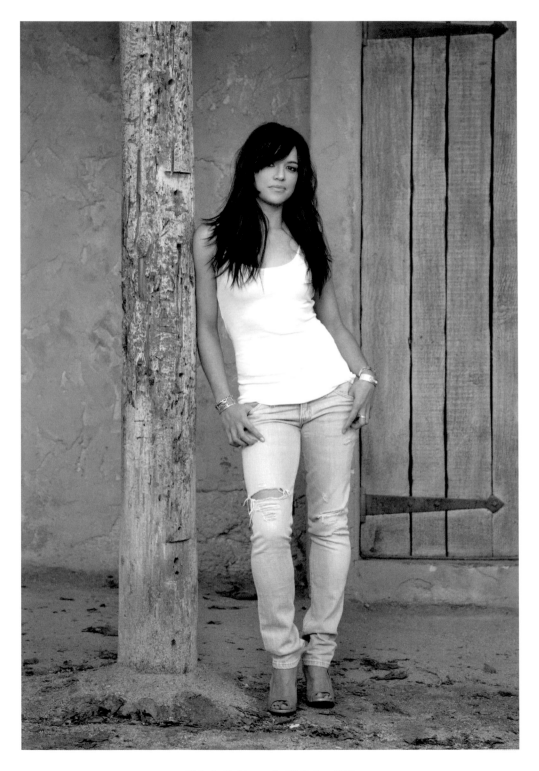

Michelle Rodriguez, *Fast & Furious*, 2009

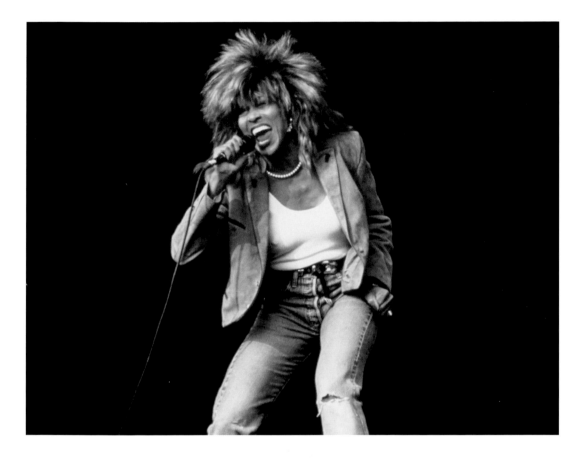

Tina Turner, 1980

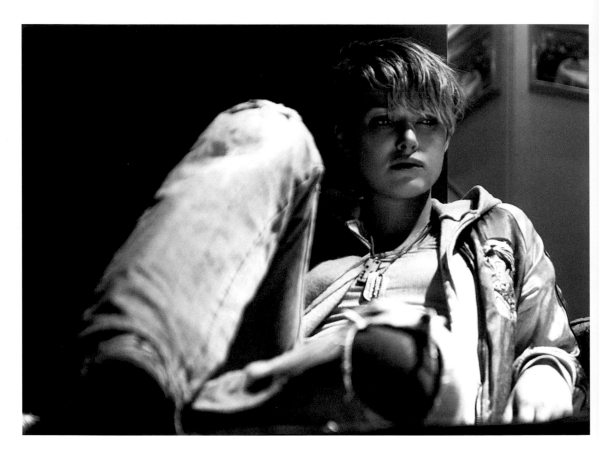

Keira Knightley, *Domino*, 2005

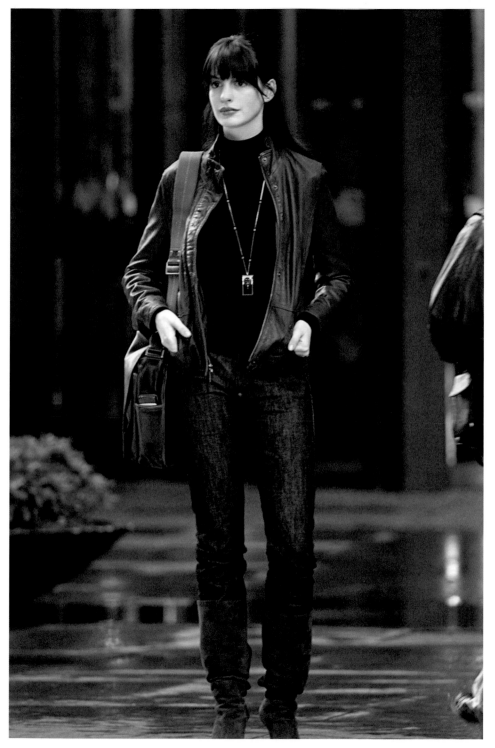

Anne Hathaway, *The Devil Wears Prada*, 2006

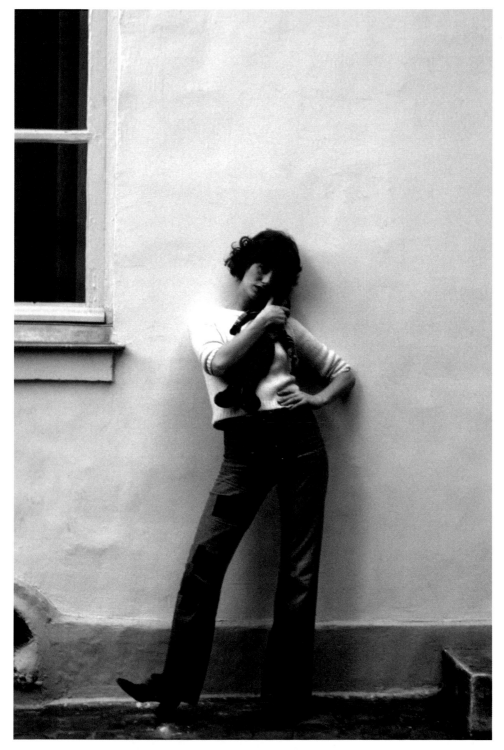

Jane Birkin, *Histoire de Melody Nelson*, 1971

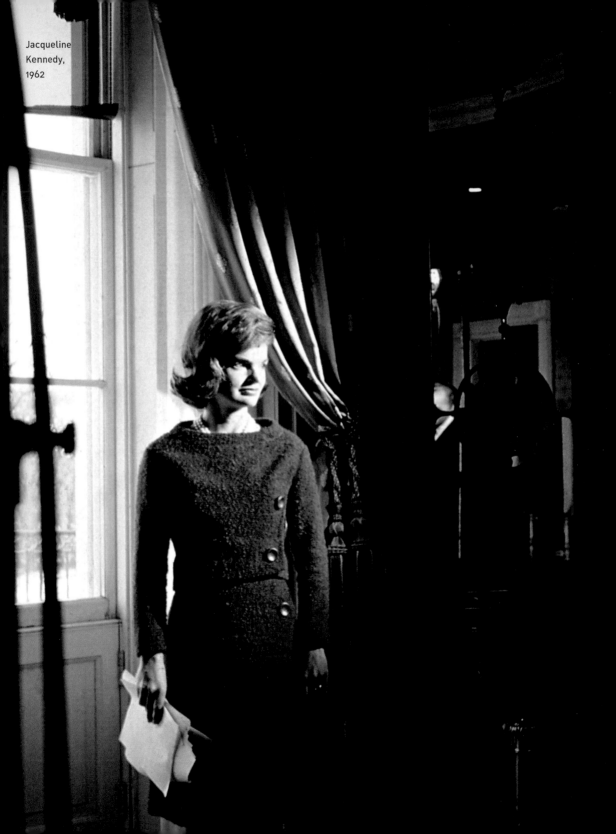

Jacqueline
Kennedy,
1962

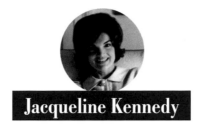

Jacqueline Kennedy

The Suit

With two black suits and three white blouses – one for the morning, one for the afternoon and one for the evening – any woman could conquer the world and the heart of the one she loves, and remain forever elegant.

COCO CHANEL

Icon Jacqueline Kennedy
Designers John Redfern, Coco Chanel
Film *Boccaccio '70: 'The Job'*, Luchino Visconti, 1962

Jacqueline Kennedy
at the White House, 1960

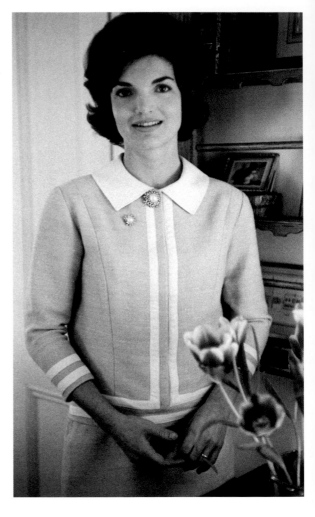

No suit in the world has remained imprinted on our collective memory more than the pink suit with blue lapels which Jacqueline Kennedy wore on 22 November 1963, the day that her husband, President John F. Kennedy, was assassinated in Dallas as he sat beside her in an open-top limousine, waving to the crowds as their motorcade passed through the city.

Jackie Kennedy was only thirty-three years old when she became First Lady, the youngest the USA had ever had. In contrast with her predecessor at the White House, she epitomized a sophisticated style that influenced women around the world. She was assisted in this by European designers such as Givenchy and Chanel, and especially Oleg Cassini, a French-born Russian–American couturier and playboy who was already famous for having transformed Grace Kelly into a creature of sinuous and refined elegance. Even before Jackie met Cassini, an instinct for apparently simple dressing with impeccable detailing, beautiful fabrics and perfect tailoring was already part of her DNA. She was naturally aristocratic; Cassini called her 'a geometric goddess', and designed hundreds of versions of the tailored suit with a boxy jacket and straight skirt for her. Buttons were the only decoration allowed.

During her first telephone call to the stylist on the day after her husband's election, Jackie is said to have asked for designs 'that I would wear if Jack were President of France.' Even today, she is still the archetype for modern First Ladies all over the world. The current leader in this regard is an Italian: Madame Sarkozy, formerly known as Carla Bruni, who, as chance would have it, *is* the wife of the President of France.

The two-piece suit itself is perhaps the most far-reaching addition to the wardrobe of modern stylish women. This classic pairing of jacket and skirt or jacket and trousers is perpetually elegant and refined, and can appear either formal or sporty depending on what it's worn with.

When it was first invented, the strict cut of a ladies' suit meant that it could only be made by a gentlemen's tailor; thus it was originally known as a 'tailor-made'. The great English tailor John Redfern is reputed to have created the first tailor-made in 1885 for Alexandra, the Princess of Wales. But it was Gabrielle 'Coco' Chanel who turned the suit into a uniform for working women. As her clients wanted to feel correctly dressed at all times but were not always able to change outfits, she developed a less formal version of the tailor-made, exchanging the traditional fabrics for soft tweed, and using

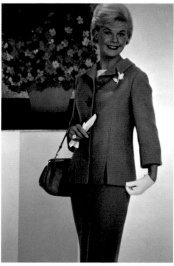

Doris Day,
Lover Come Back,
1961

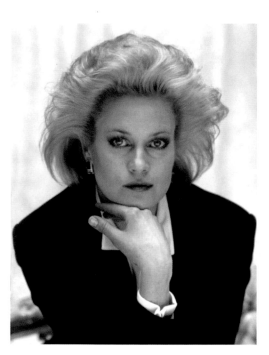

Melanie Griffith, *Working Girl*, 1988

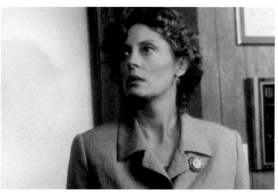

Susan Sarandon, *The Client*, 1994

gold buttons and chains as decoration. In the late 1960s, the suit revelled in its androgynous nature and subtle ambiguity when Yves Saint Laurent turned it into evening wear. Paradoxically pigeonholed as conservative in the decade that followed, it was only with Giorgio Armani that the suit became the essential element in every woman's wardrobe which had needed a new item of clothing in a post-feminist world where women could now take their place in the boardrooms of power. The new 'power suit' became a symbol of female authority. At the movies, it was worn by Sigourney Weaver in *Working Girl* (Mike Nichols, 1988), where she played the boss of the downtrodden Melanie

Griffith, by Glenn Close in *Fatal Attraction* (Adrian Lyne, 1987), by Susan Sarandon when she played a lawyer in *The Client* (Joel Schumacher, 1994) and by Meryl Streep in the role of the slave-driving magazine editor in *The Devil Wears Prada* (David Frankel, 2006).

The suit has come a long way from the candy-coloured ensembles worn by Doris Day, or the bourgeois primness of Romy Schneider's outfits in Luchino Visconti's segment of *Boccaccio '70* (1962). Indeed, it has led countless lives. The basic combination of a jacket, shirt and skirt is still a classic but can always break the rules, creating an infinite number of new looks and variations.

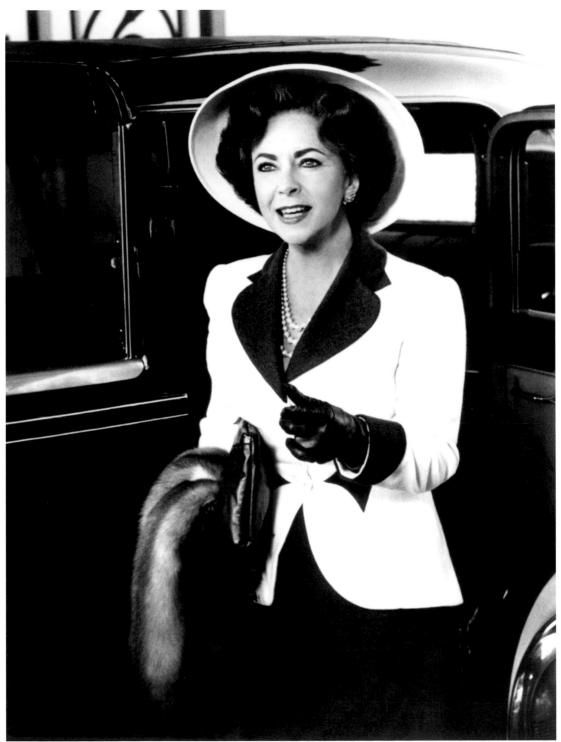

Elizabeth Taylor, *Malice in Wonderland*, 1985

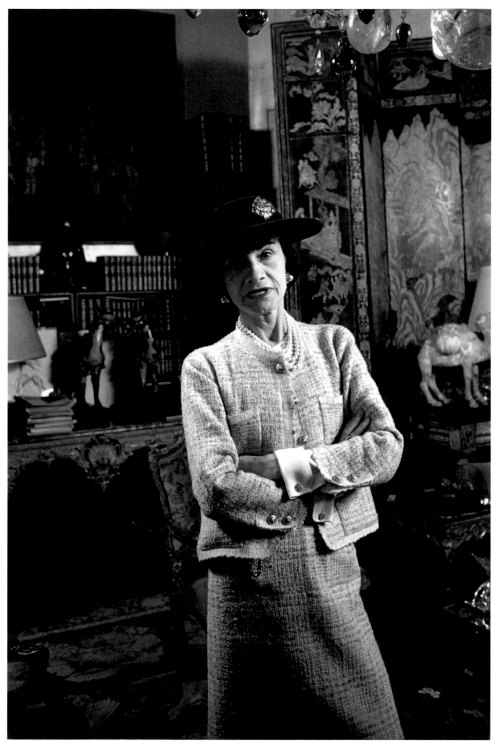

Coco Chanel, Paris, 1960s

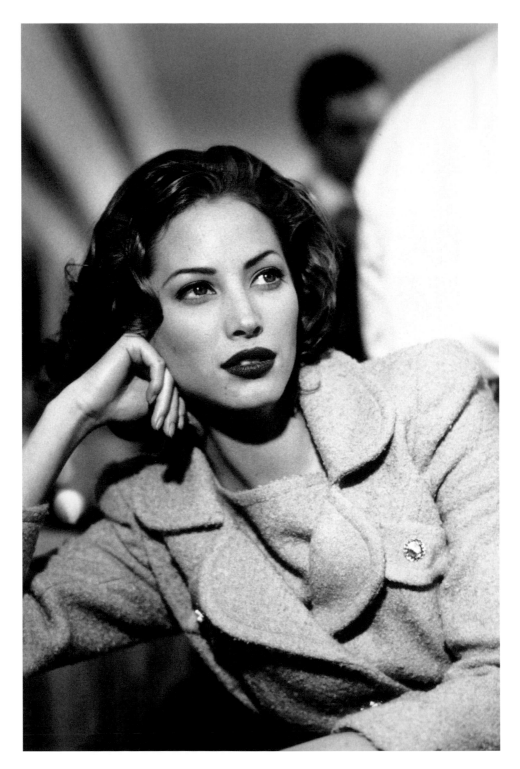

Christy Turlington, 2003

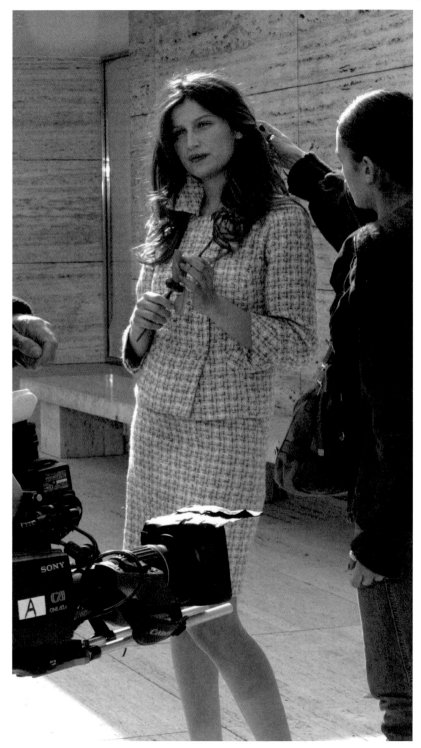

Laetitia Casta, 2004

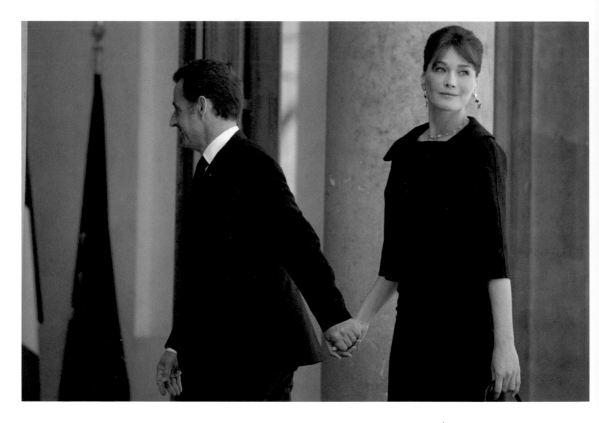

Nicolas Sarkozy, President of France, and his wife Carla Bruni-Sarkozy, Palais de l'Élysée, Paris, 2008

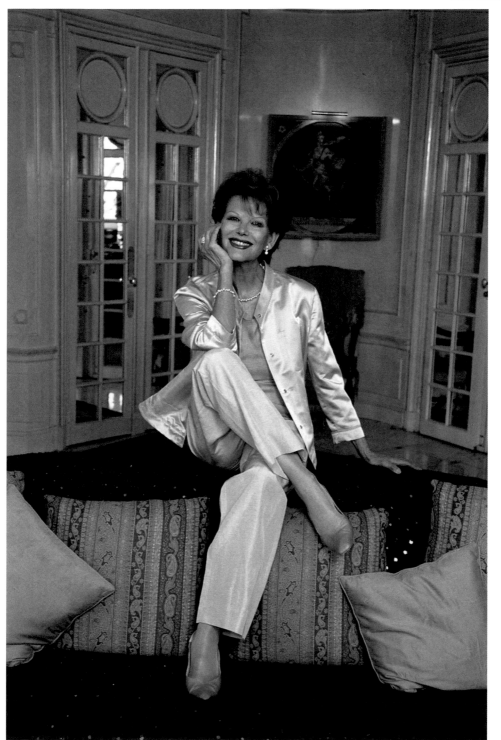

Claudia Cardinale, Rome, 2010

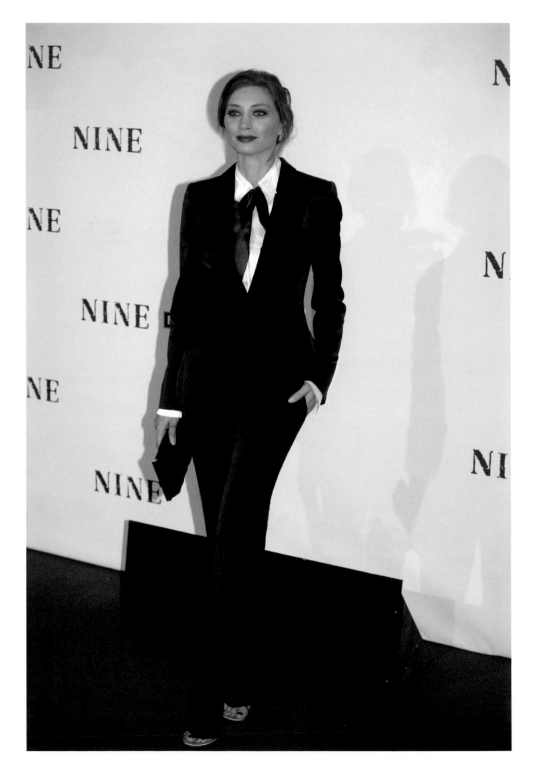

Margareth Mad, Rome, 2010

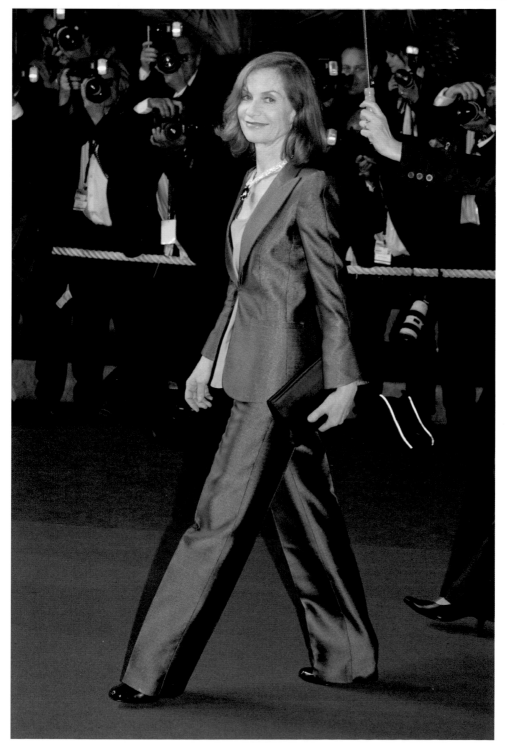

Isabelle Huppert, Cannes, 2009

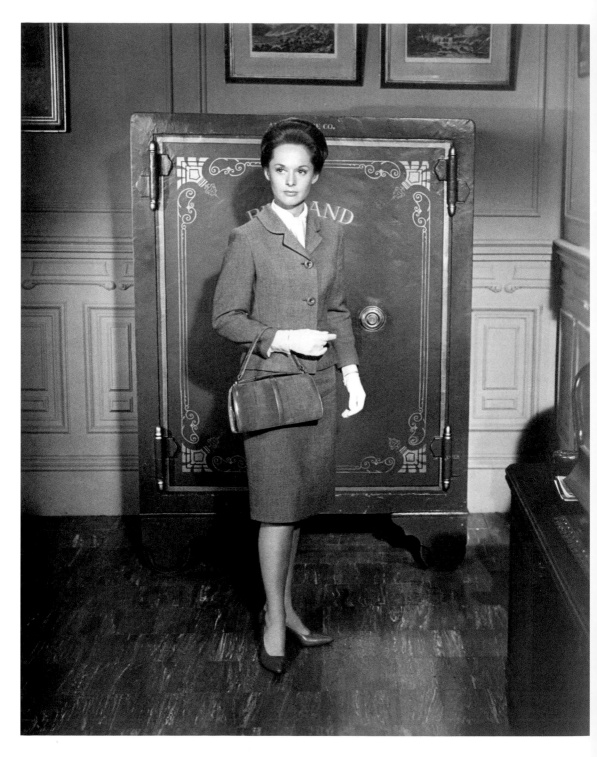

Tippi Hedren, *Marnie*, 1964

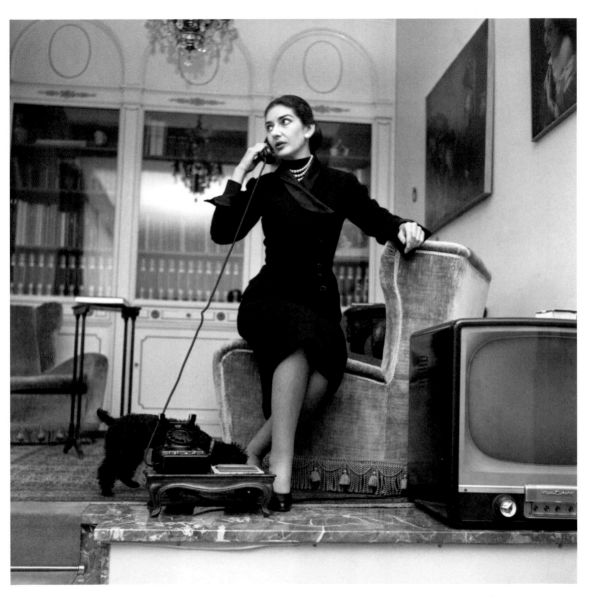

The soprano Maria Callas at home, Milan, 1956

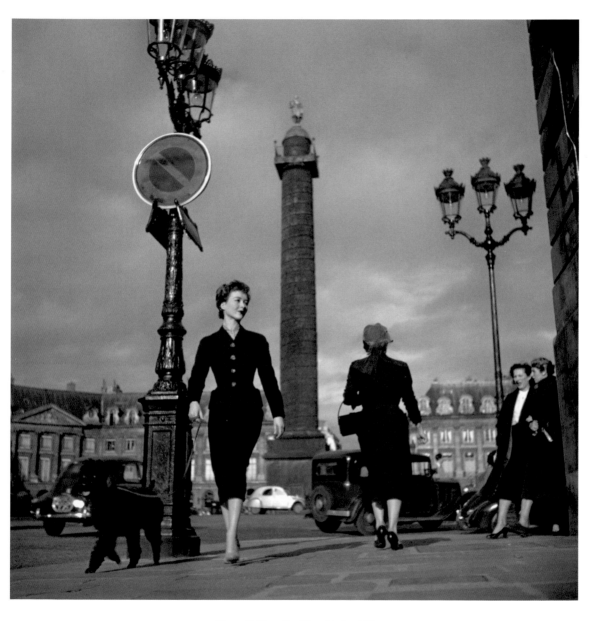

Dior suit, Place Vendôme, Paris, 1948

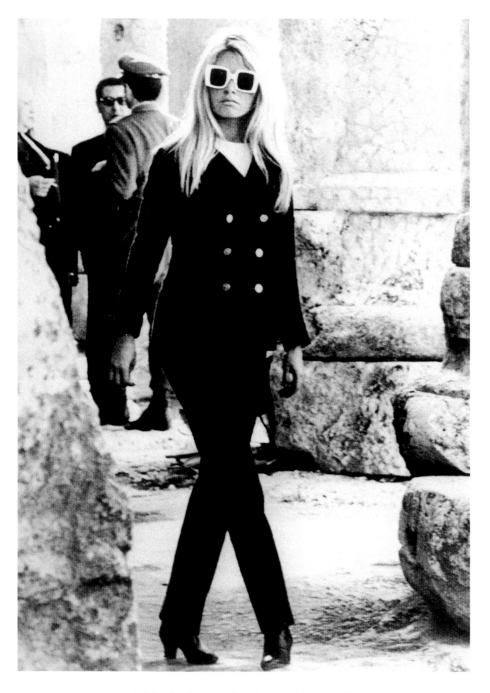

Brigitte Bardot in Yves Saint Laurent, Lebanon, 1967

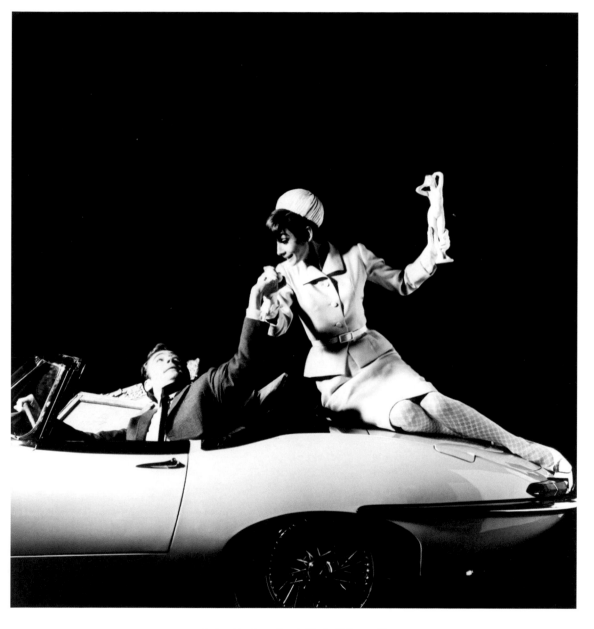

Audrey Hepburn, *How to Steal a Million*, 1966

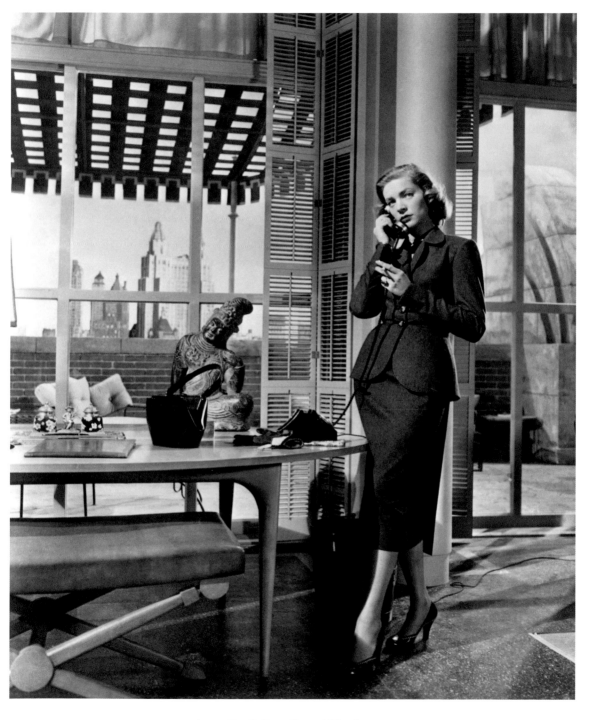

Lauren Bacall, *How to Marry a Millionaire*, 1953

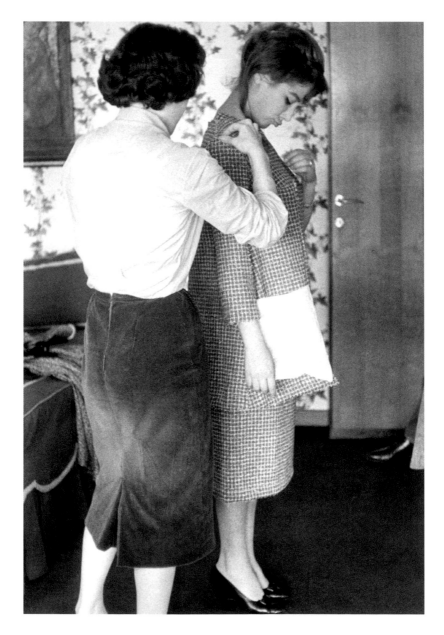

Cosetta Greco, Rome, 1959

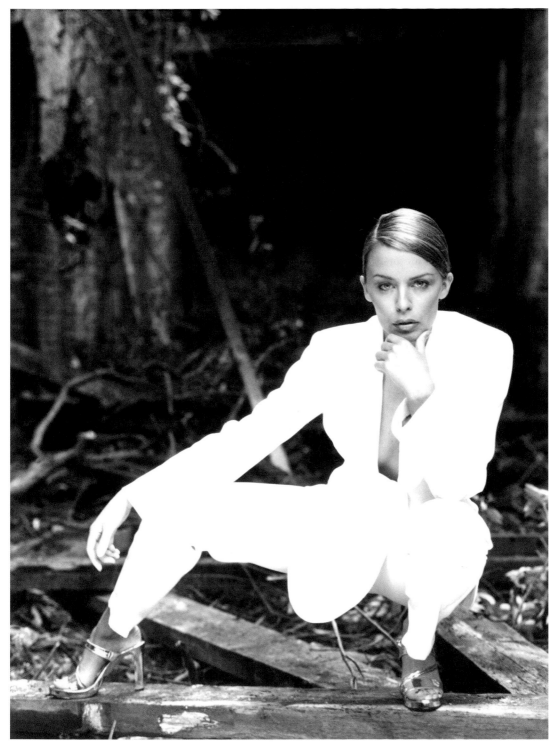

Kylie Minogue, 1990s

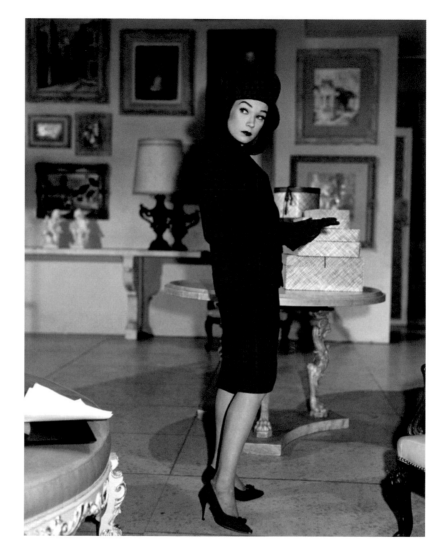

Shirley MacLaine, *What a Way to Go!*, 1964

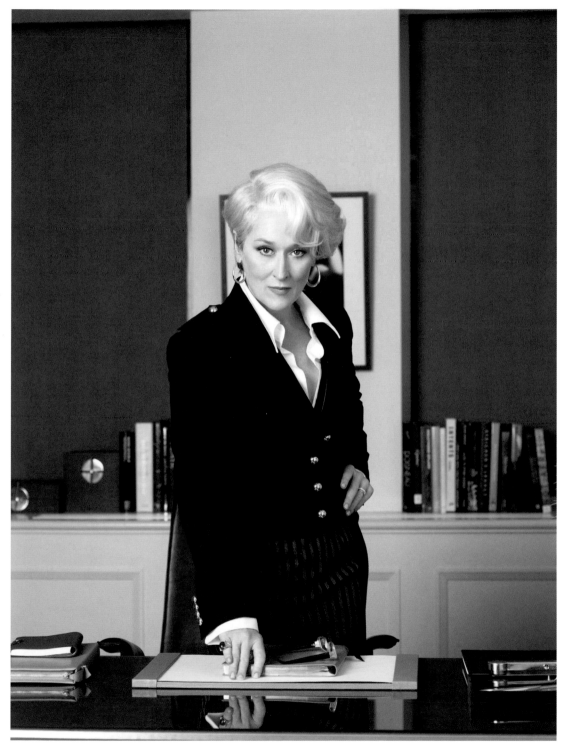

Meryl Streep, *The Devil Wears Prada*, 2006

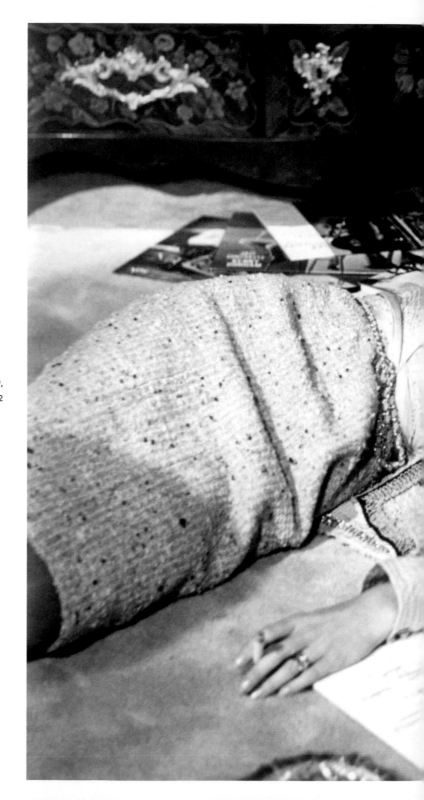

Romy Schneider, *Boccaccio '70*, 1962

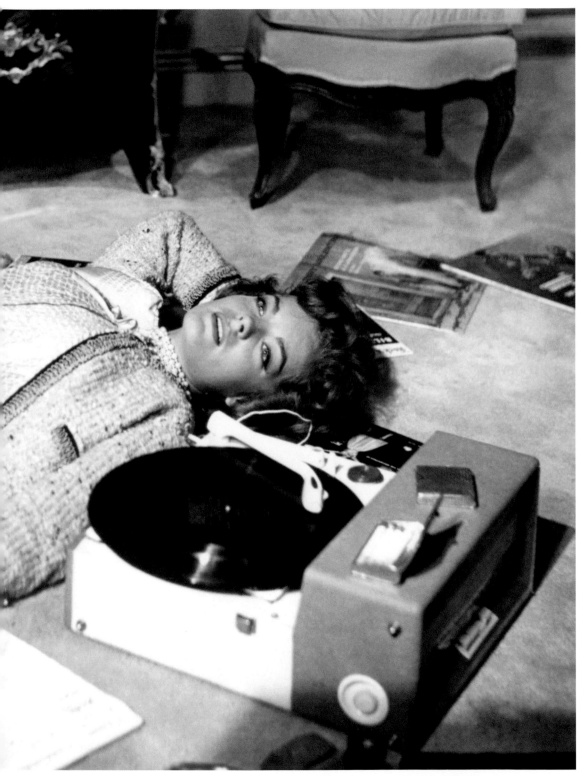

Ursula Andress, *Dr No*, 1962

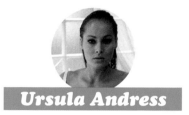

Ursula Andress

The Bikini

Statistics are like a bikini. What they reveal is suggestive,
but what they conceal is vital.

AARON LEVENSTEIN

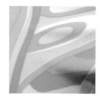

Icon Ursula Andress
Designer Louis Réard
Film *Dr No*, Terence Young, 1962

128

Ursula Andress, 1962

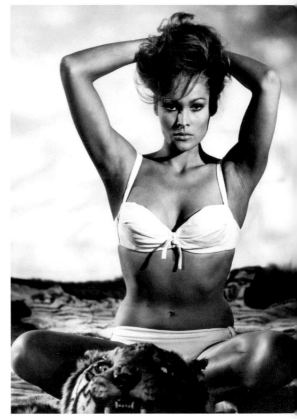

'It was the bikini that made me a star.' That's Ursula
Andress's honest explanation for her fame today,
and she makes no attempt to hide it. Indeed,
how could she hide anything in such a costume?
That bikini became legendary, and in 2001 it fetched
£35,000 at auction in London. The scene in which
Bond girl Honey Ryder emerges out of the ocean
to seduce Sean Connery as Agent 007 in *Dr No*
(Terence Young, 1962) has such an erotic charge that
it was recreated in *Die Another Day* (Lee Tamahori,
2002) when Halle Berry stepped out of the ocean
in a similar bikini to seduce 007, played this time
by Pierce Brosnan.

It is hard to believe that in 1951 competitors
in the Miss World beauty pageant were forbidden
to wear bikinis, for fear of offending the public.
Decency is still a hurdle today: in the USA, the trailer
for the film *Into the Blue* (John Stockwell, 2005)
was digitally manipulated to make Jessica Alba's
bikini less skimpy and to ensure that no laws were
infringed. Not bad for a garment that first appeared
during Roman times, but which in its current form
has a precise date of birth: 1946. This was the year
when the French designer Louis Réard invented
it and named it after Bikini Atoll in the Marshall
Islands where the USA was conducting nuclear tests.
Réard predicted that this new type of swimsuit would
have an explosive, even devastating effect, and he
was right. His version is a refinement of work of
Jacques Heim who, two months earlier, had
introduced the 'Atome' (so called because of its tiny
dimensions) which was advertised as the smallest
bathing suit in the world. Réard's version was smaller
still, but at first he could not find a model who
would dare to wear it. Eventually he hired Micheline
Bernardini, a nude dancer at the Casino de Paris,
as a model. He wanted the bikini to become a part

of everyday life, but he lit a fuse that provoked
outrage from the churches and conservative
members of society. It took another fifteen years
for the bikini to be accepted in the USA.

Brigitte Bardot in Roger Vadim's 1956 movie
And God Created Woman, followed by the hit song
'Itsy Bitsy Teenie Weenie Yellow Polka Dot Bikini',
sung by Brian Hyland in 1960, caused a stampede
of bikini buying. In America, the bikini was
endorsed by such stars as Marilyn Monroe, Rita
Hayworth and Jayne Mansfield, the latter being
immortalized wearing one on the cover of *Life*
magazine in 1957. In the 1960s, the two-piece
outfit went mass market: *Beach Party* (William
Asher, 1963) was the first in a series of films that
made it an icon of pop culture, although its star,
Annette Funicello, did not wear a bikini herself
at the express request of Walt Disney.

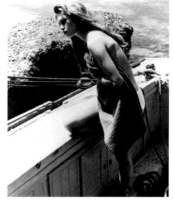

Brigitte Bardot,
And God Created Woman,
1956

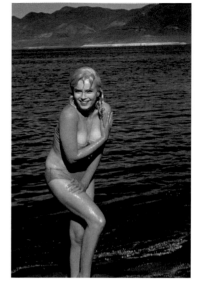

Marilyn Monroe after a
swim, Pyramid Lake,
Nevada, 1960

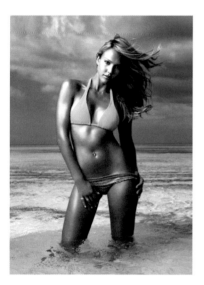

Jessica Alba,
Into the Blue,
2005

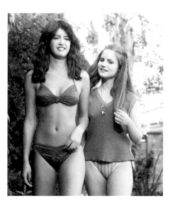

Phoebe Cates and
Jennifer Jason
Leigh, *Fast Times
at Ridgemont High*,
1982

Once the bikini had reached mainsteam acceptability, its obvious sex appeal made it a key element of many hit film and television shows, from the surf movies of the 1960s to the series *Baywatch* in the 1980s. Other bikini-wearing cinematic icons include Raquel Welch as the prehistoric heroine of the film *One Million Years B.C.* (Don Chaffey, 1966), Phoebe Cates in *Fast Times at Ridgemont High* (Amy Heckerling, 1982) and Charlize Theron in *Æon Flux* (Karyn Kusama, 2005), who wears a bikini while beating up her enemies. Although the bikini has now become *de rigeur* for television stars as well as dancers and showgirls, it should always be remembered that any woman who stands in front of a mirror and tries one on is bravely carrying out her own 'bikini test'.

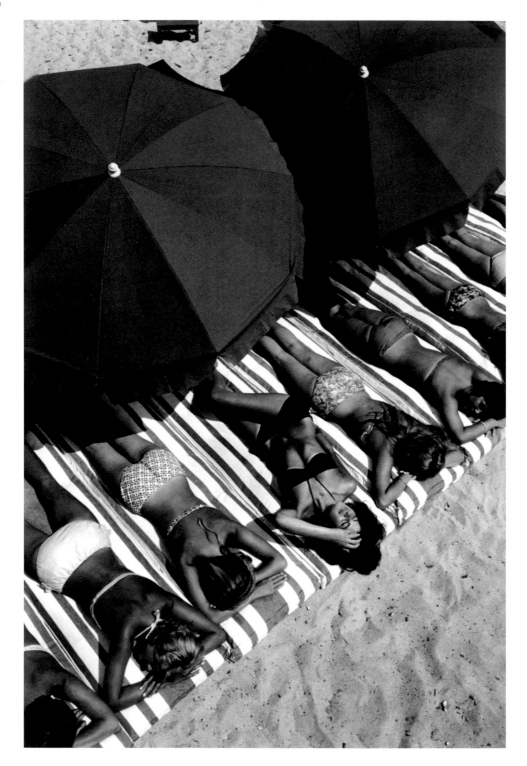

Beach in Saint-Tropez, France, 1959

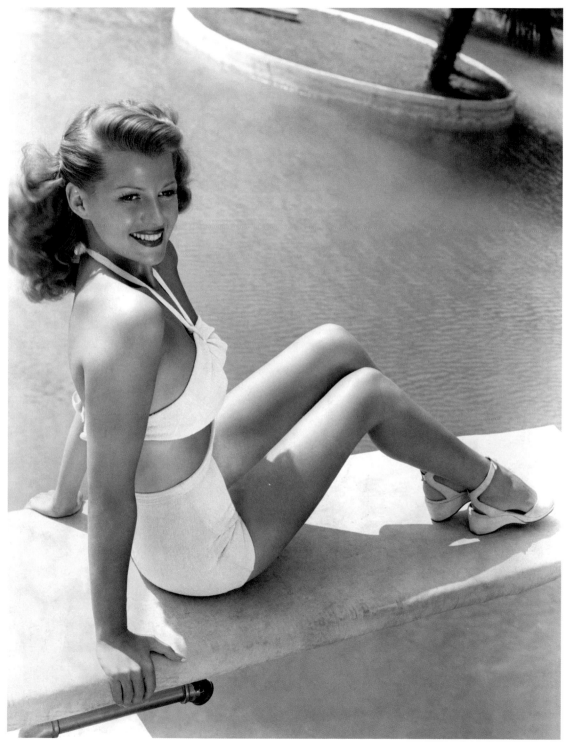

Rita Hayworth, 1947

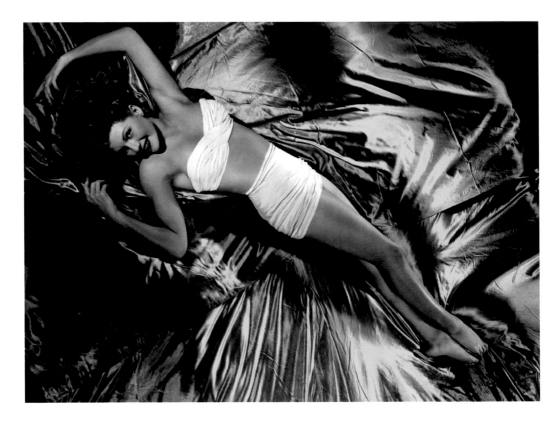

Rita Hayworth, 1940s

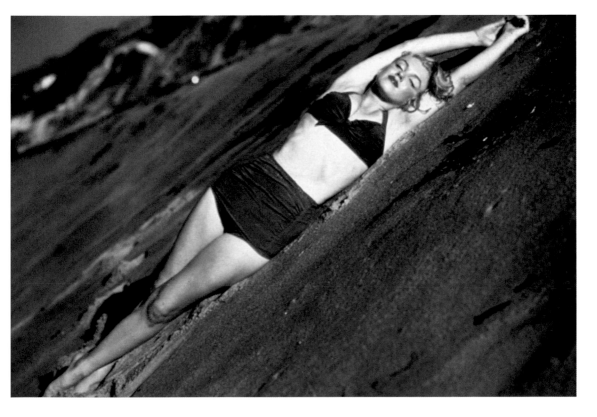

Marilyn Monroe, 1940s

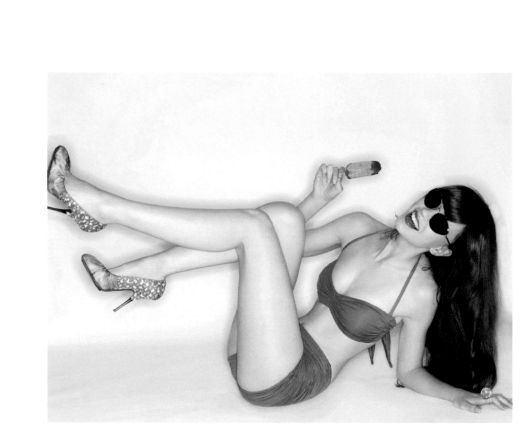

Model wearing a retro bikini, New York, 2008

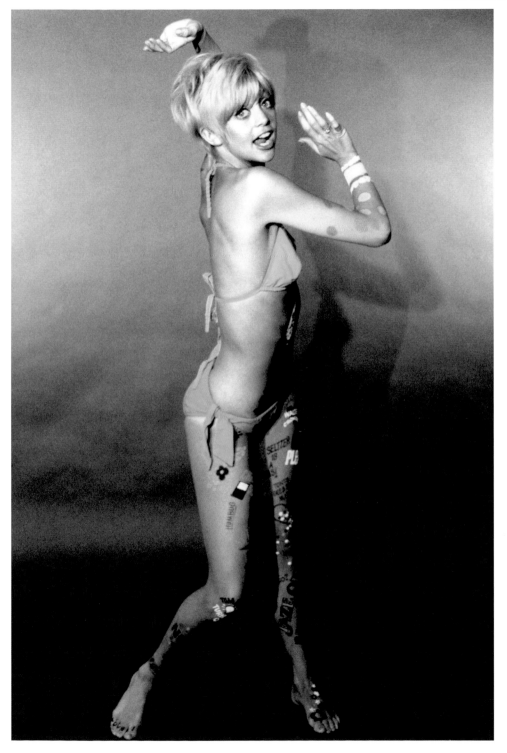

Goldie Hawn, *Rowan & Martin's Laugh-In*, 1968–70

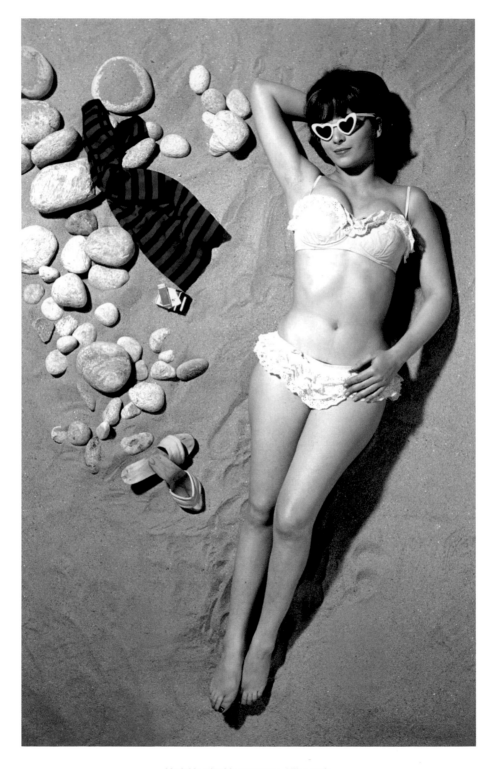

Model in a bathing costume, Milan, 1964

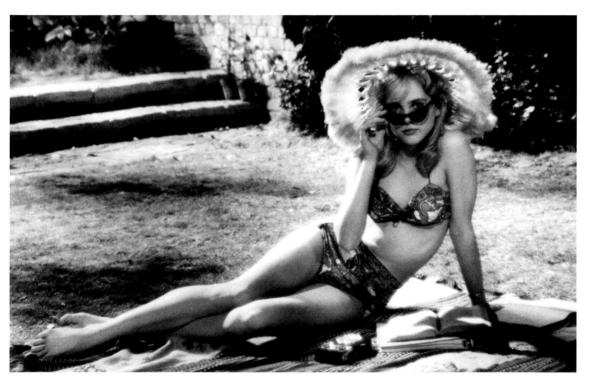

Sue Lyon, *Lolita*, 1962

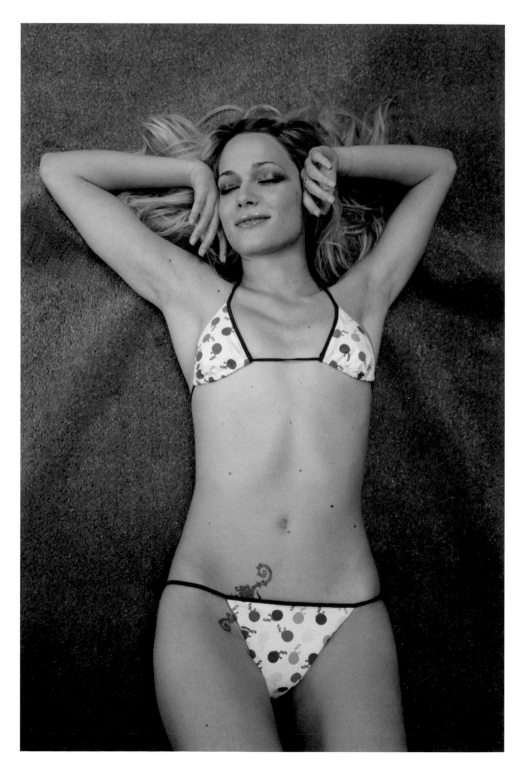

Laura Chiatti, Rome, 2006

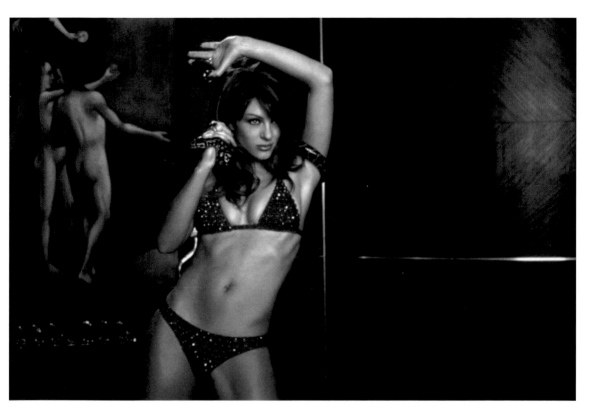

Elizabeth Hurley, *Bedazzled*, 2000

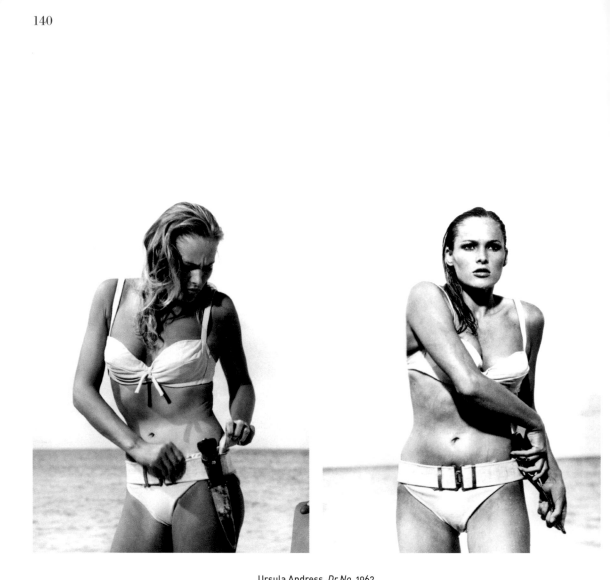

Ursula Andress, *Dr No*, 1962

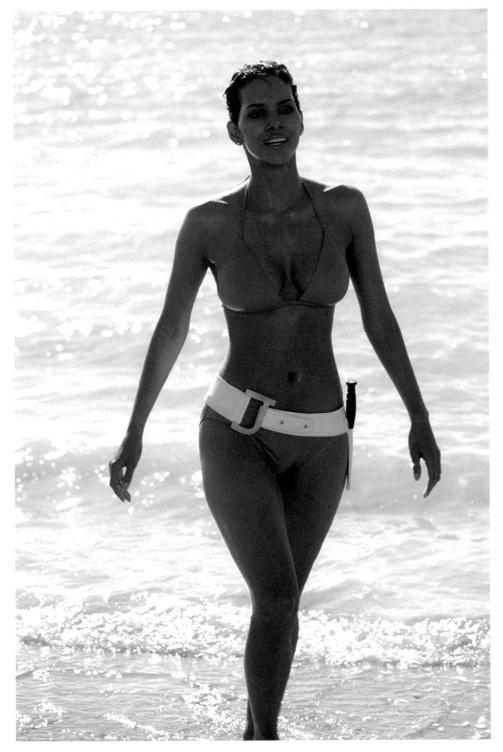

Halle Berry, *Die Another Day*, 2002

Veruschka in Richard Avedon's
studio, New York, 1966

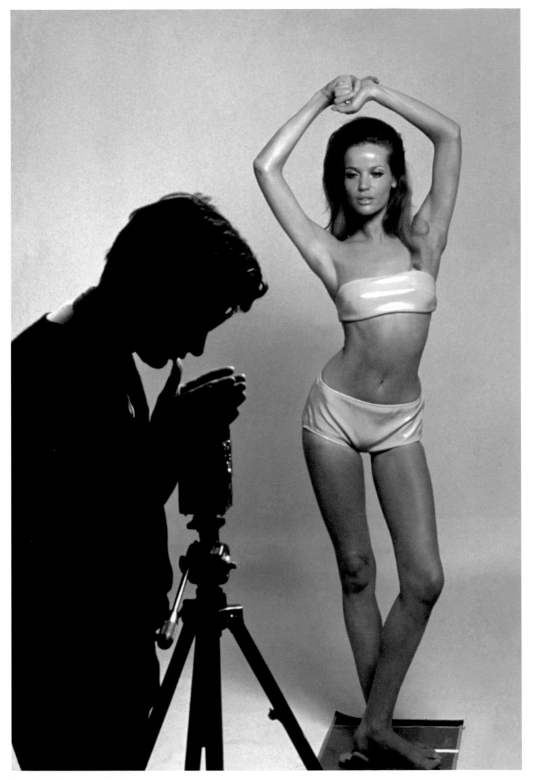

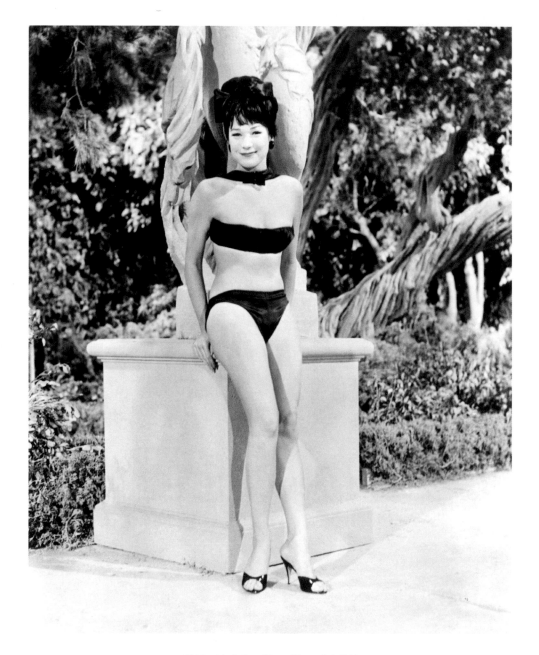

Shirley MacLaine, *What a Way to Go!*, 1964

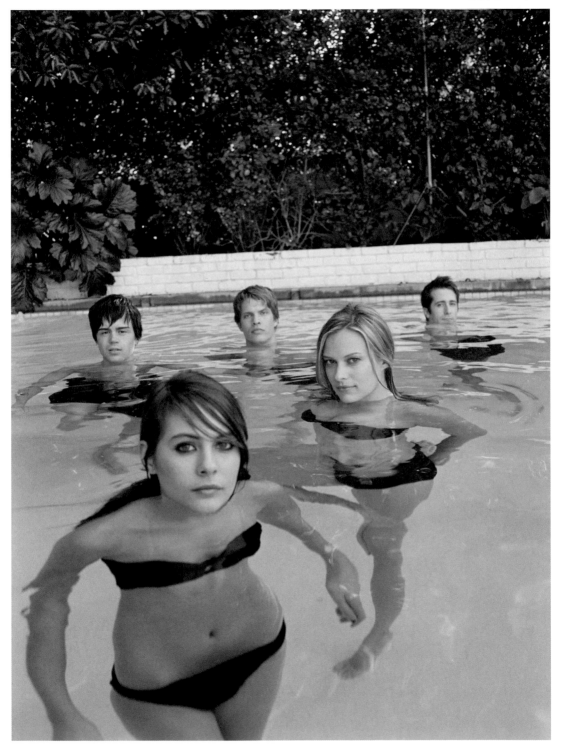

Willa Holland, Erik Smith, Alexander Cendese, Richard Gunn and Vinessa Shaw, *Garden Party*, 2008

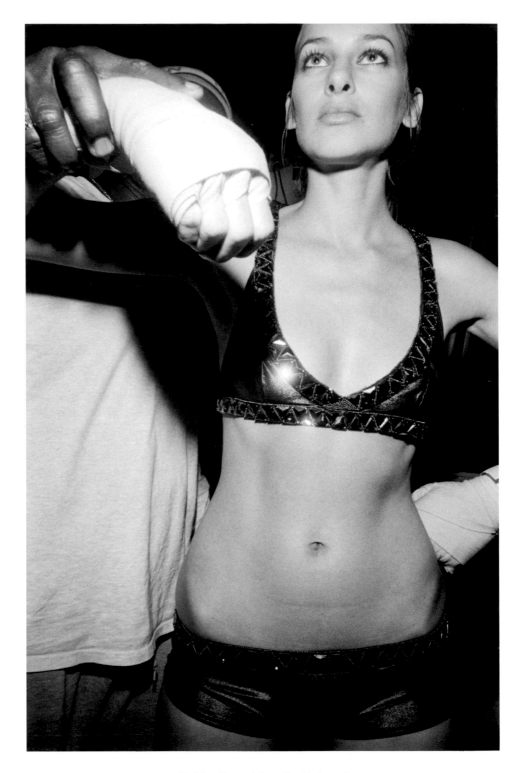

Model at Gleason's Gym, New York, 2006

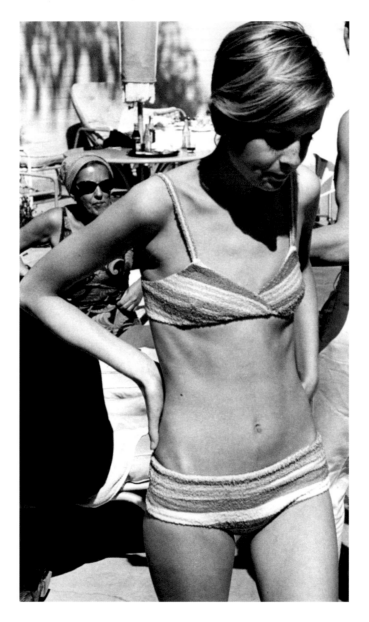

Twiggy, 1967

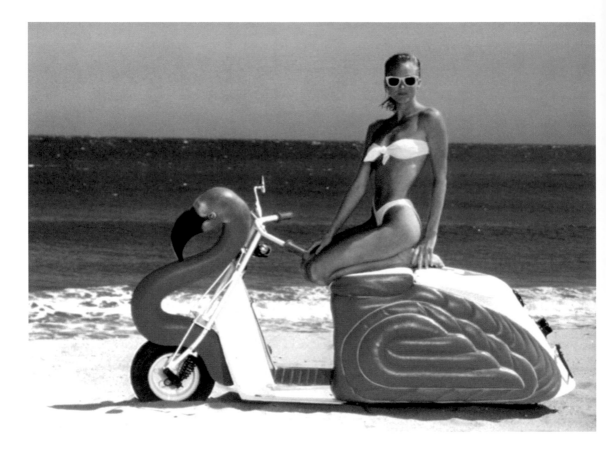

Janet Jones, *The Flamingo Kid*, 1984

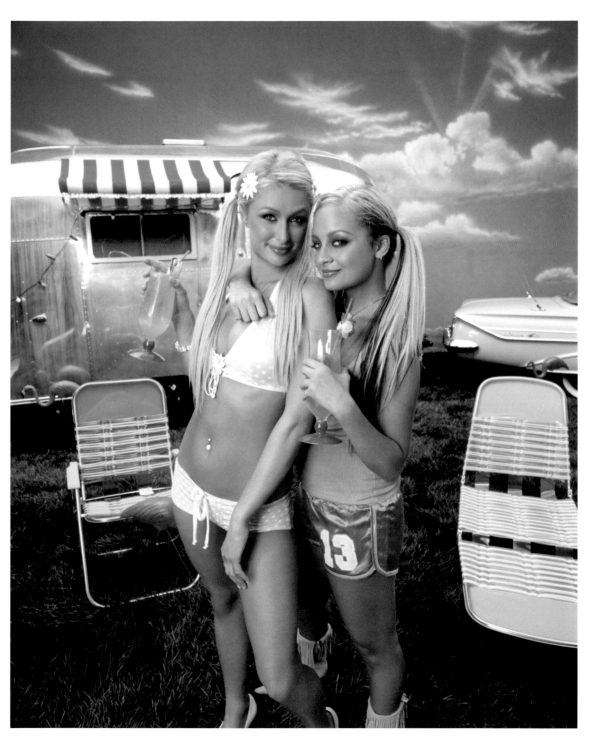

Paris Hilton and Nicole Richie, *The Simple Life*, 2004

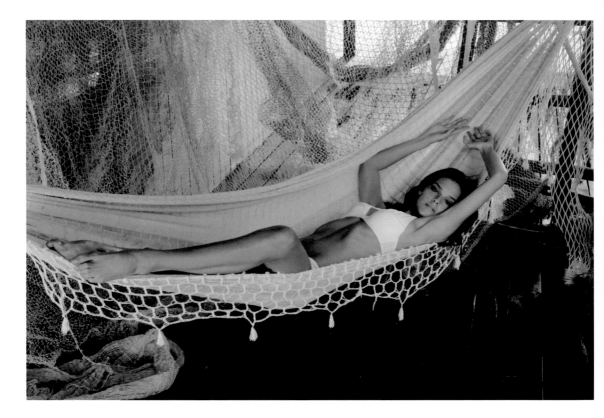

Kathy Saunders, Rome, 2008

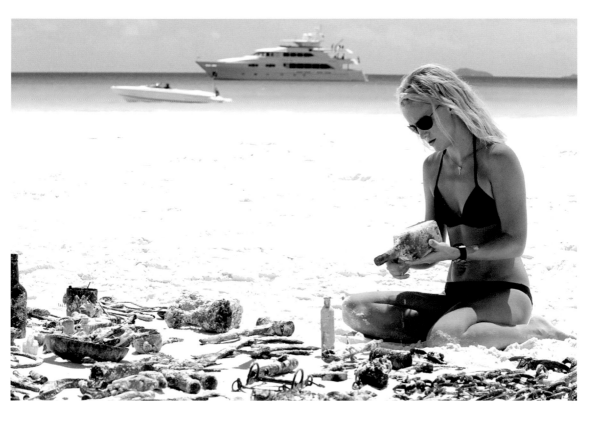

Kate Hudson, *Fool's Gold*, 2008

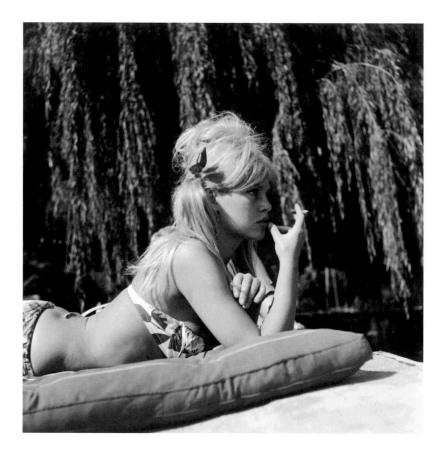

Brigitte Bardot, Spoleto, Italy, 1961

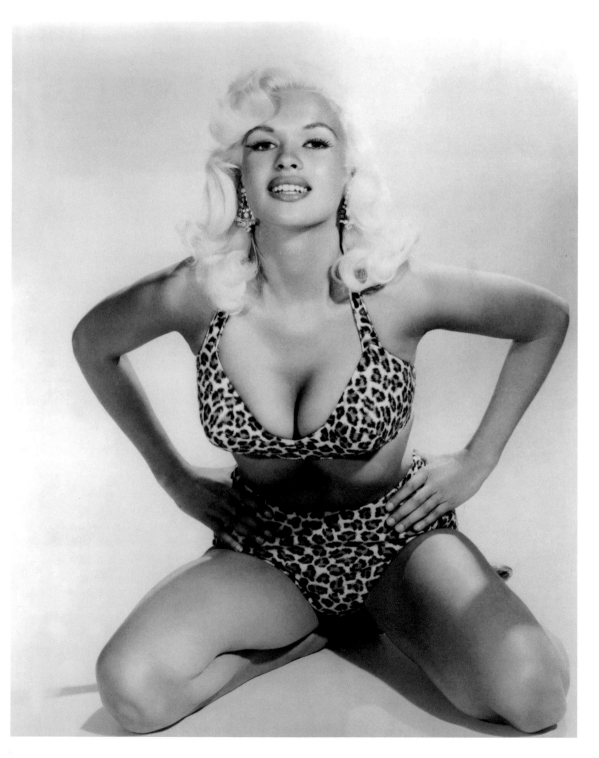

Jayne Mansfield, 1950s

Jeanne Moreau on the set of *The Sailor from Gibraltar*, 1965

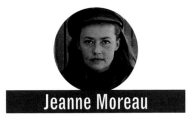

Jeanne Moreau

The Turtleneck

The black cashmere turtleneck is a perfect garment.

DAVID MAMET

Icon Jeanne Moreau
Designer Emanuel Ungaro
Film *Jules et Jim*, François Truffaut, 1962

Jeanne Moreau, *Jules et Jim*, 1962

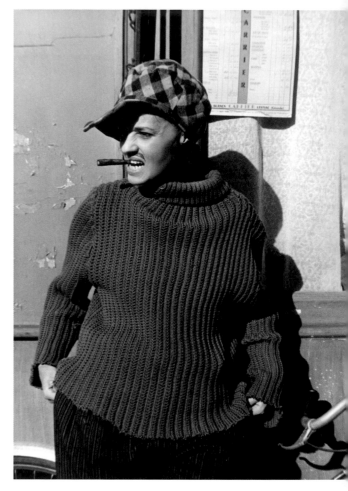

For more than thirty years, the beautiful Catherine has charmed and challenged society with her scandalous *ménage à trois*: she is equally and inextricably in love with two friends, the eponymous heroes of François Truffaut's 1962 film *Jules et Jim*. Her complicated and complex character is torn between the joy of living and the fear of dying, and this is represented by her clothes, which alternate between feminine and masculine. It is only when she is dressed as a boy and goes running with her two lovers that she feels, as do the viewers, that it is possible to be truly happy. The turtleneck pullover creates the perfect frame for actress Jeanne Moreau's fascinating, tormented and magnetic face.

A very different version of the turtleneck was popularized by the 'sweater girls' of the 1940s and 50s, who often wore it two sizes too small in order to emphasize their busts and so enhance their allure. Think of Lana Turner and Jane Russell in their signature pullovers, living advertisements for the engineering of the latest brassiere designs. According to Lou Valentino, the author of *The Films of Lana Turner*, Turner's debut in the role of a sexy student in *They Won't Forget* (Mervyn LeRoy, 1937) 'made an impact not only on her but on the sweater industry. Lana brought sweaters into vogue. Every American girl built her wardrobe around them.'

It was in the 1960s, with the advent of existentialism, that the turtleneck or polo neck – always in severe black – became part of the uniform of every self-respecting leftist intellectual, accompanied by straight-leg pants and flat-soled shoes, required wearing in the basement wine bars frequented by the readers of Jean-Paul Sartre and Albert Camus. Even Marilyn Monroe tested out this new fashion trend in her dance routine for 'My Heart Belongs to Daddy' in *Let's Make Love* (George Cukor, 1960), wearing a maxi pullover over black leggings.

Sophia Loren gave the turtleneck a classic elegance in films such as *Operation Crossbow* (Michael Anderson, 1965) and *Yesterday, Today and Tomorrow* (Vittorio De Sica, 1963), as well as in the television series *Anna*, in which she wore a very chic taupe grey pullover with a belted waist designed by

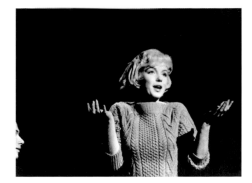

Marilyn Monroe,
Let's Make Love, 1960

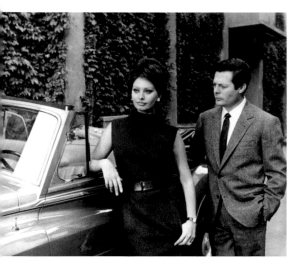

Sophia Loren and Marcello Mastroianni,
Yesterday, Today and Tomorrow, 1963

Diane Keaton, Kristin Griffith
and Marybeth Hurt, *Interiors*,
1978

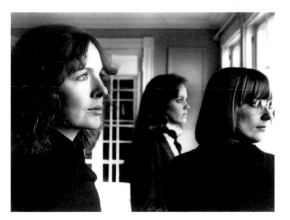

Marc Bohan for Dior. The turtleneck became the symbol of Bergmanesque family drama in Woody Allen's *Interiors* (1978), a powerful story of three sisters – all dressed in black – caught up in their parents' painful divorce. In *The Ice Storm* (Ang Lee, 1997) Sigourney Weaver wore an open-necked version of the sweater in a 1970s style, emphasizing her character's carefree attitude. When playing the difficult role of Sylvia in *The Burning Plain* (Guillermo Arriaga, 2008), it took all of Charlize Theron's innate style to give her high-necked sweater a shabby chic.

Celebrities love the turtleneck: the neck can be pulled up to hide any wrinkles; it sets off the face; and, above all, it does not distract the gaze. An evening dress may allow you to be regal for just one night, but the turtleneck can transform you into a queen every day. David Mamet has called the turtleneck 'a perfect garment', and, as his description suggests, there's no way to improve on it.

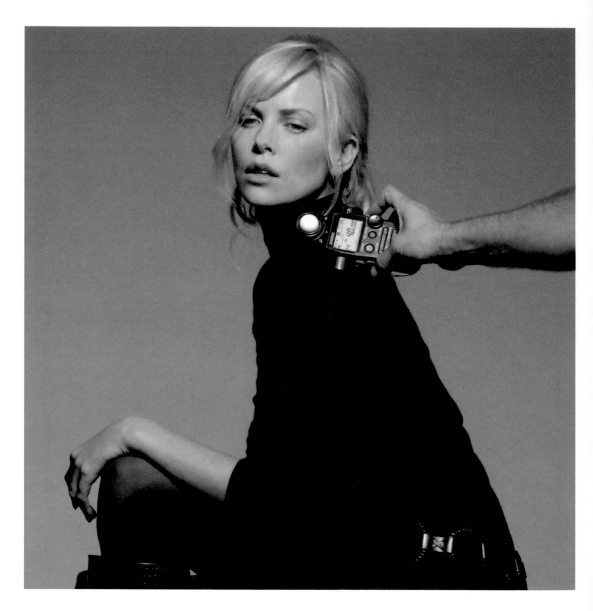

Charlize Theron, Los Angeles, 2006

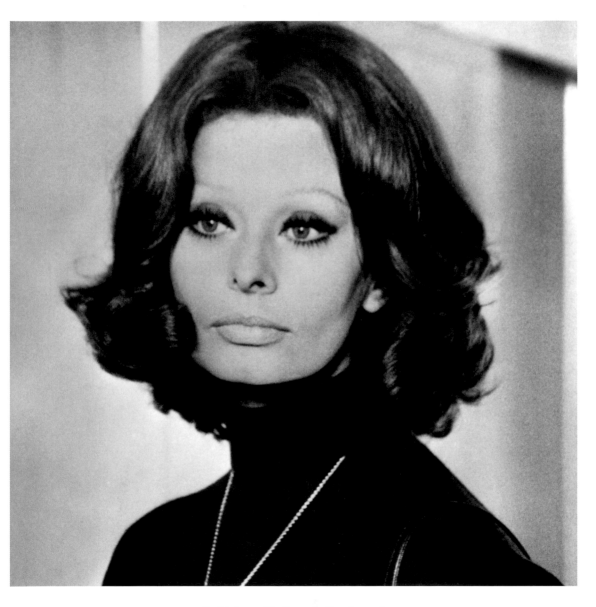

Sophia Loren, *The Cassandra Crossing*, 1976

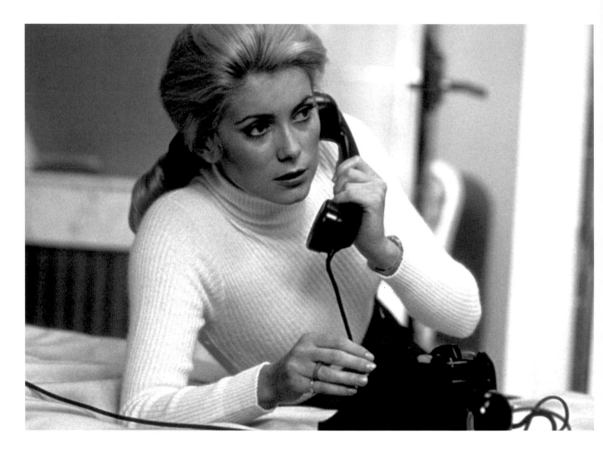

Catherine Deneuve, *La chamade*, 1968

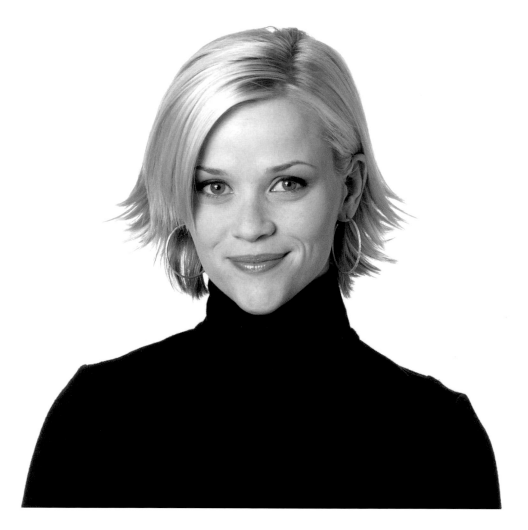

Reese Witherspoon, *Sweet Home Alabama*, 2002

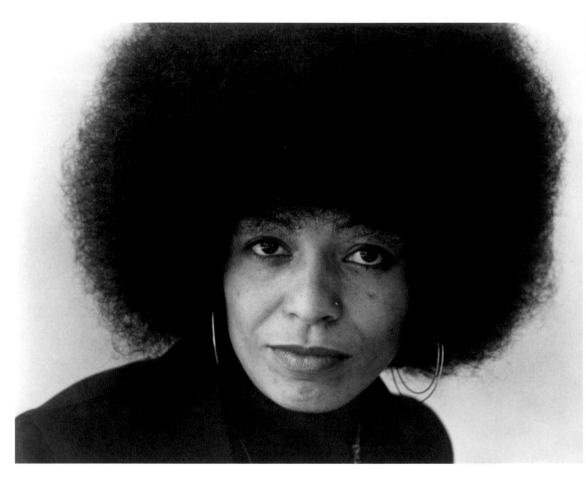

Angela Davis, 1975

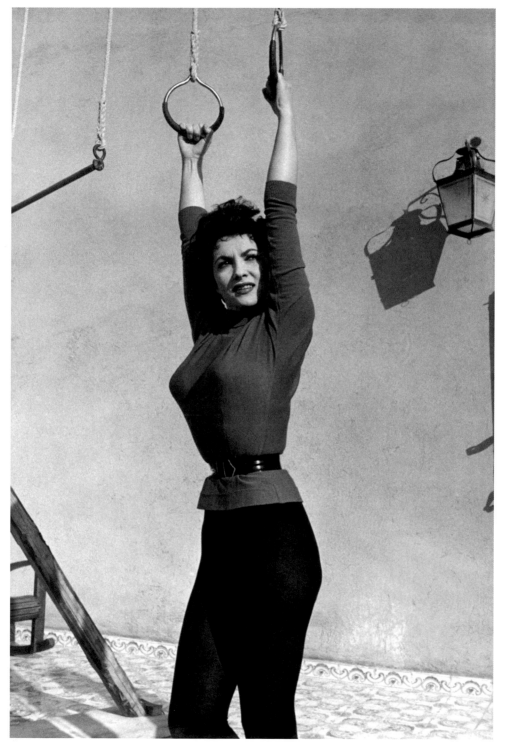

Gina Lollobrigida, Venice, 1954

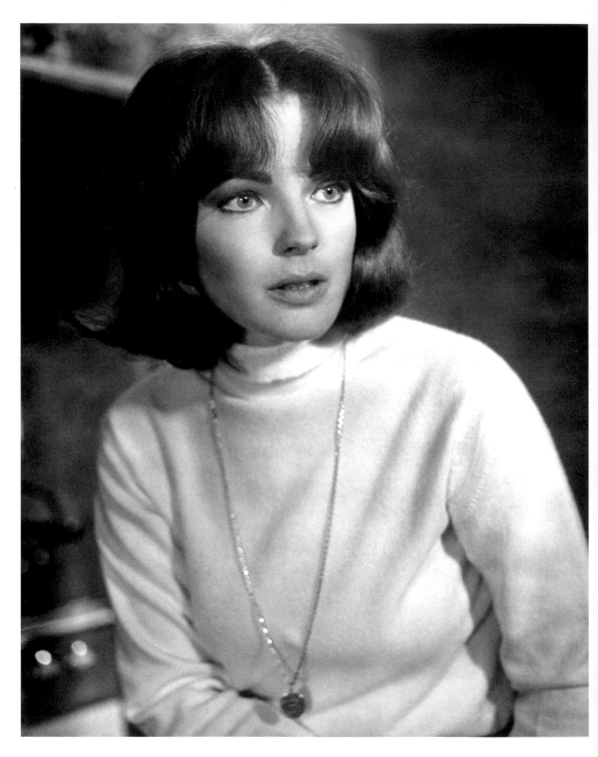

Romy Schneider, *Otley*, 1968

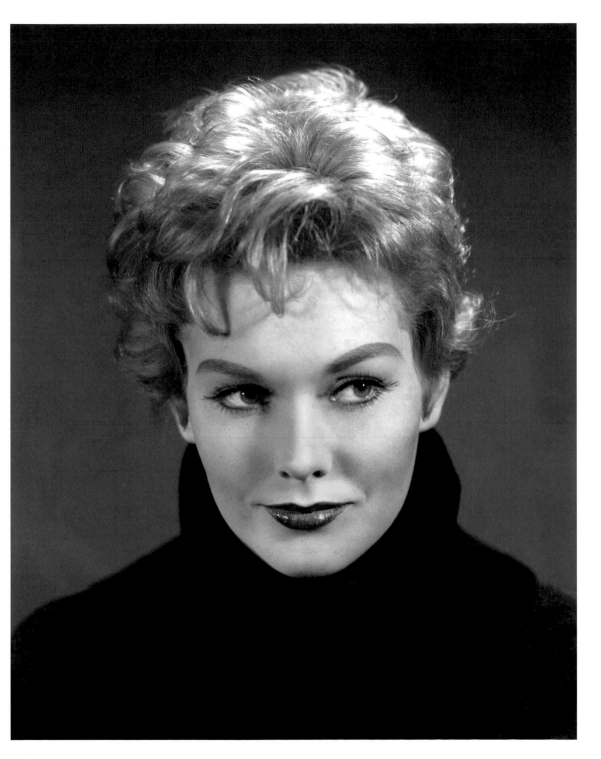

Kim Novak, 1950s

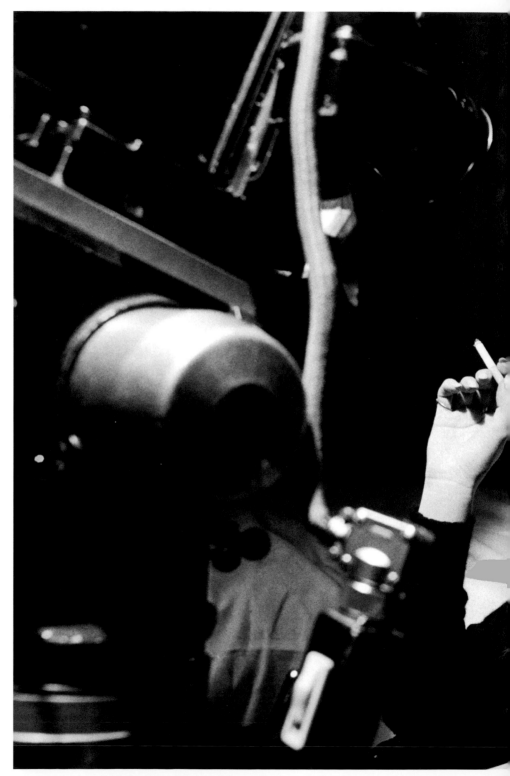

Brigitte Bardot,
Les femmes,
1969

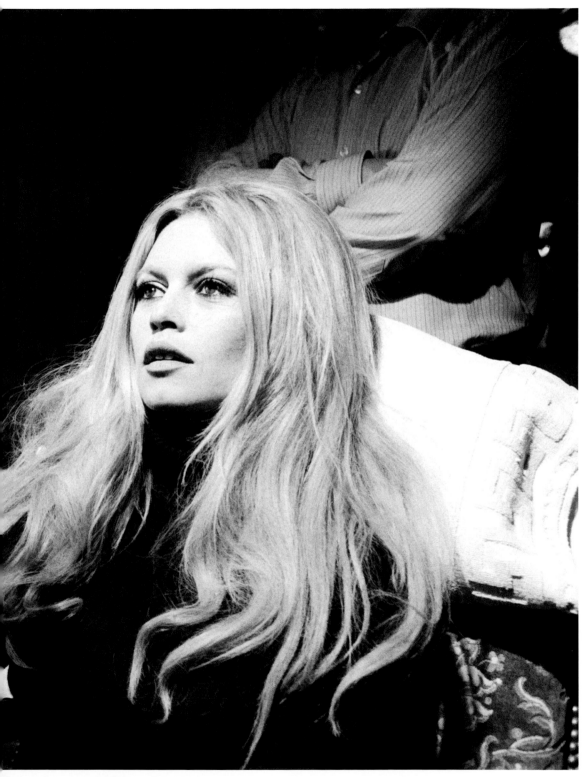

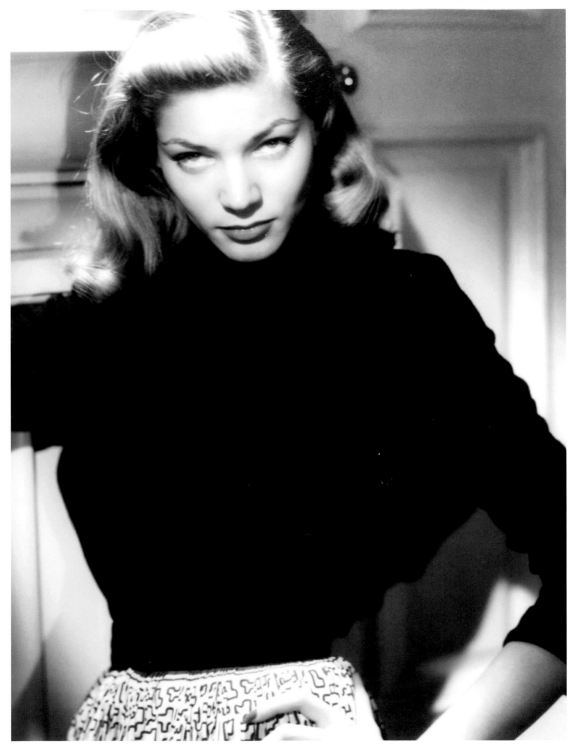

Lauren Bacall, 1950s

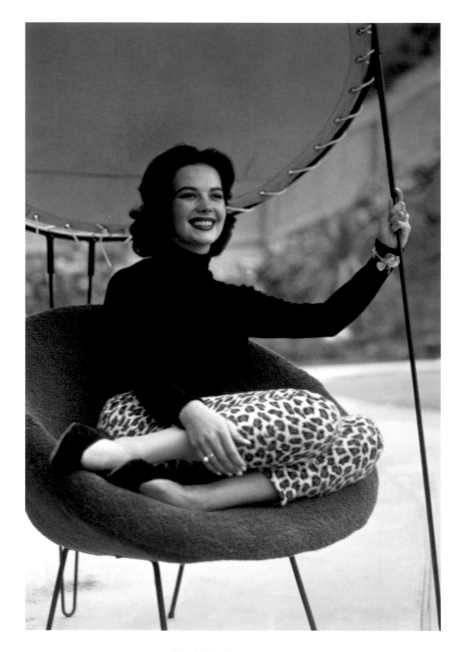

Natalie Wood at home, 1950s

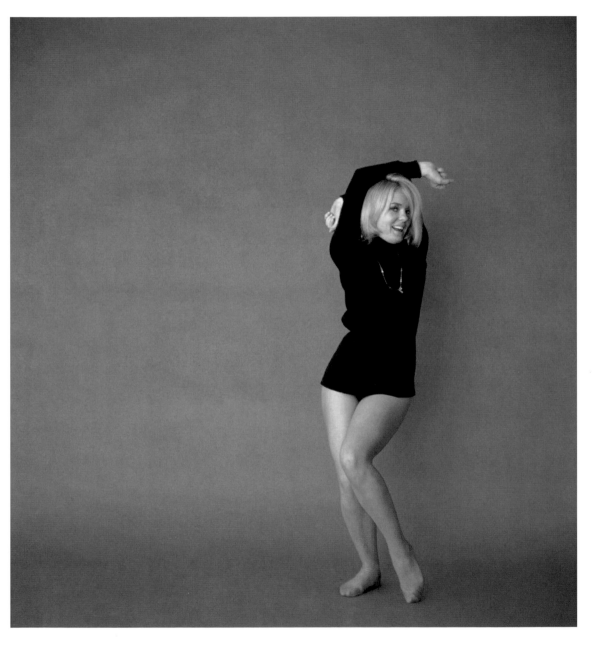

Joey Heatherton, 1960s

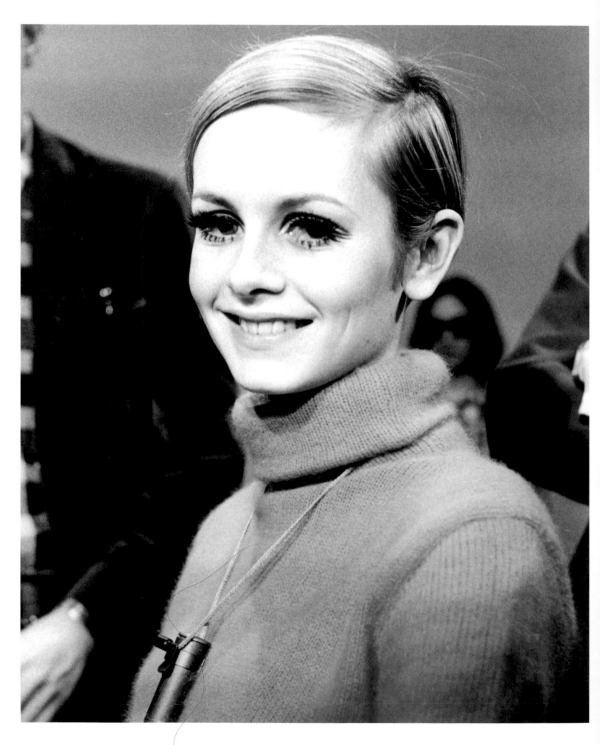

Twiggy, 1967

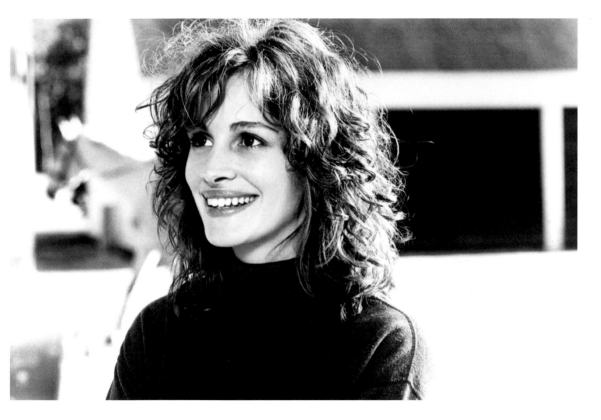

Julia Roberts, *Something to Talk About*, 1995

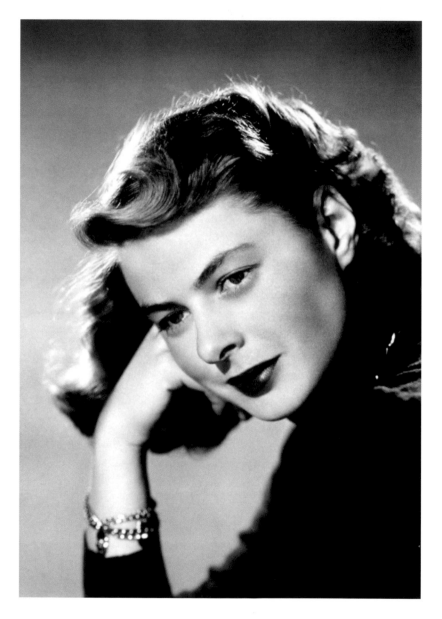

Ingrid Bergman, 1950s

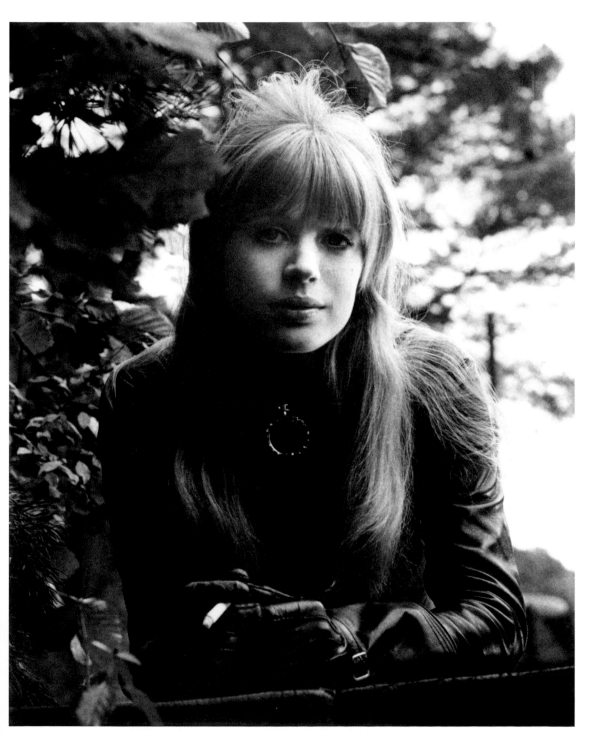

Marianne Faithfull, *Girl on a Motorcycle*, 1968

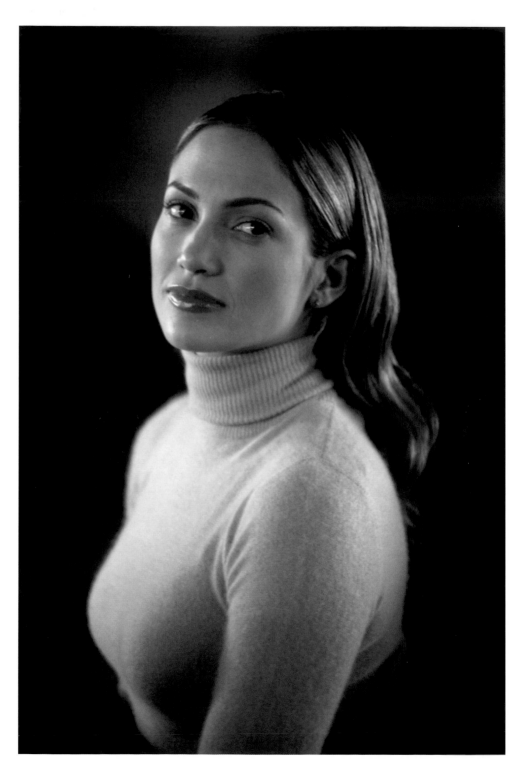

Jennifer Lopez, *The Wedding Planner*, 2001

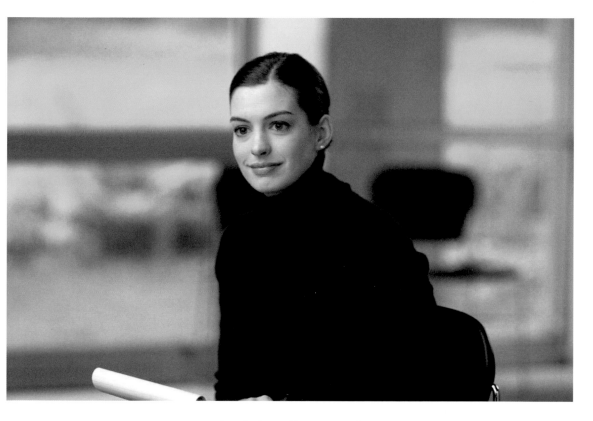

Anne Hathaway, *Passengers*, 2008

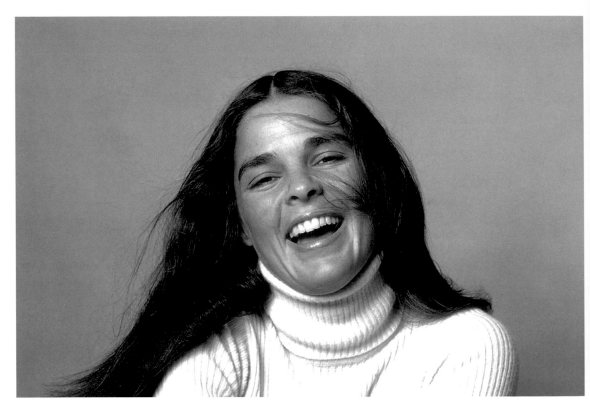

Ali MacGraw, *Love Story*, 1970

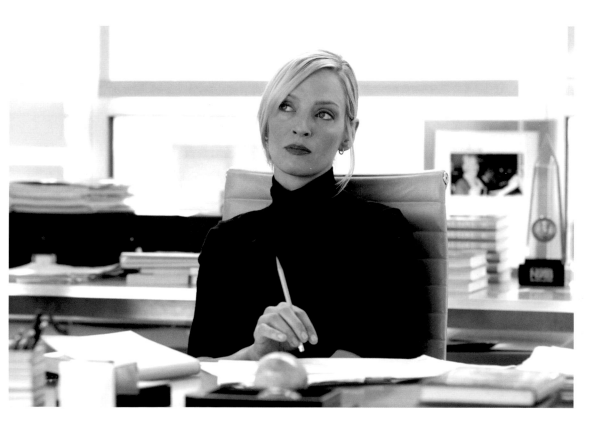

Uma Thurman, *The Accidental Husband*, 2008

Audrey Hepburn during filming of
Sabrina, 1954

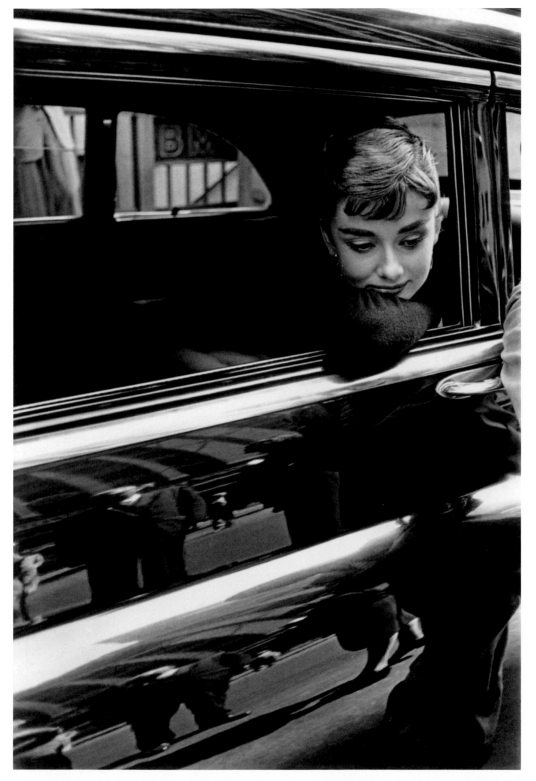

Silvana Mangano, *Bitter Rice*, 1949

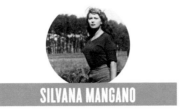

SILVANA MANGANO

Hot Pants

Hot pants, hey hot pants
Hot pants, smokin' that hot pants
That's where it's at
And that's where it's at
Take your fine self home
It looks much better than time
My fever keeps growin'
Girl you're blowin' my mind.

JAMES BROWN, 'HOT PANTS'

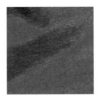

Icon Silvana Mangano
Designer Betsey Johnson
Film *Bitter Rice*, Giuseppe De Santis, 1949

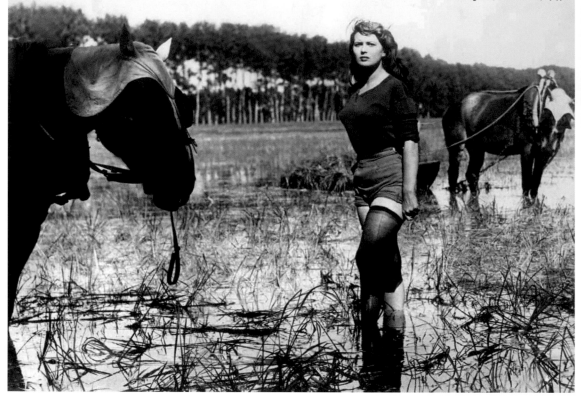

Silvana Mangano, *Bitter Rice*, 1949

In Giuseppe De Santis's film *Bitter Rice* (1949), nineteen-year-old Silvana Mangano is a supreme embodiment of sensuality. When Italo Calvino visited the set as a reporter, he described her as having 'an expression which is both beguiling and proud, dark eyes, shoulders which open out with the sweetness of a cameo portrait, a boldly harmonious bust which is both triumphant and streamlined, a waist like a slim stem, and an admirable rhythm of full curves and long-limbed artistry.' An Aphrodite of the rice fields, Mangano was exuberant Neo-Realist femininity incarnate in her practical but sexy shorts.

At that time, no one could have anticipated that hot pants would become a craze, first for the hippie generation and later for the punks. Oliviero Toscani designed a memorable ad campaign for the Italian fashion label Jesus Jeans, featuring a shapely female bottom clad in the tightest and tiniest pair of blue denim shorts, emblazoned with the slogan: 'Chi mi ama mi segua' ('He who loves me follows me'). These provocative garments were not just for summer wear. As they moved from the catwalk to the street they became shorter with each passing season. Hot pants came to symbolize youth at its most irrepressible, whether they were peeping out from long overcoats or worn with smart and serious blazers. They disappeared in the 1980s, but reappeared in the late 1990s in a more unconventional reinterpretation, signalling a newly assertive femininity and an explicit declaration of sexual power.

In the female iconography of the 20th century very few women have made such a powerful impression as Wonder Woman. Millions of little girls around the world grew up watching the 1970s television series in

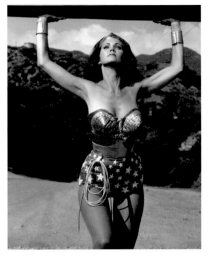

Lynda Carter,
Wonder Woman,
1976–79

Angelina Jolie,
*Lara Croft:
Tomb Raider*, 2001

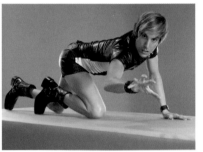

Sacha Baron Cohen,
Brüno, 2009

which the superheroine was played by Lynda Carter, fighting the bad guys in her hot pants and red boots and casually lifting up cars without ever spoiling her nail varnish. In *Charlie's Angels: Full Throttle* (McG, 2003) Cameron Diaz, Drew Barrymore and Lucy Liu delivered kung-fu kicks while wearing short shorts and Jimmy Choo heels. Still enormously popular amongst girls (not to mention boys) today, hot pants challenge our sense of modesty and thumb a nose at middle-class stuffiness. Their cause has been helped by the boom in synthetic fabrics since the 1980s which has created extreme variations such as the elastic micro-shorts Madonna is often photographed wearing when out jogging. And it is no surprise that the highlight of *Kylie: The Exhibition* at the Victoria and Albert Museum in London was the infamous pair of gold lamé hot pants that Ms Minogue wore in her video 'Spinning Around' in 2000.

Hot pants have come a long way, from Jodie Foster's teenage prostitute in *Taxi Driver* (Martin Scorsese, 1976) to the gutsy Angelina Jolie in *Lara Croft: Tomb Raider* (Simon West, 2001). But no one has worn them more memorably than Brüno in Larry Charles's 2009 film of the same name. Brüno, a gay Austrian fashion journalist, 'the star of the biggest German-speaking show on television in every single German-speaking country, except Germany', is one of the many faces of comedian Sacha Baron Cohen. At one point in the film he appears as a Hasidic Jew dressed in hot pants; the furious reactions prove that the shortest of shorts have not yet lost their power to shock.

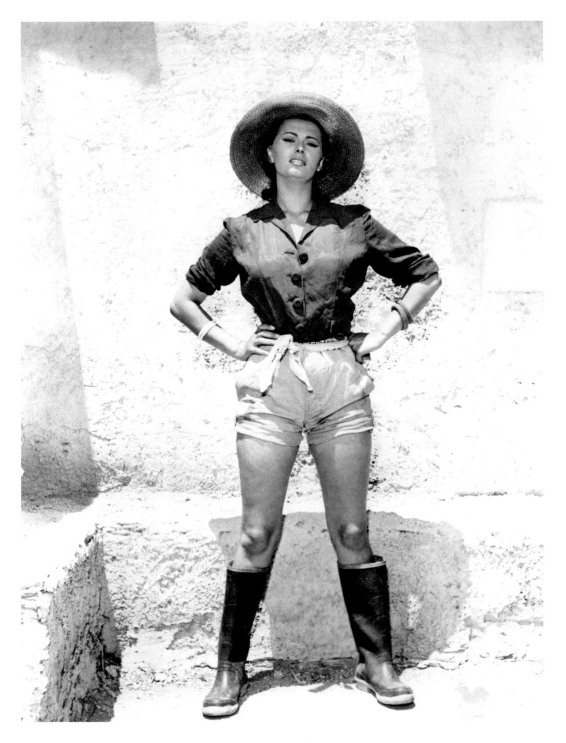

Sophia Loren, *The River Girl*, 1954

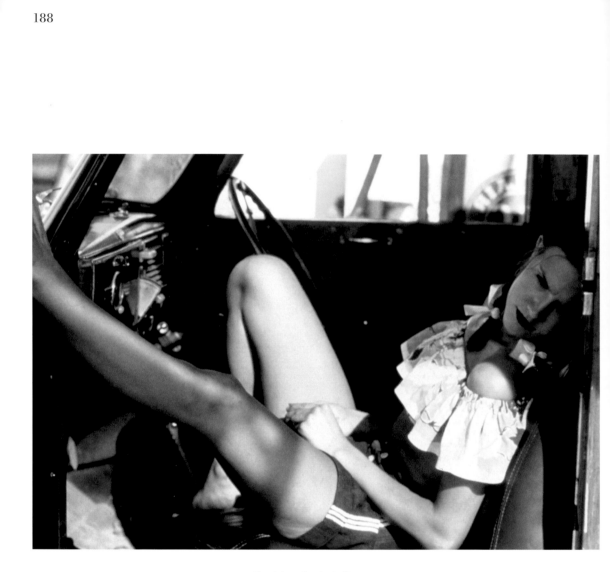

Dominique Swain, *Lolita*, 1997

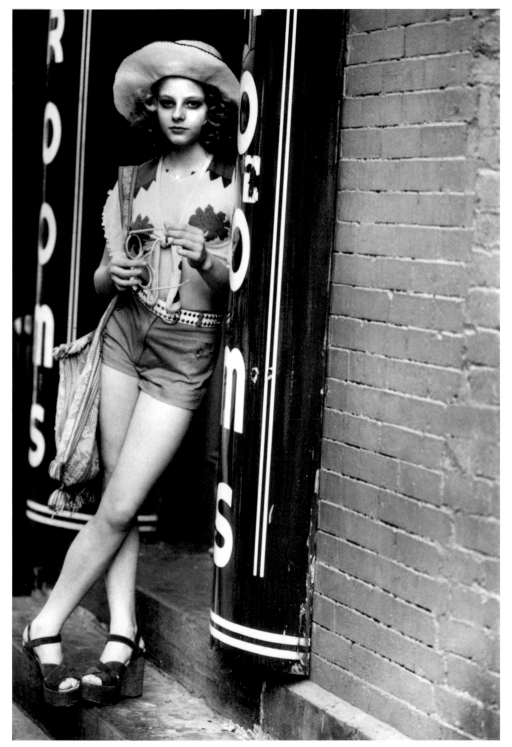

Jodie Foster, *Taxi Driver*, 1976

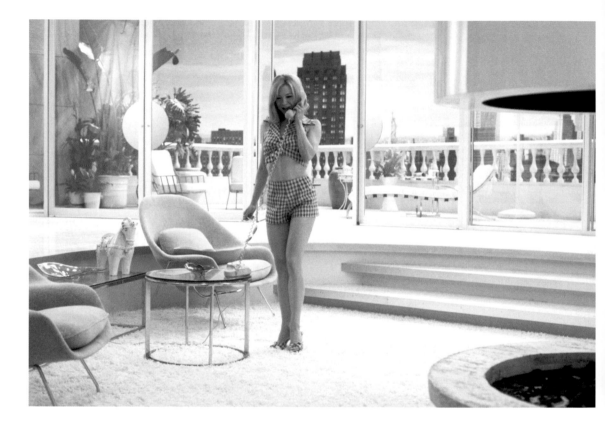

Renee Zellweger, *Down With Love*, 2003

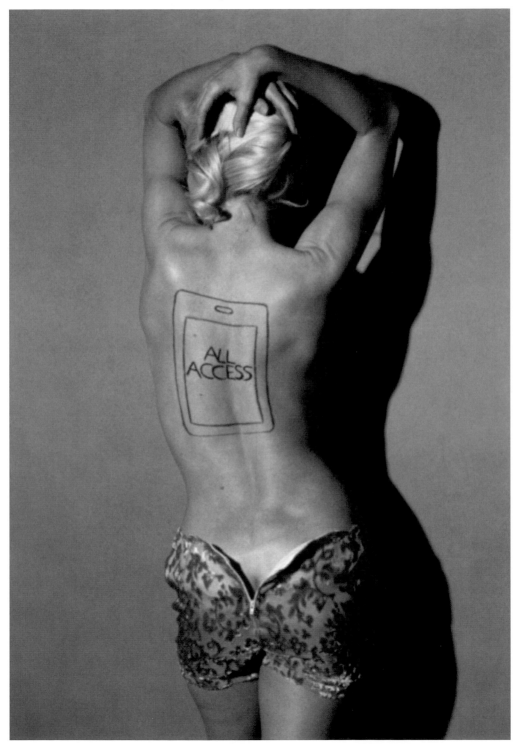

Madonna, *Truth or Dare*, 1991

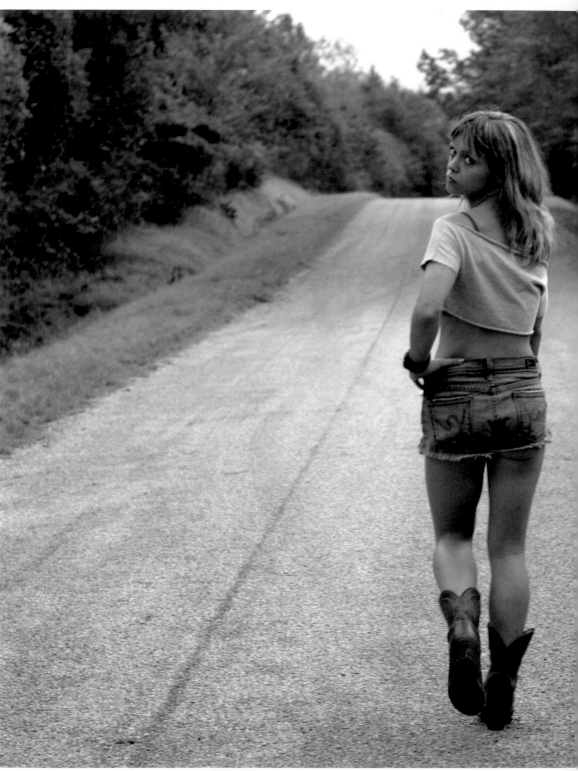

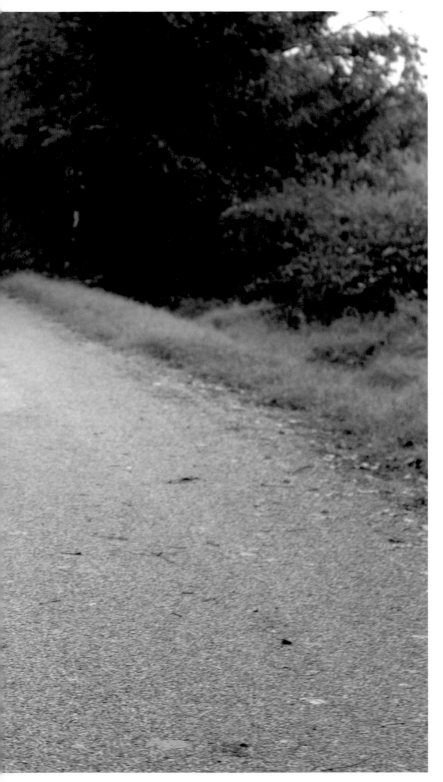

Christina Ricci,
Black Snake Moan, 2006

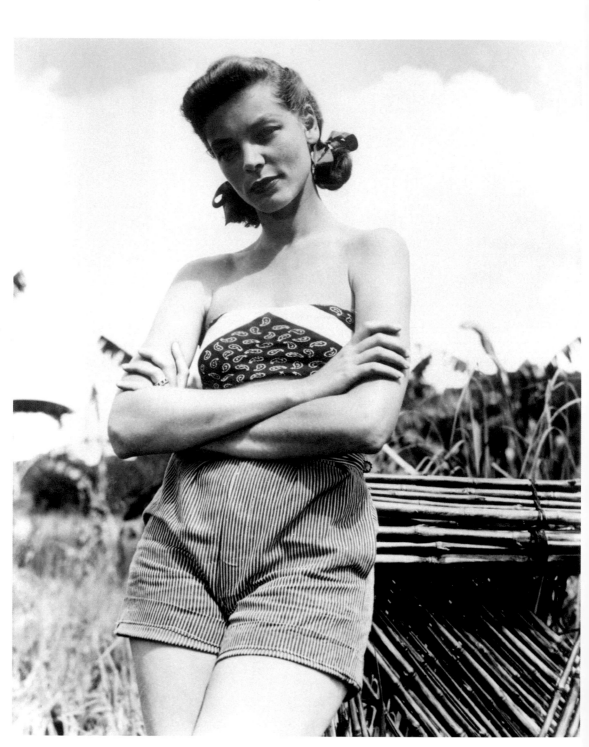

Lauren Bacall on the set of *The African Queen*, 1951

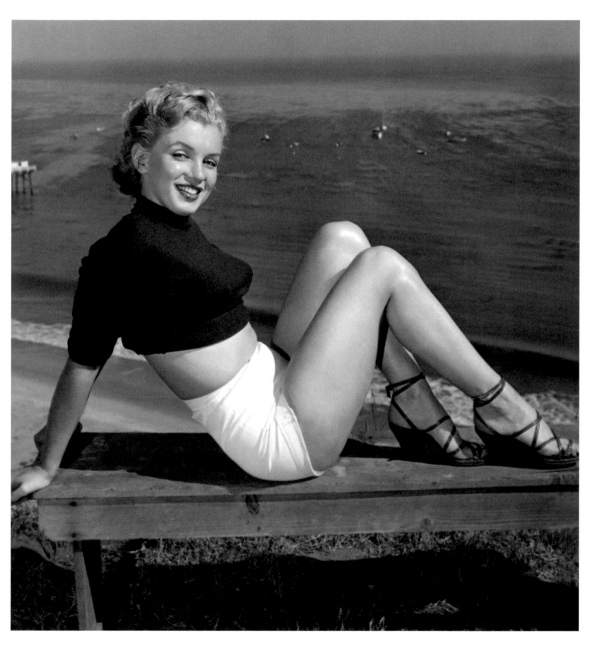

Marilyn Monroe, 1950s

Serge Gainsbourg and Jane Birkin, 1970

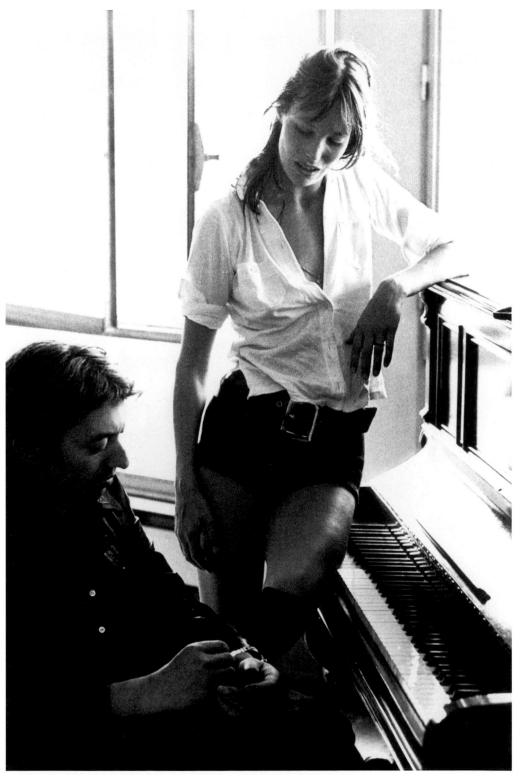

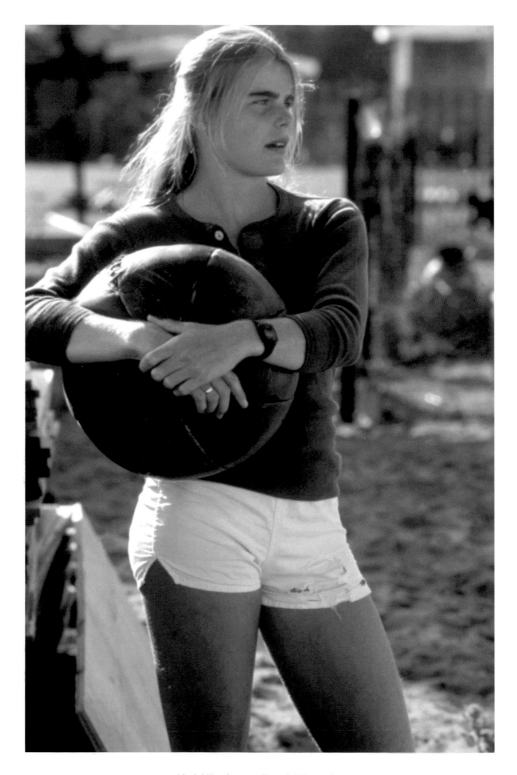

Mariel Hemingway, *Personal Best*, 1982

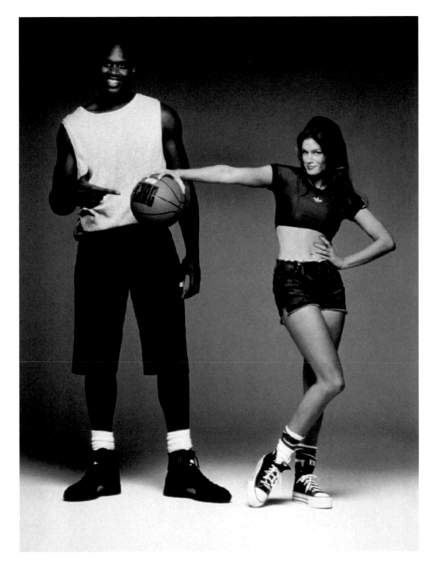

Cindy Crawford and Shaquille O'Neal, 1994

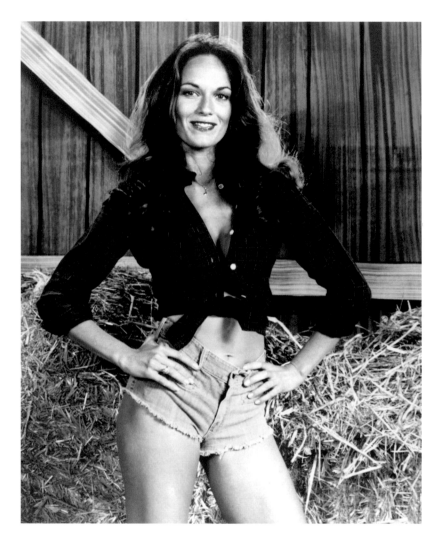

Catherine Bach, *The Dukes of Hazzard*, 1979–85

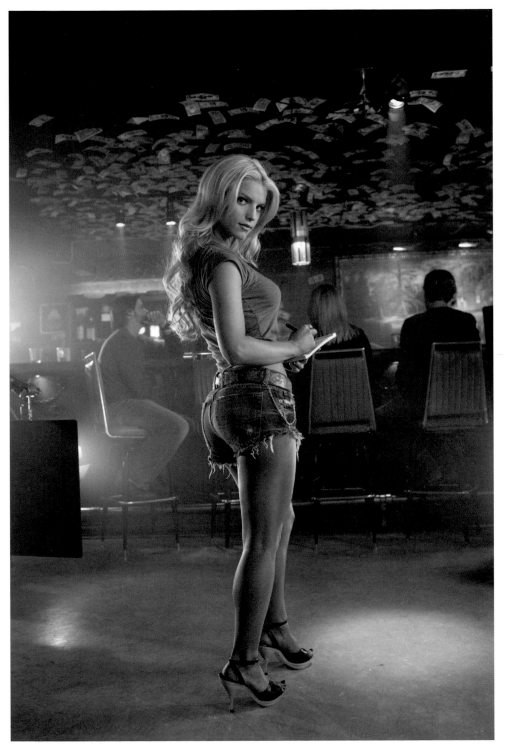

Jessica Simpson, *The Dukes of Hazzard*, 2005

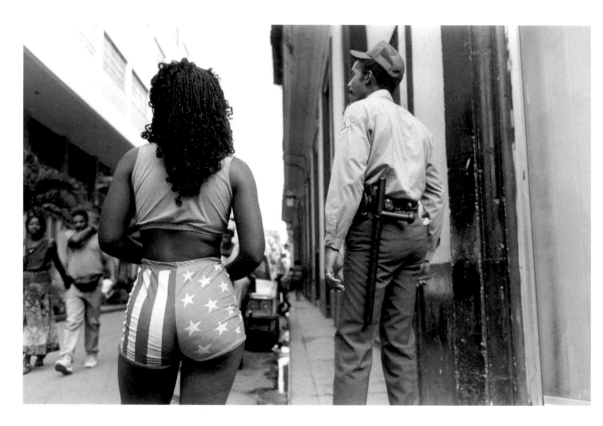

Havana, 1998

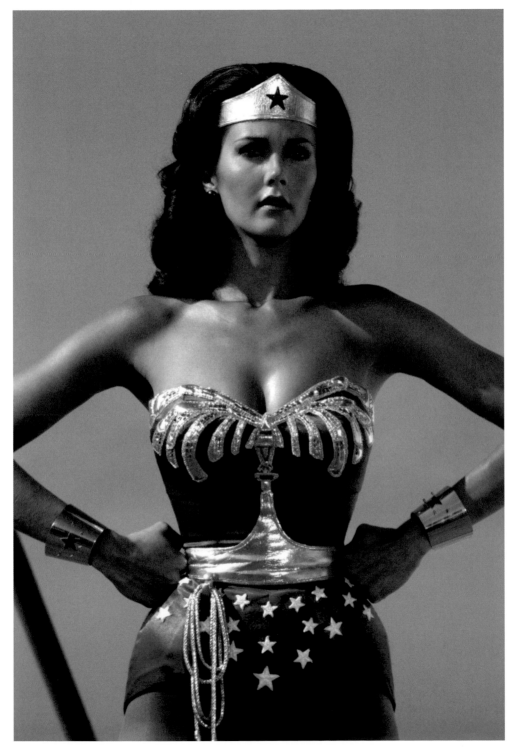

Lynda Carter, *Wonder Woman*, 1976–79

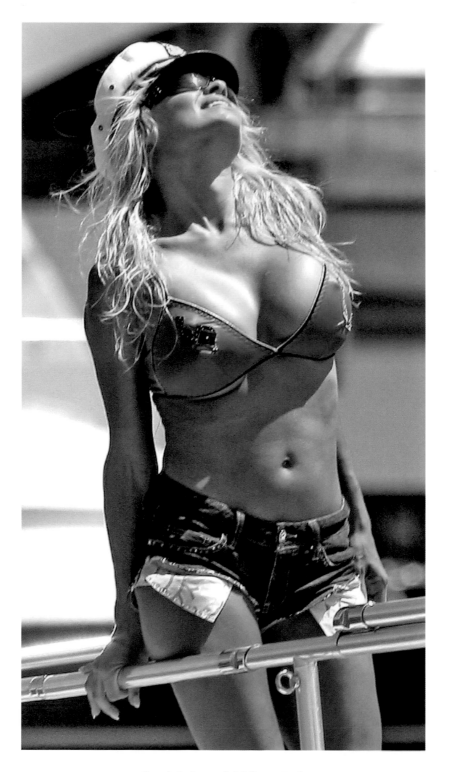

Pamela Anderson, Saint-Tropez, 2006

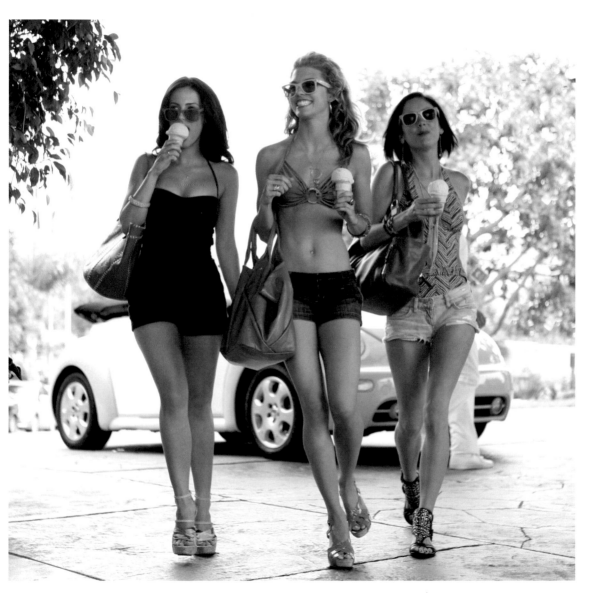

Jessica Lowndes, AnnaLynne McCord and Jessica Stroup, *90210*, 2008

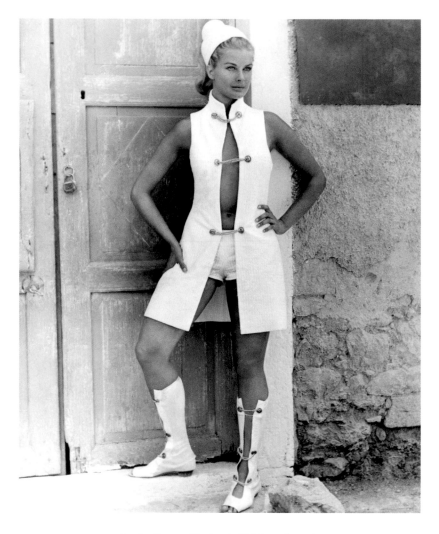

Candice Bergen, *The Day the Fish Came Out*, 1967

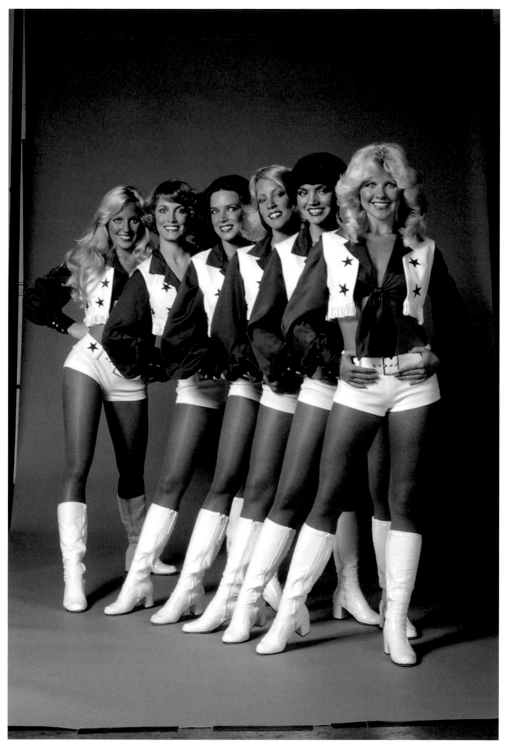

The Dallas Cowboys Cheerleaders, 1978

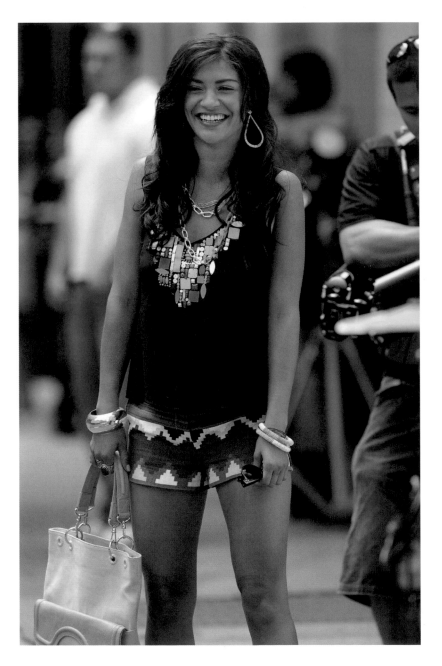

Jessica Szohr on the set of *Gossip Girl*, New York, 2009

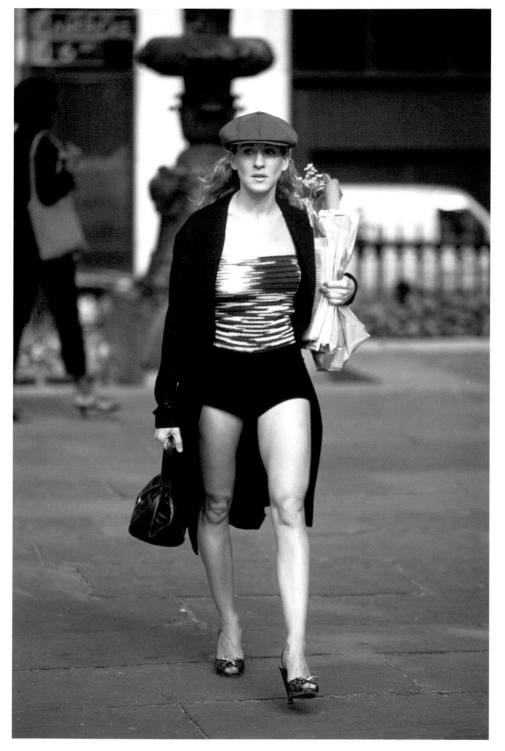

Sarah Jessica Parker, *Sex and the City*, 2001

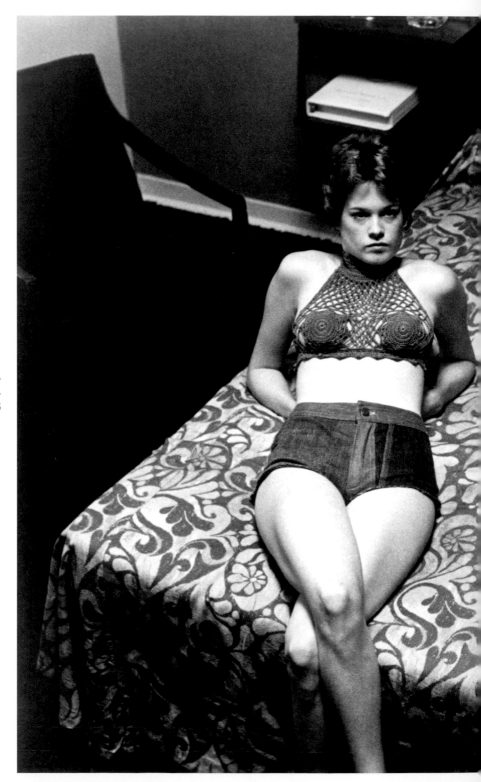

Melanie Griffith,
The Drowning Pool,
1975

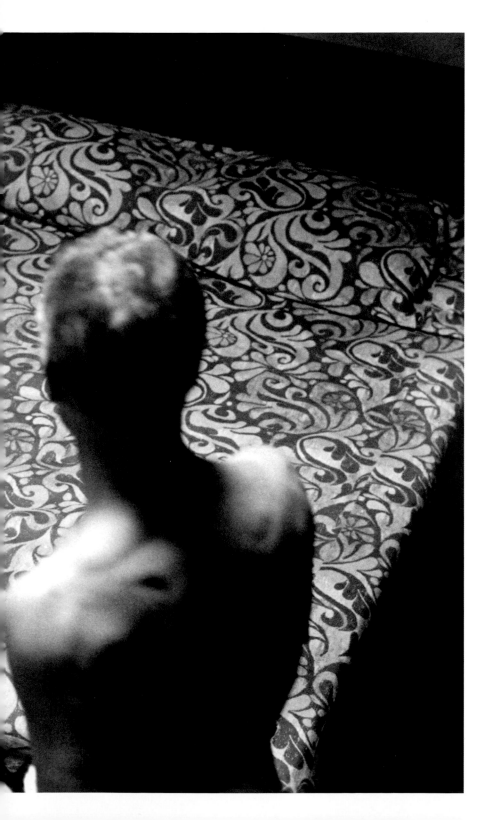

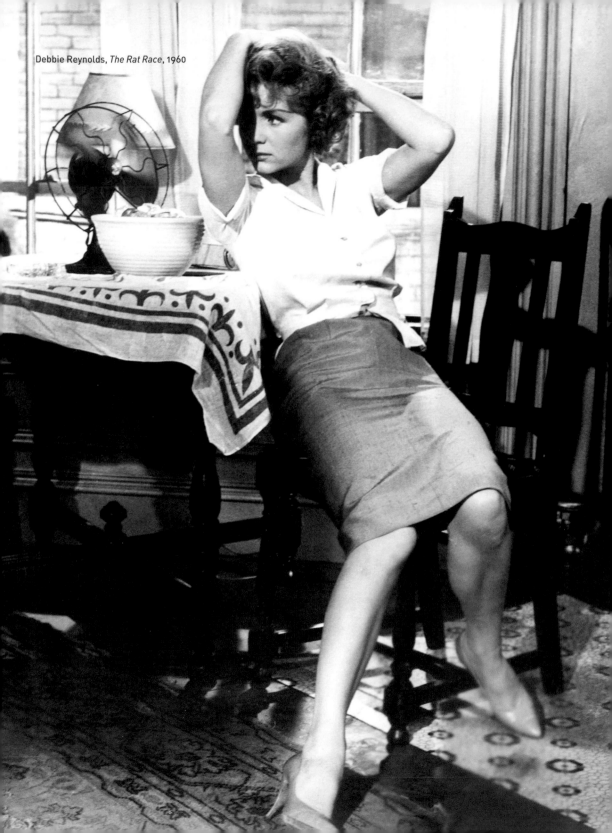

Debbie Reynolds, *The Rat Race*, 1960

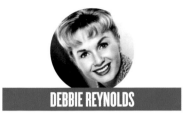

DEBBIE REYNOLDS

The Pencil Skirt

It is not a fine arm or a fine leg that makes a beautiful woman,
but the graceful symmetry of the whole, which takes away the
admiration of any singular part.

SENECA

Icon **Debbie Reynolds**
Designer **Christian Dior**
Film ***The Rat Race***, Robert Mulligan, 1960

214

Debbie Reynolds and Tony Randall,
The Mating Game, 1959

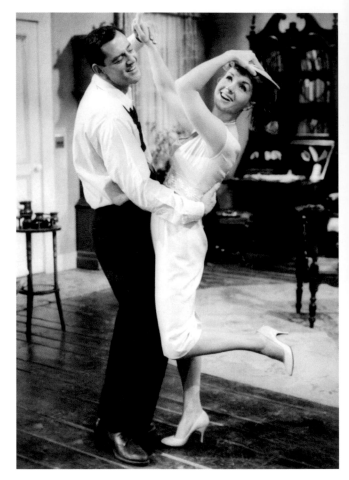

W̲ho better than America's eternal sweetheart to represent the dual nature of the long, tight pencil skirt? Debbie Reynolds played it smart and sensible alongside Gene Kelly in *Singin' in The Rain* (1952), starred in a wealth of musicals and was nominated for an Oscar as the lead in *The Unsinkable Molly Brown* (1964). More recently she turned in a high-spirited performance as Bobbi Adler, Grace's mother, in the sitcom *Will & Grace*.

The pencil skirt is characterized by its clever but apparently simple construction: a tube of varying length. It was created by Christian Dior in the 1950s as an alternative to the full or flared skirts of the New Look style. Since then, the pencil skirt has become a wardrobe staple for every woman who enjoys implying without showing, arousing interest without giving anything away: this is, quite simply, sensuality in its purest form. The modern-day queen of burlesque Dita Von Teese often wears a pencil skirt for a sexy retro look, a style that harks back to a time when the clothed body could arouse far more hot-blooded ideas than any pornographic film. The same sense of nostalgia is evoked by the brooding sexuality of the ultra-bourgeois Catherine Deneuve in *Belle*

de jour (Luis Buñuel, 1967). Her character is defined by the costumes designed by Yves Saint Laurent, which convey her longing to transgress via a wardrobe of geometric perfection: soft boxy little jackets worn over skirts that taper but do not restrict. It is as if the prostitute inside the proper lady is elegantly fooling first herself, and then the whole world.

It's true that the pencil skirt, especially when combined with high heels, can inhibit movement, forcing the wearer to adopt a sinuous and swaying walk that can have a hypnotic effect on male eyes. But there is little in common between the skirts worn by

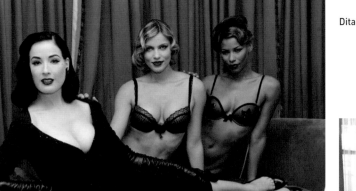

Dita Von Teese, London, 2009

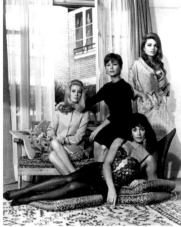

Françoise Fabian, Catherine Deneuve,
Genevieve Page and Maria Latour,
Belle de jour, 1967

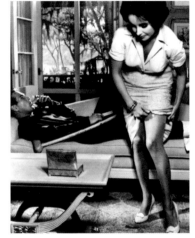

Elizabeth Taylor and Paul Newman,
Cat on a Hot Tin Roof, 1958

Carol Burnett's comedy character Mrs Wiggins, a frumpy and incompetent secretary, and those worn by Elizabeth Taylor in *Cat on a Hot Tin Roof* (Richard Brooks, 1958) playing a passionate woman who is prepared to do anything to win back the man she loves. Her character Maggie cannot believe the true reason for her husband's disinterest – he is more attracted to other men – and so tries to reawaken his fading desire with the inflammatory act of pulling up her skirt to change her stockings. In the 21st century, Angelina Jolie made a bid to become the new queen of the pencil skirt when the film *Mr & Mrs Smith* (Doug Liman) was released in 2005.

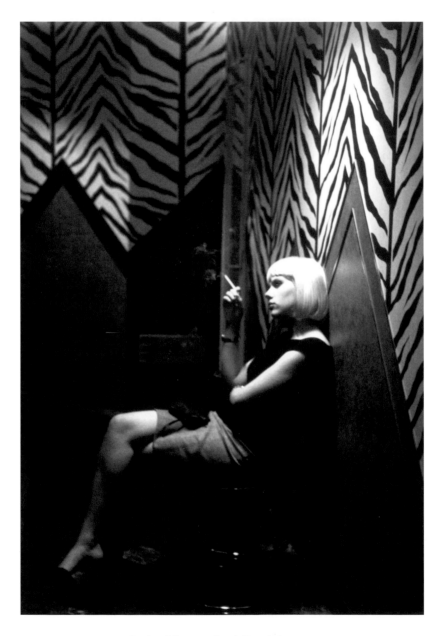

Scarlett Johansson, *Lost in Translation*, 2003

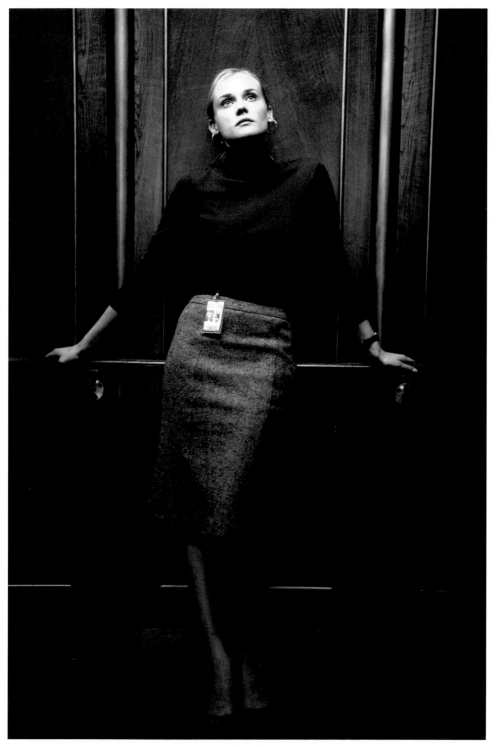

Diane Kruger, *National Treasure*, 2004

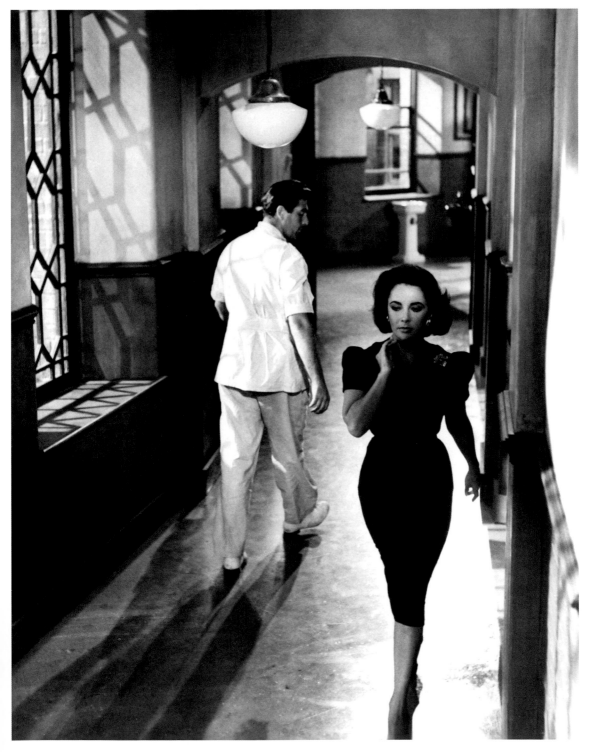

Elizabeth Taylor, *Suddenly, Last Summer*, 1959

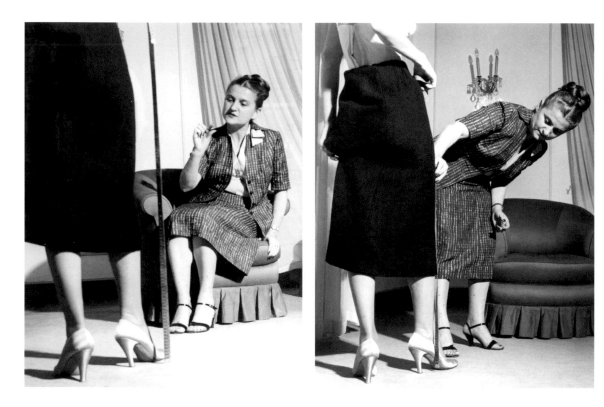

Zoe Fontana deciding the best length for a skirt, Rome, 1952

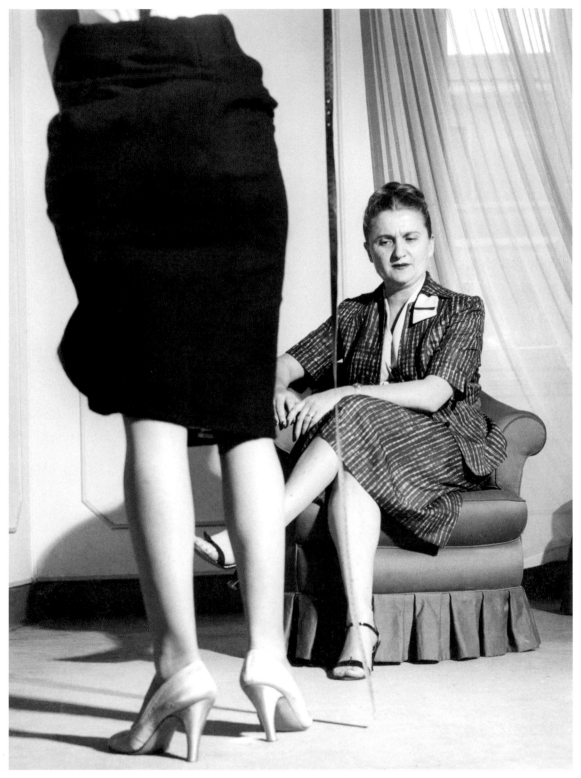

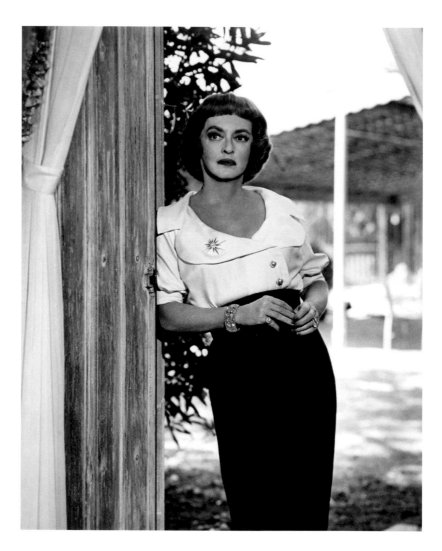

Bette Davis, *Dead Ringer*, 1964

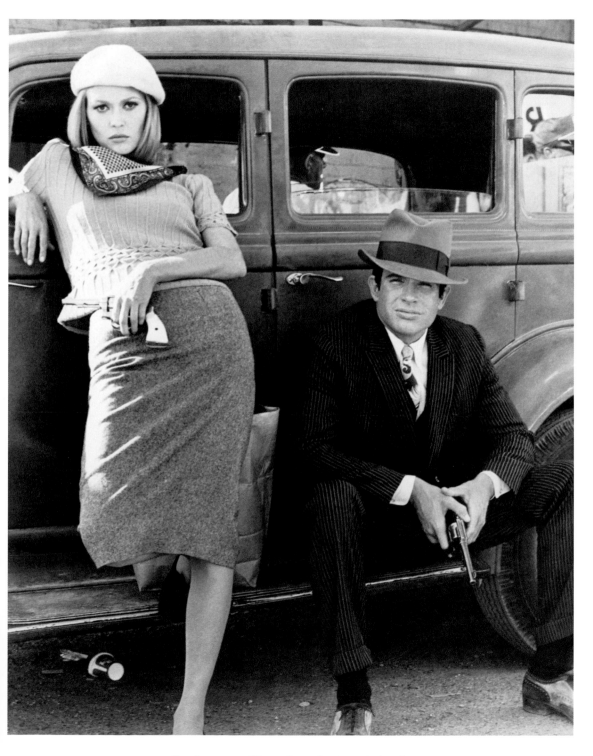

Faye Dunaway and Warren Beatty, *Bonnie and Clyde*, 1967

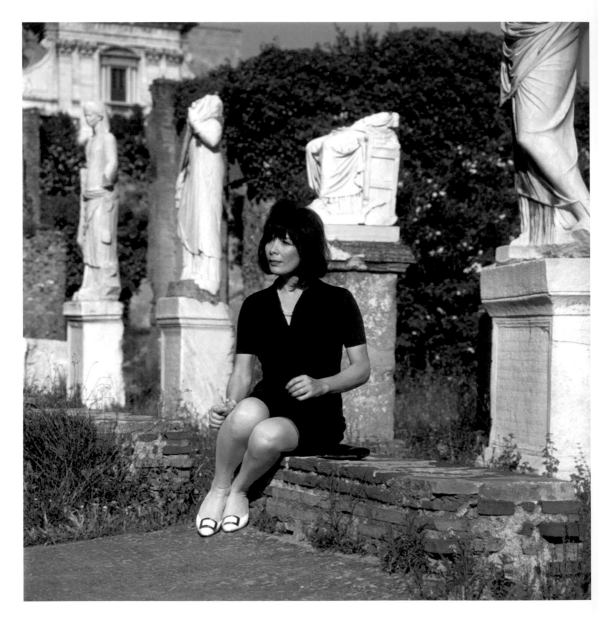

Juliette Greco, Rome, 1967

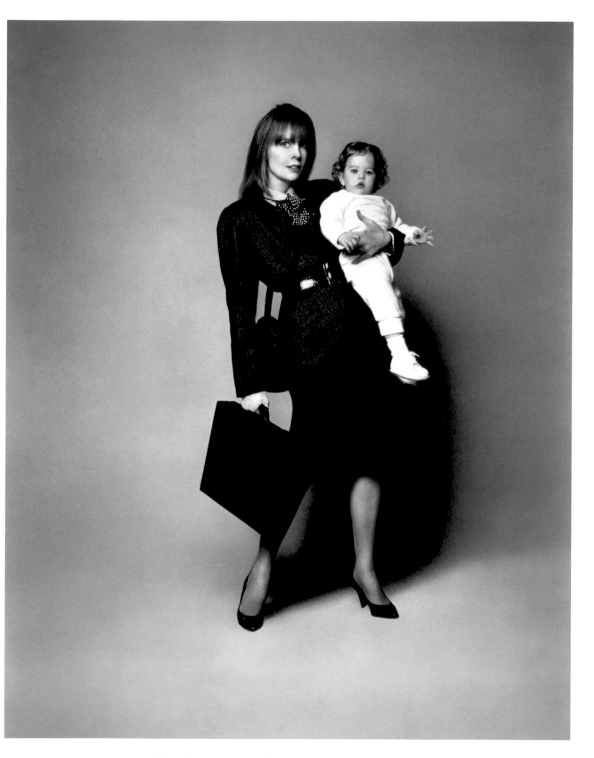

Diane Keaton and Kristina/Michelle Kennedy, *Baby Boom*, 1987

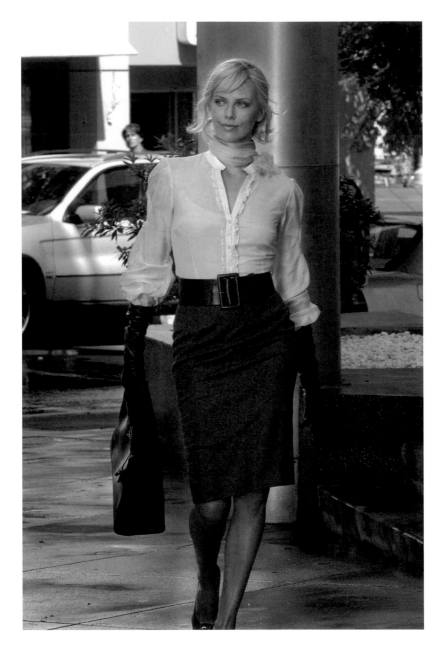

Charlize Theron, Los Angeles, 2006

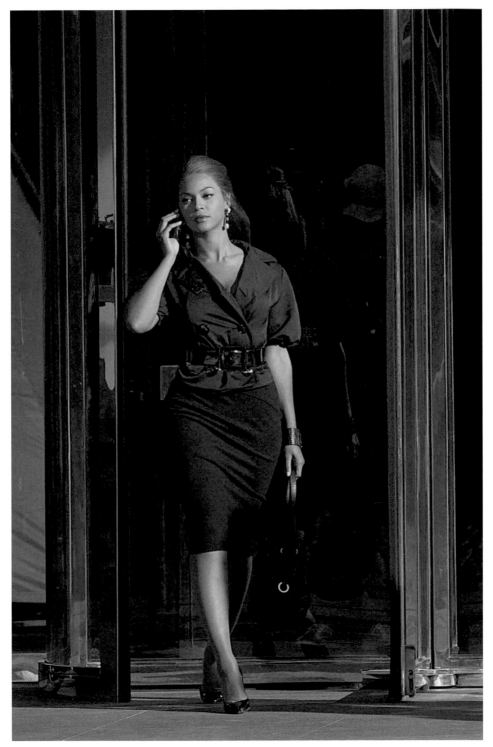

Beyoncé Knowles, New York, 2007

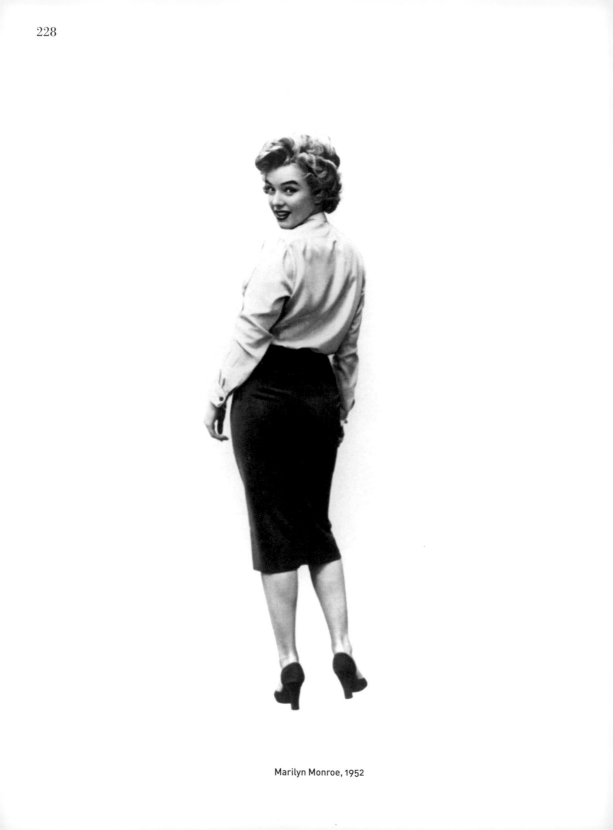

Marilyn Monroe, 1952

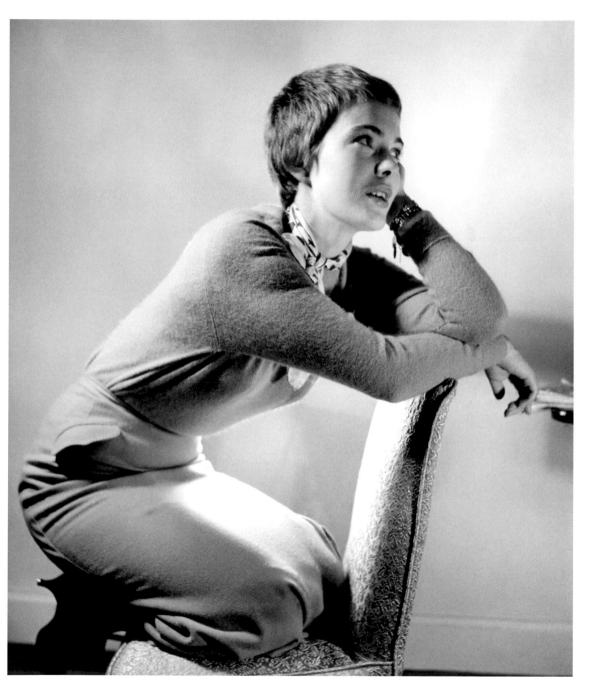

Jean Seberg, 1958

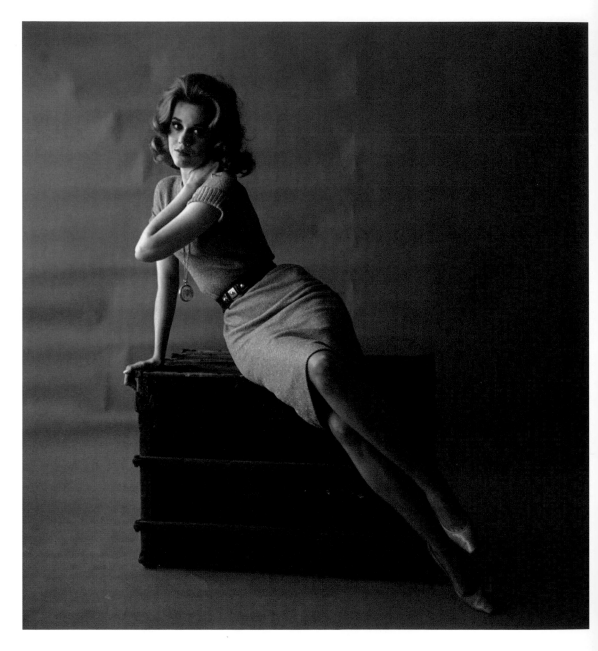

Jane Fonda, 1963

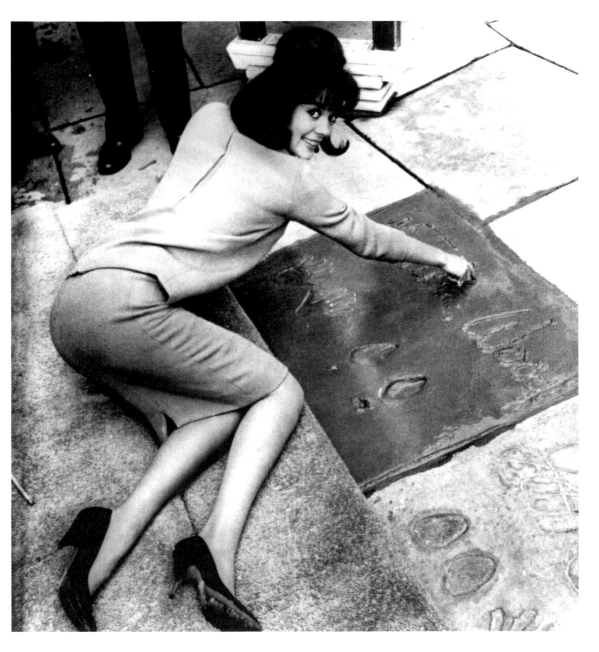

Natalie Wood in front of Grauman's Chinese Theatre, Los Angeles, 1961

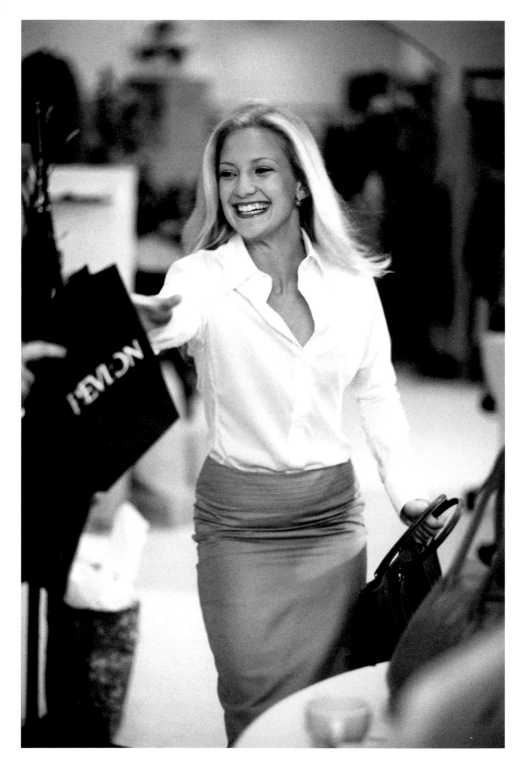

Kate Hudson, *How to Lose a Guy in 10 Days*, 2003

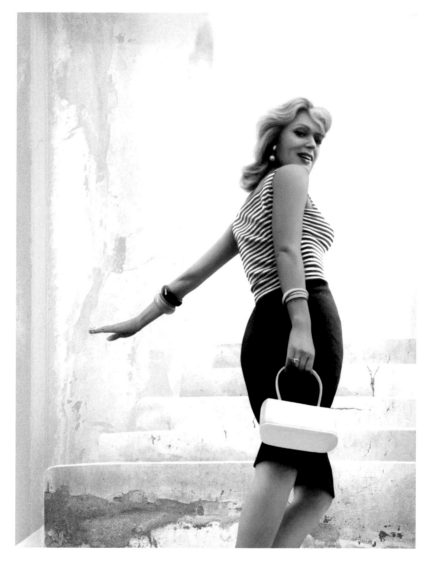

Melina Mercouri, *Never on Sunday*, 1960

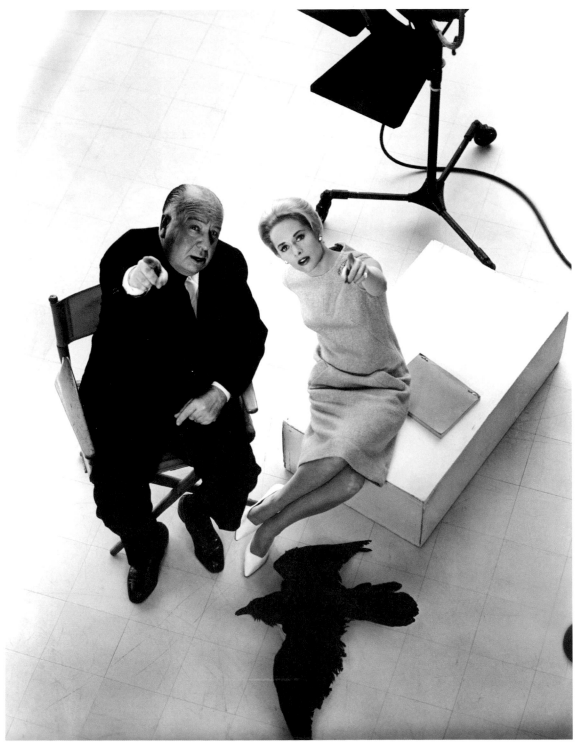

Alfred Hitchcock and Tippi Hedren in a promotional shot for *The Birds*, 1963

Jane Birkin, 1970s

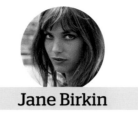

Jane Birkin

The T-Shirt

Who can live without them? I have quite a variety,
ranging from Saint Laurent to Gap. I wear them at the beach,
at the house, on people's boats, wherever I am.
I am cuckoo about my white T-shirts.

NAN KEMPNER

Icon Jane Birkin
Designer Calvin Klein
Film *Je t'aime...moi non plus*, Serge Gainsbourg, 1976

Jane Birkin, 1970s

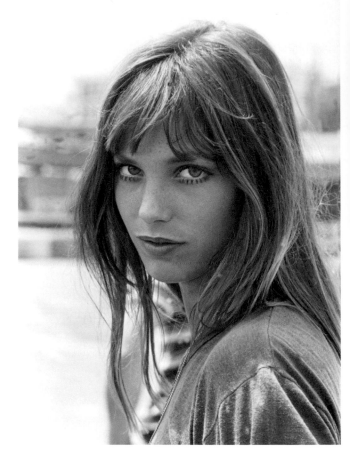

In *Je t'aime…moi non plus*, directed by her lover Serge Gainsbourg in 1976, Jane Birkin wore a T-shirt that was pure white, oversized and worn with ultra-straight jeans. Her role as Johnny in that movie was scandalous: Johnny radiates such an ambiguous sexuality that she arouses the desire of Krassky (Joe Dallesandro) who is already involved in a gay relationship with the objectionable Padovan (Hugues Quester). Both her T-shirt and her face simultaneously evoked innocence and debauchery, desire and punishment, love and death: they could say anything and contradict everything without fear of deceit or hypocrisy. Before Jane Birkin, the androgynous and beautiful Jean Seberg became the standard-bearer of French New Wave cinema in Jean-Luc Godard's 1960 film *À bout de souffle* in her immaculate T-shirt with rolled-up sleeves, emblazoned with the logo of the *New York Herald Tribune*. In *Babette Goes to War* (Christian-Jaque, 1959) Brigitte Bardot wore a white T-shirt that clung like a second skin; as did Demi Moore in *G.I. Jane* (Ridley Scott, 1997), this time as a defiant symbol of her muscular and feisty allure.

Whether it is a protest, a non-conformist gesture or a rejection of frivolousness, the T-shirt never lies. Taking its name from the simple shape of the letter T, its very history is bound up with the written expression of feelings, passions and sensations. Its design is not derived from military clothing, as many people think, but from men's underwear. As is often the case with clothing from previous centuries, it originated in the world of physical labour, in the cotton shirts that workers wore beneath their jackets in the early 20th century. With almost three billion sold around the world every year, it can be seen as an allegory of globalization, but it is also a metaphor for individual identity, as it can be printed, decorated and designed.

It tells more stories about us than we can for ourselves. It can be a souvenir or a manifesto, transmitting political, witty or even literary messages.

The T-shirt carries its greatest erotic charge in its simplest, purest form: just think of the tight-fitting versions worn by Marlon Brando, James Dean and Madonna. Calvin Klein declared that a woman wearing her boyfriend's T-shirt and underwear is an amazingly sexy sight. And all this from a garment that doesn't cost much, can be found everywhere, and has the simple air of one of those understated things that accompanies us throughout our lives. This may be why the world's top designers are among the T-shirt's most enthusiastic

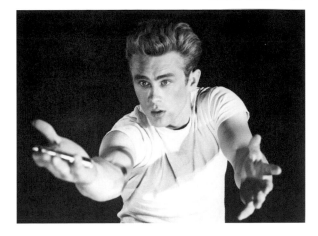

James Dean, *Rebel Without A Cause*, 1955

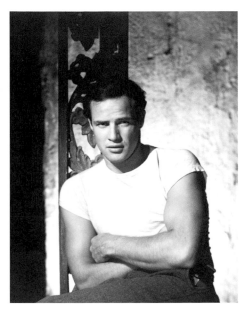

Marlo Brando,
A Streetcar Named Desire, 1951

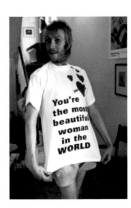

Rhys Ifans, *Notting Hill*, 1999

fans, the greatest of them being Giorgio Armani, who has long described himself as a 'T-shirt addict'.

The significance of the T-shirt, just like that of jeans, goes far beyond self-definition to become a commentary on society itself. Accessible to everyone, it has the universality of a work of art. Casual fashion has covered the T-shirt with so much writing, so many designs and messages that it has virtually been turned into a work of literature. The romantic comedy *Notting Hill* (1999) includes a scene in which the hero's best friend tries to choose which T-shirt to wear and eventually bases his decision on which tasteless slogan is most appropriate for a first date. Julia Roberts, the female lead in the

same film, is also a T-shirt fanatic: in 1992 she was photographed by Herb Ritts as she emerged out of the sea wearing only a white T-shirt and men's underpants. A year earlier, Susan Sarandon and Geena Davis's T-shirts became symbols of rediscovered sisterhood in Ridley Scott's *Thelma & Louise*.

T-shirts: we love them because they are the way they are, and because we can make them our own.

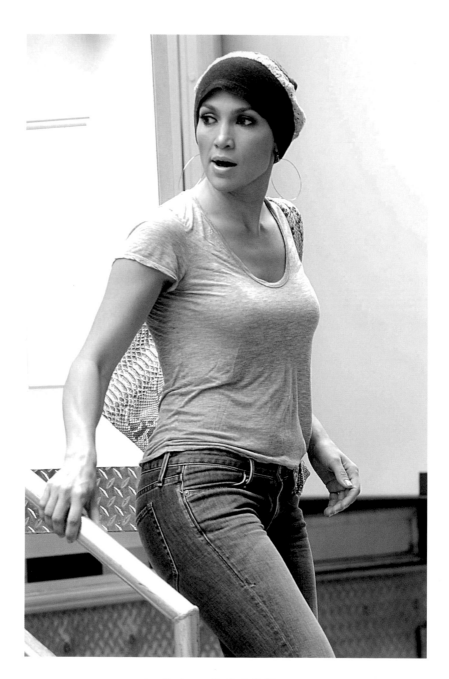

Jennifer Lopez, *The Back-Up Plan*, 2009

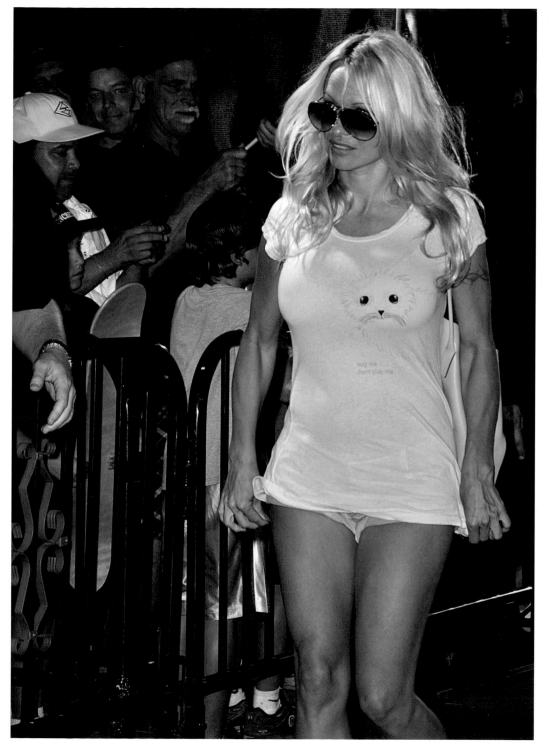

Pamela Anderson, Los Angeles, 2009

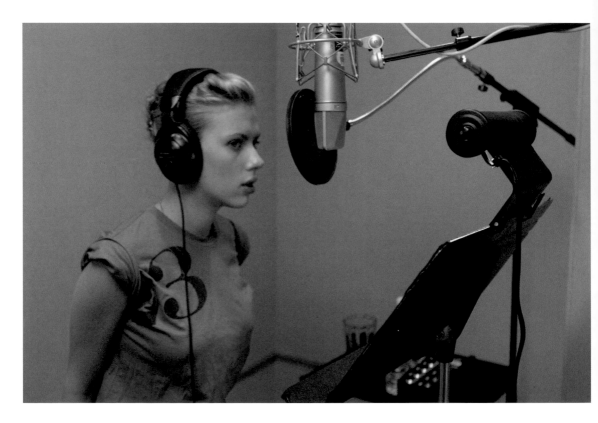

Scarlett Johansson recording the soundtrack for *The SpongeBob SquarePants Movie*, 2004

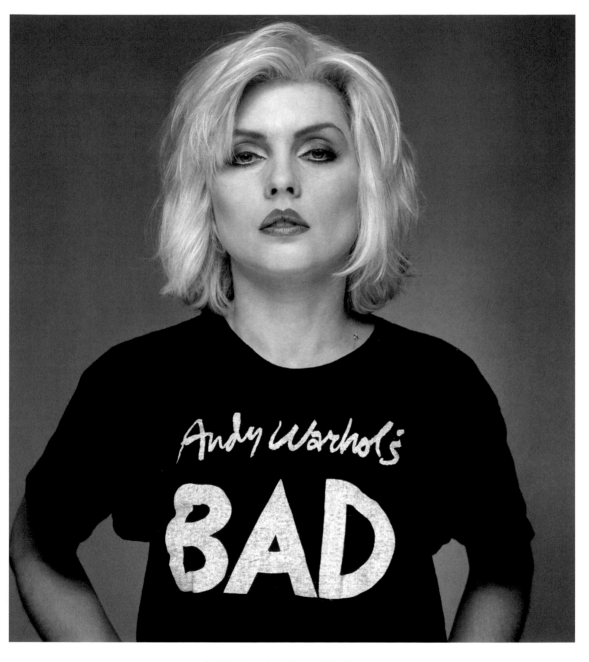

Debbie Harry, lead singer of Blondie, 1979

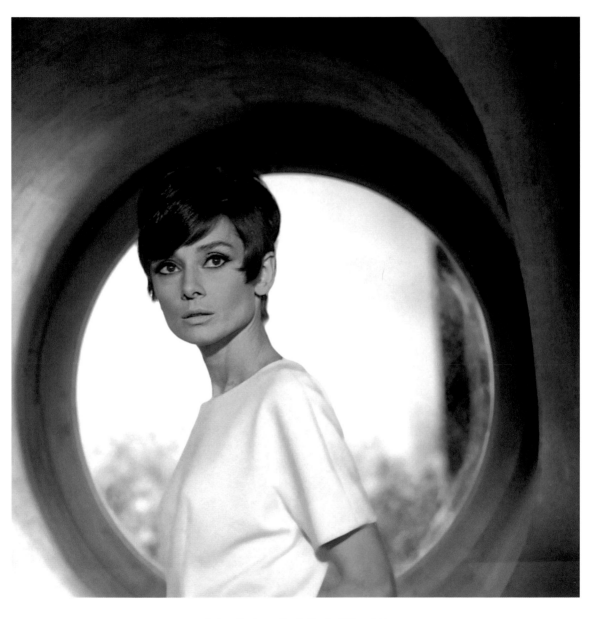

Audrey Hepburn, *How to Steal a Million*, 1966

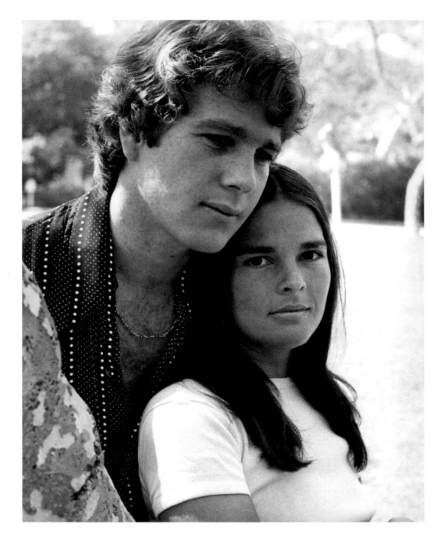

Ali MacGraw and Ryan O'Neal, *Love Story*, 1970

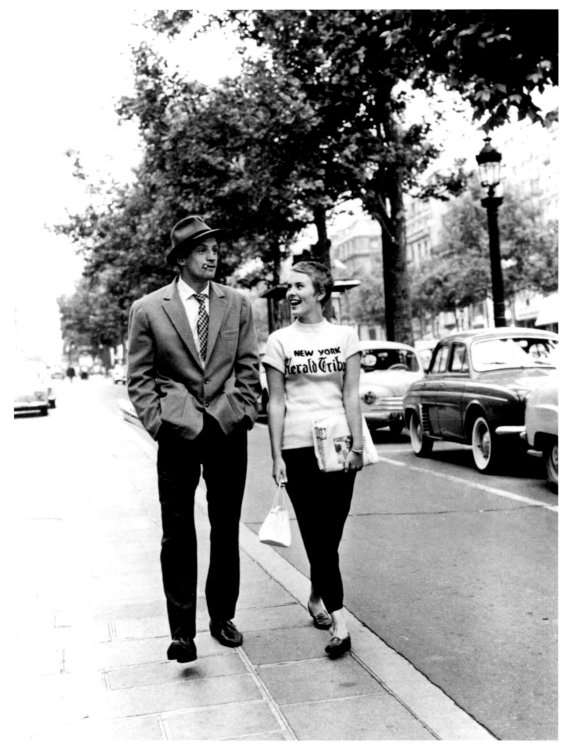

Jean Seberg and Jean-Paul Belmondo, *À bout de souffle*, 1960

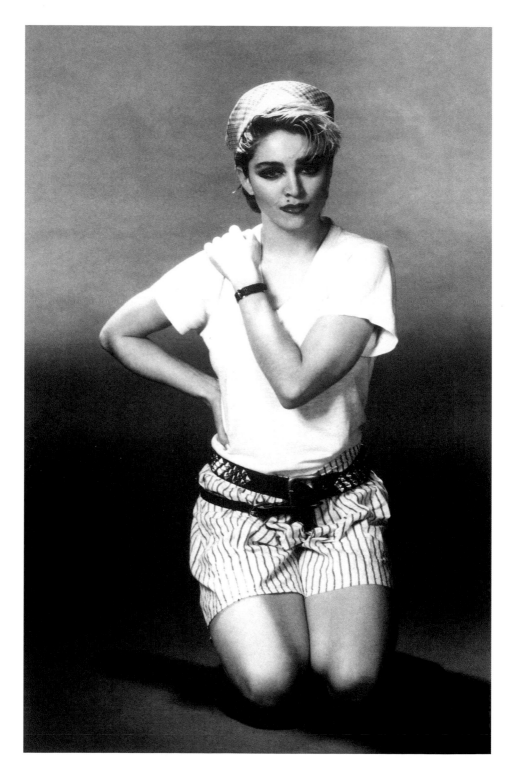

Madonna, 1980s

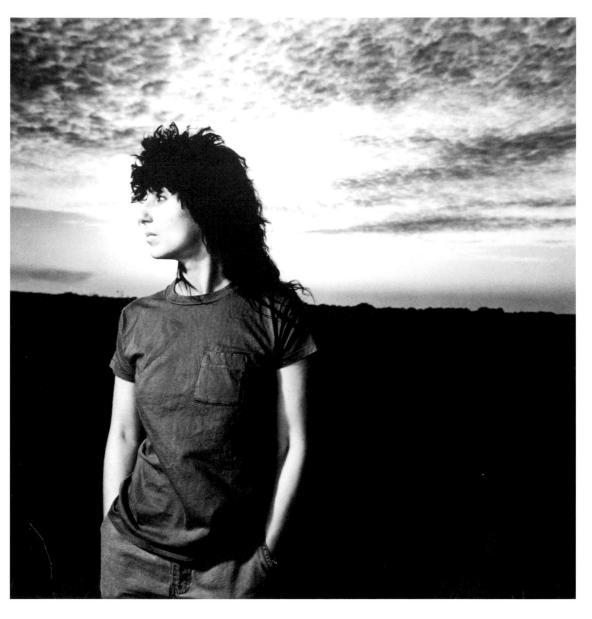

Cher, *Silkwood*, 1983

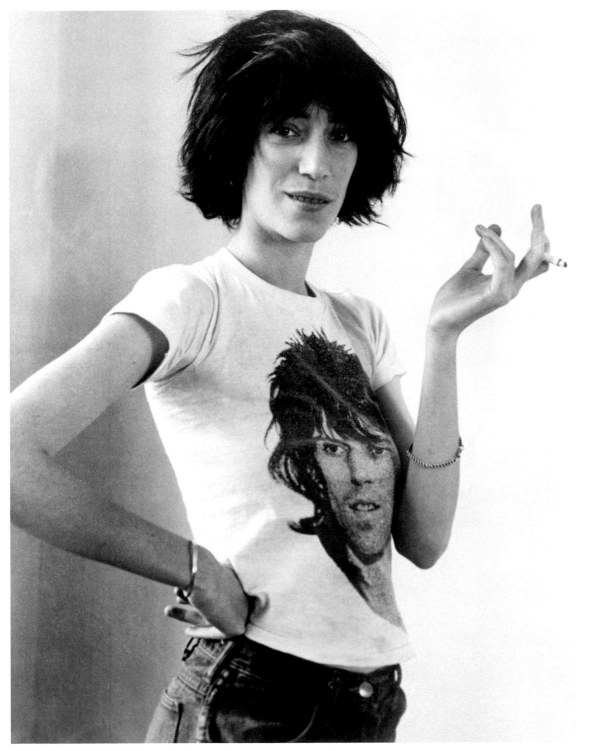

Patti Smith, 1980s

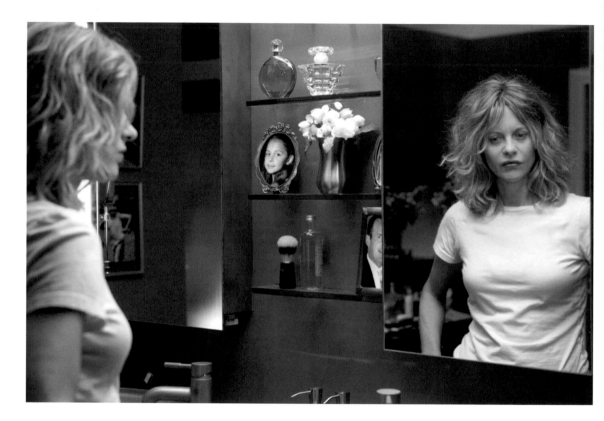

Meg Ryan, *In the Land of Women*, 2007

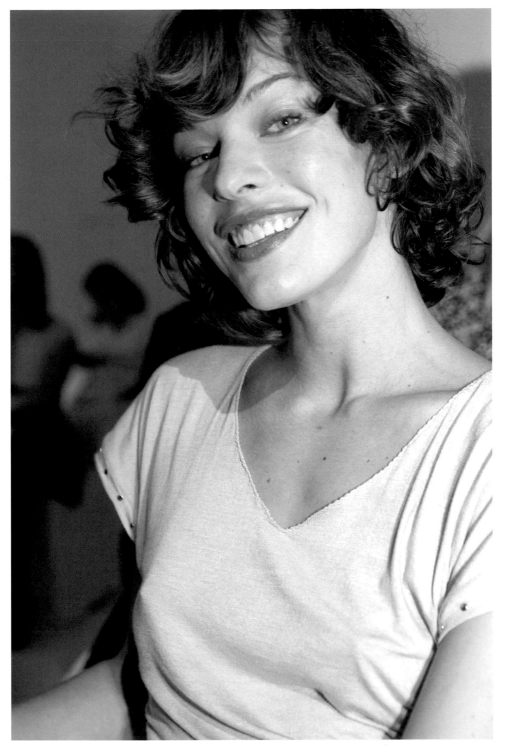

Milla Jovovich, New York, 2004

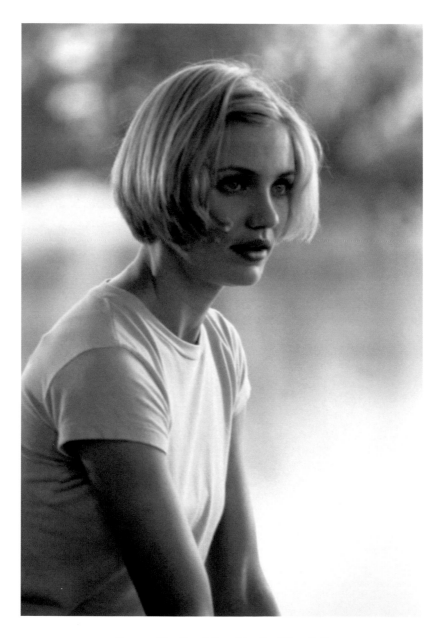

Cameron Diaz, *There's Something About Mary*, 1998

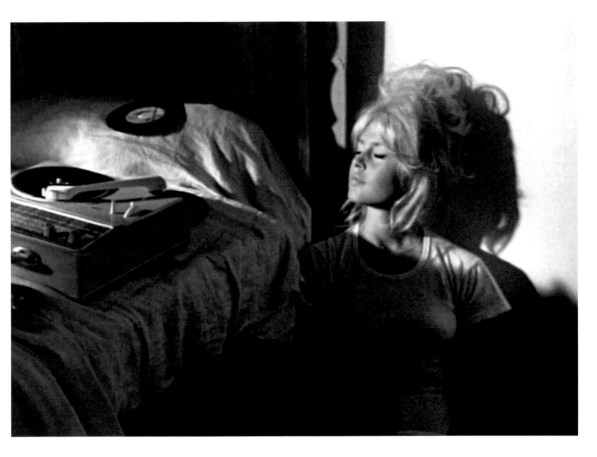

Brigitte Bardot, *A Very Private Affair*, 1962

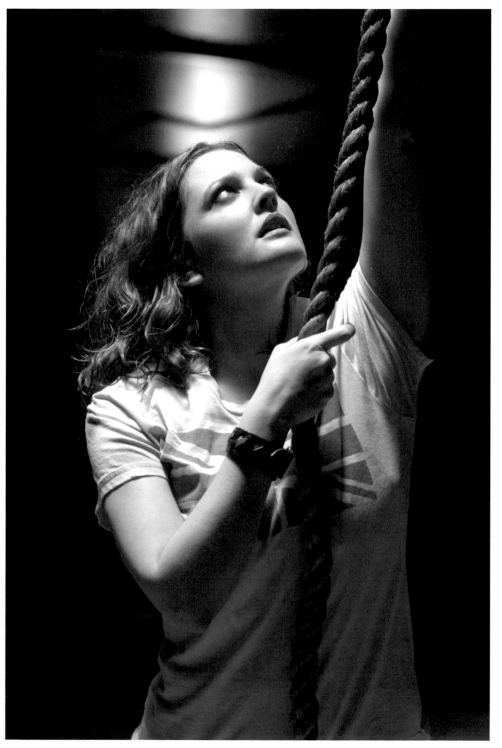

Drew Barrymore, *Charlie's Angels: Full Throttle*, 2003

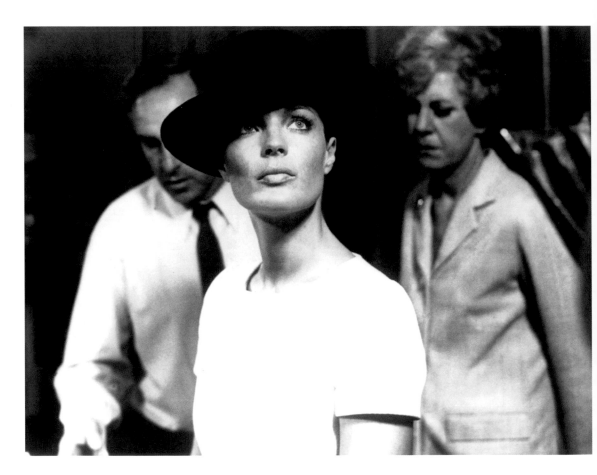

Romy Schneider, *Les choses de la vie*, 1969

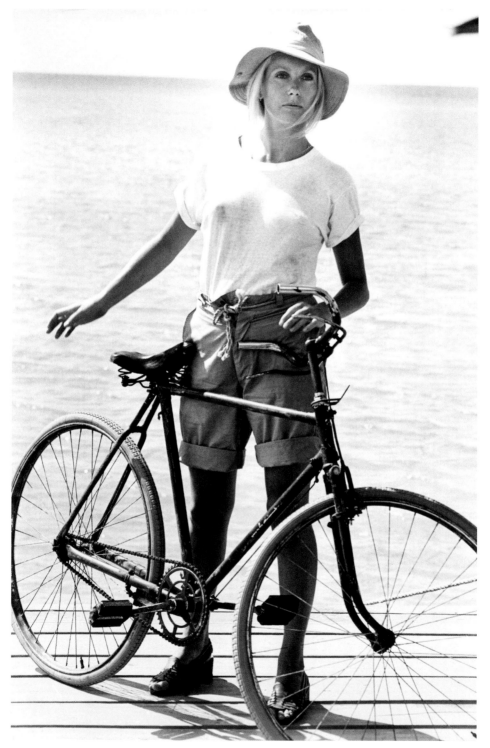

Catherine Deneuve, Bahamas, 1975

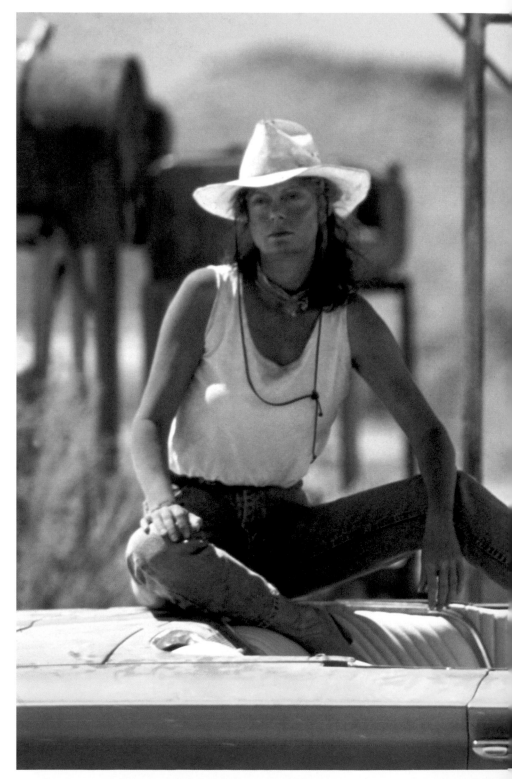

Susan Sarandon
and Geena Davis,
Thelma & Louise,
1991

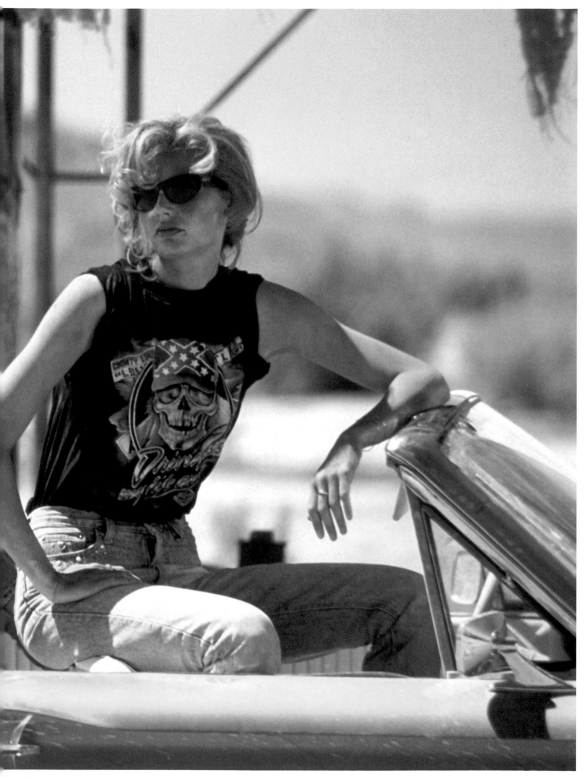

Marlene Dietrich,
A Foreign Affair, 1948

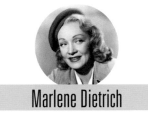

Marlene Dietrich

The Trench Coat

The man in the trench coat
Badge out, laid off
Says he's got a bad cough
Wants to get it paid off.

BOB DYLAN, *SUBTERRANEAN HOMESICK BLUES*

Icon **Marlene Dietrich**
Designer **Burberry**
Film ***Witness for the Prosecution***, Billy Wilder, 1957

Marlene Dietrich, *Manpower*, 1941

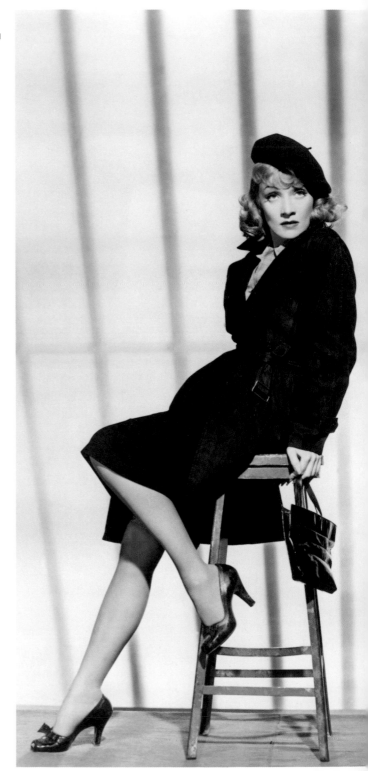

Enigmatic, independent, with a complex and fascinating personality: the adjectives we use to describe both the trench coat and Marlene Dietrich, the original ice goddess, are nearly identical. Both have an attraction characterized first and foremost by the word 'ambiguous'. In her role as the enigmatic Christine Vole in *Witness for the Prosecution* (Billy Wilder, 1957), Dietrich is languidly – almost diabolically – enshrouded in a trench coat for most of the film, as if to underline the fact that neither her personality nor her clothes are anything to joke about. The trench coat is simultaneously protective and highly erotic: it makes a man look more masculine and enhances the feminine shape of a woman when it is nipped in at the waist with a belt, as it creates an hourglass silhouette. The trench coat is associated with strong emotions: Audrey Hepburn's longing to change her life in *Funny Face* (Stanley Donen, 1957), or Humphrey Bogart's sense of resignation at the end of *Casablanca* (Michael Curtiz, 1942). Worn buttoned-up, it can also convey resentment, as it did for the young Meryl Streep in *Kramer vs. Kramer* (Robert Benton, 1979), or symbolize desire, as worn by Jane Fonda in *Klute* (Alan J. Pakula, 1971) and Kim Basinger in *9½ Weeks* (Adrian Lyne, 1986).

The trench coat can hide the secret of a person who plans to carry out a dangerous or symbolic act. The trench coats worn by the protagonists in *The Matrix* (Andy and Larry Wachowski, 1999) are said to have inspired Eric Harris and Dylan Klebold, the high-school seniors who carried out the

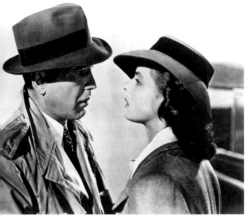

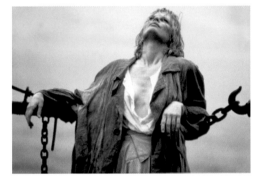

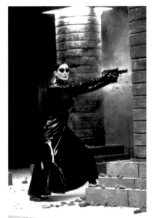

Audrey Hepburn on the
set of *Funny Face*, 1957

Carrie-Anne Moss,
The Matrix Reloaded, 2003

Humphrey Bogart and
Ingrid Bergman, *Casablanca*, 1942

Kim Basinger,
9½ Weeks, 1986

Columbine High School massacre in 1999 and were reputedly associated with the Trench Coat Mafia, a teenage gang that took its name from its members' uniform.

This ambiguous garment was created with practical intentions as a lightweight coat for military officers in the First World War. Thomas Burberry was commissioned to produce the coats by the British War Office in 1914. The Burberry company is still in dispute today with Mackintosh and Aquascutum over which firm was the first to invent the waterproofing process that makes the cotton rain-resistant. From its earliest days, Burberry's design was a consummate example of garment-making, with its deep yoke at the back, military epaulettes, cuffs closed by straps and buckles, pockets, belted waist and D-rings from which to hang tools and utensils.

Because it had such direct wartime associations, it was later adopted by Hollywood as part of the uniform of film noir. It has appeared in many colour variations over the years, but the trench coat still looks its best in shades of beige. As Alison Lurie explains in her book *The Language of Clothes*: 'Beige is the most neutral of all colors, the least communicative … Neither cheerful nor sad, neither active nor passive.' It is perfect for people who need or want to hide their emotions: it protects them from the eyes of others. Its most alluring characteristic is that it allows us to turn ourselves into enigmas.

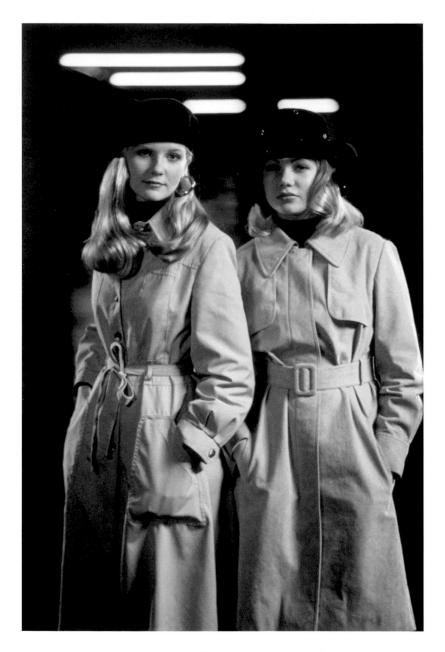

Kirsten Dunst and Michelle Williams, *Dick*, 1999

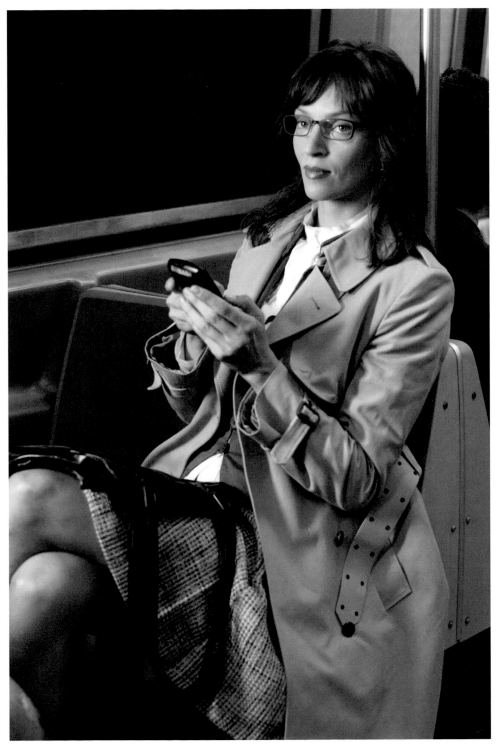

Uma Thurman, *My Super Ex-Girlfriend*, 2006

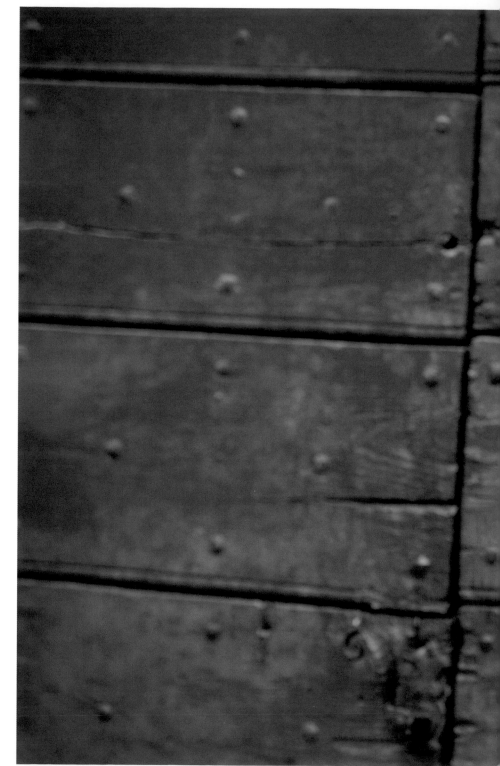

Valeria Solarino,
Rome, 2006

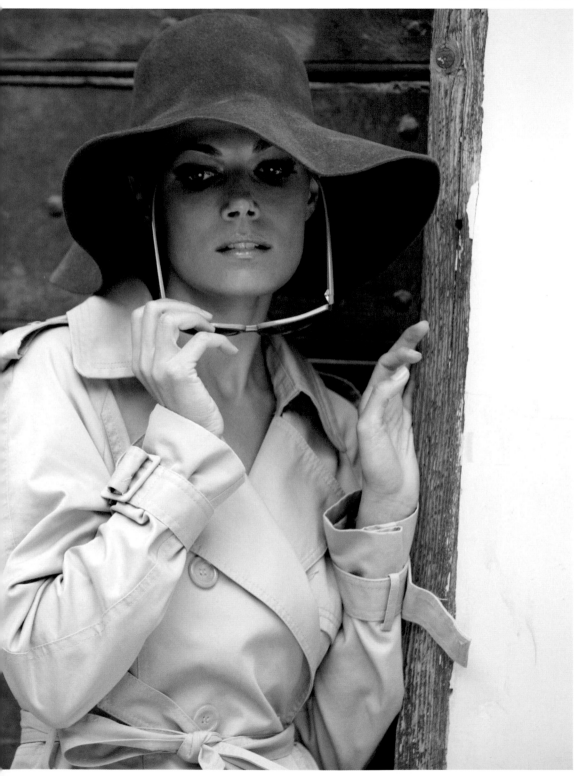

Brigitte Bardot, 1963

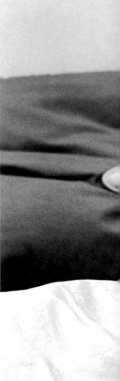

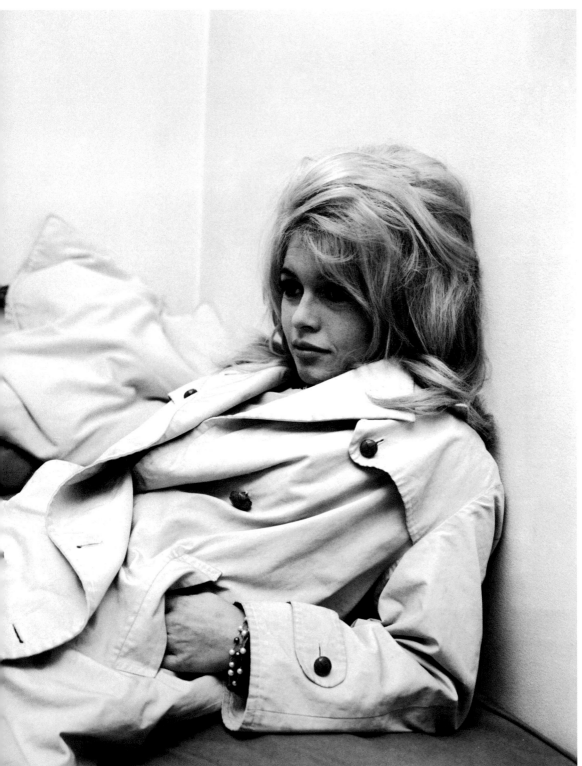

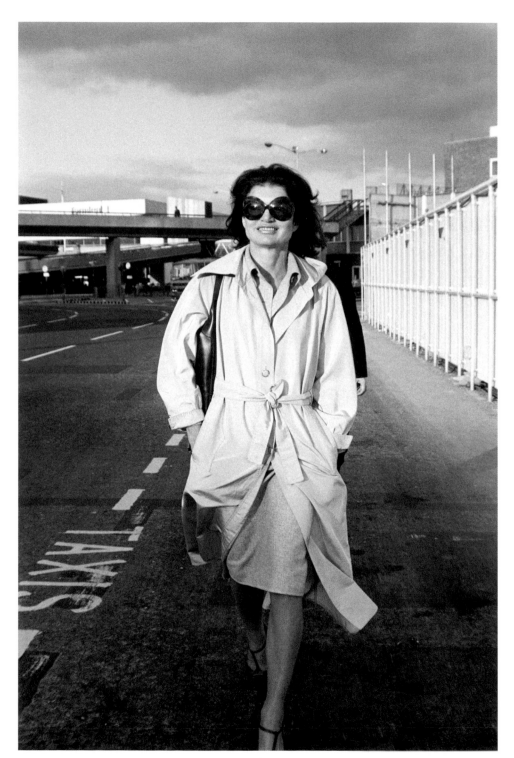

Jackie Onassis, London, 1975

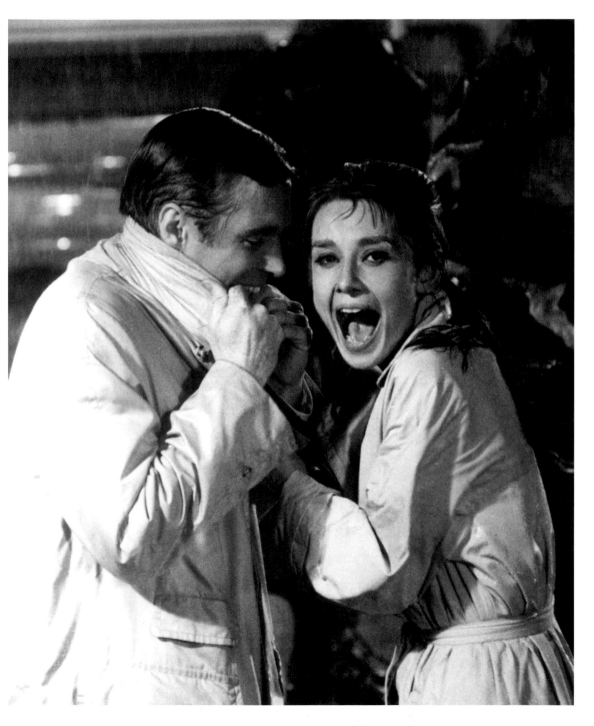

Audrey Hepburn and George Peppard, *Breakfast at Tiffany's*, 1961

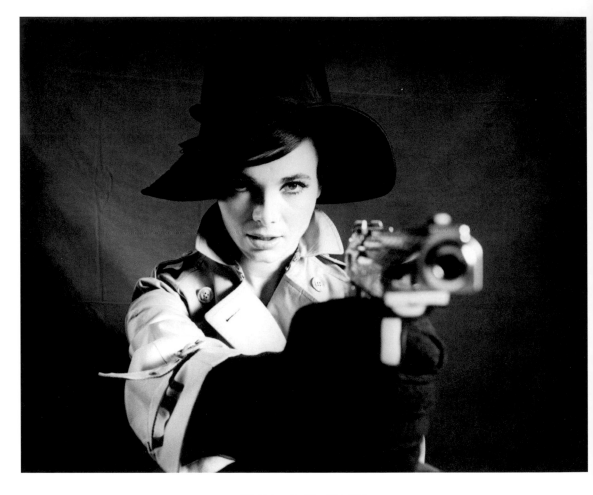

Gila Golan, *Our Man Flint*, 1966

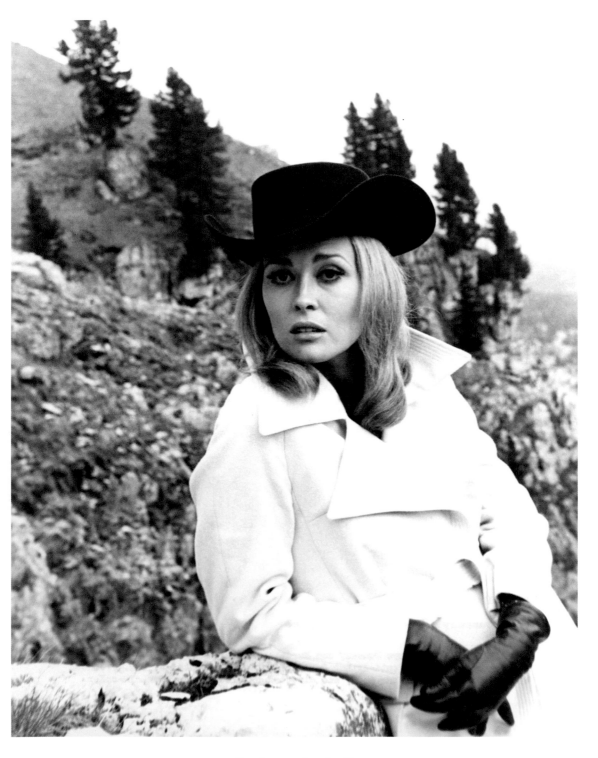

Faye Dunaway, *Amanti*, 1968

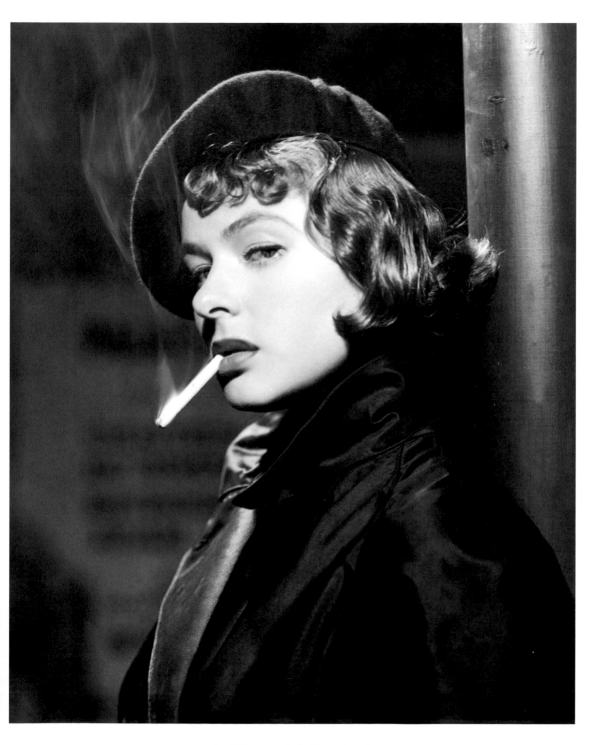

Ingrid Bergman, *Arch of Triumph*, 1948

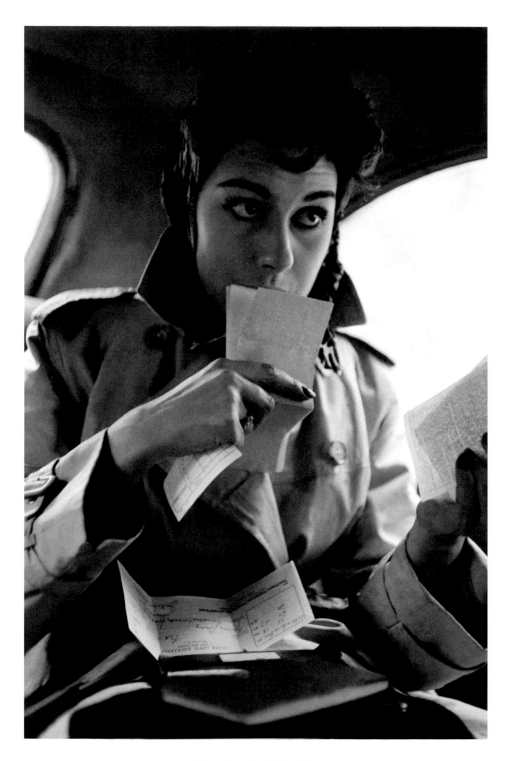

Nancy Berg, New York, 1956

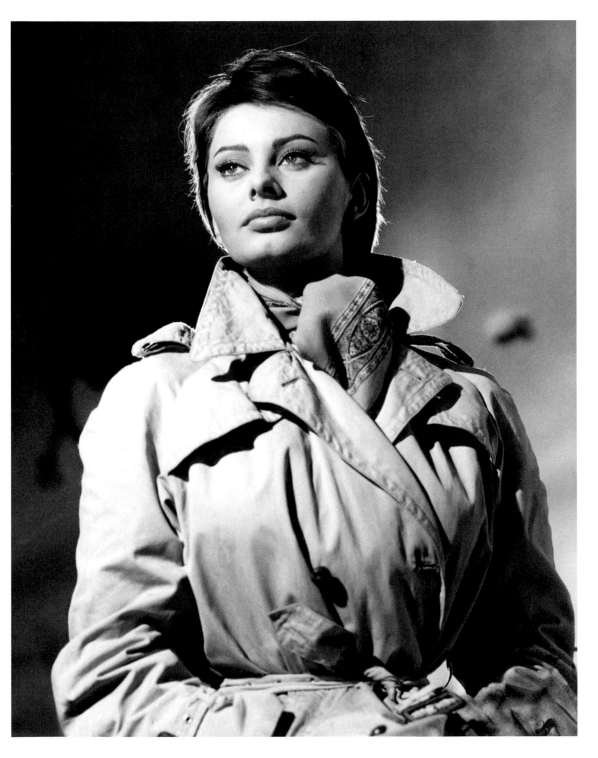

Sophia Loren, *The Key*, 1958

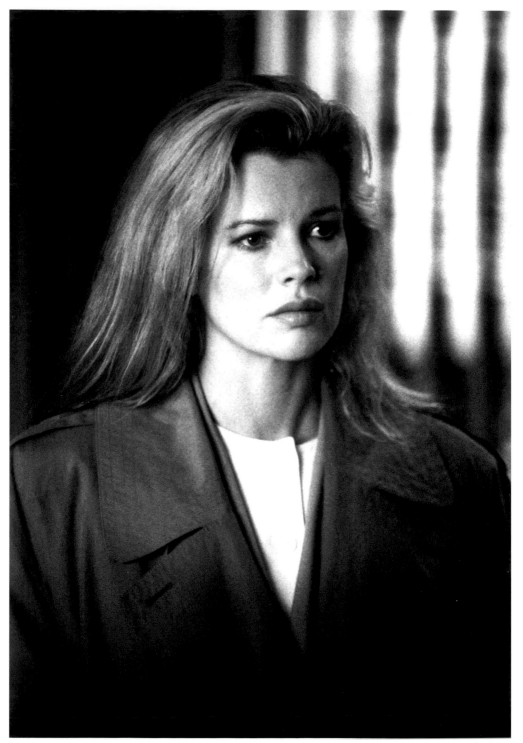

Kim Basinger, *Final Analysis*, 1992

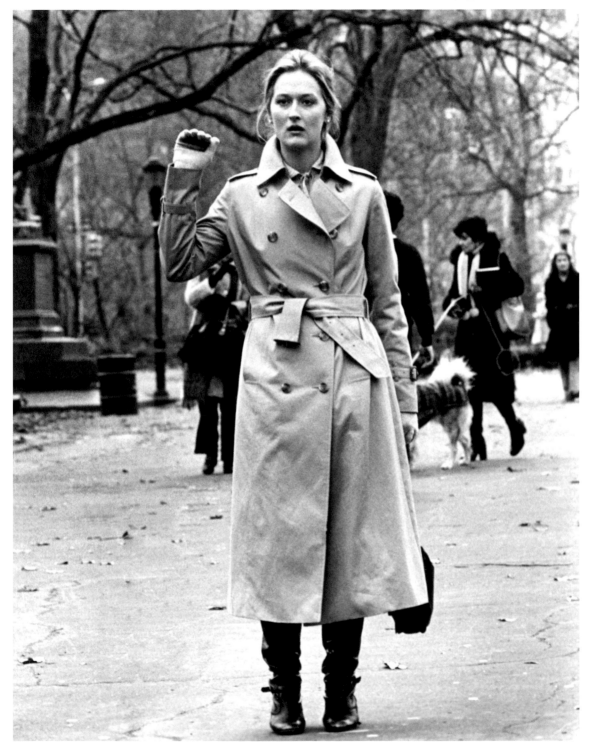

Meryl Streep, *Kramer vs. Kramer*, 1979

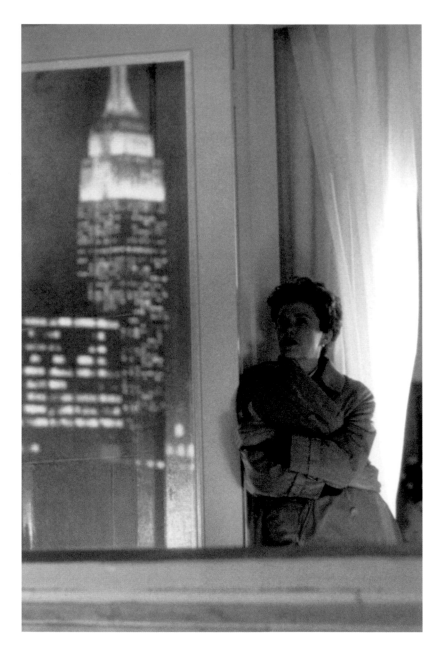

Annette Bening, *Love Affair*, 1994

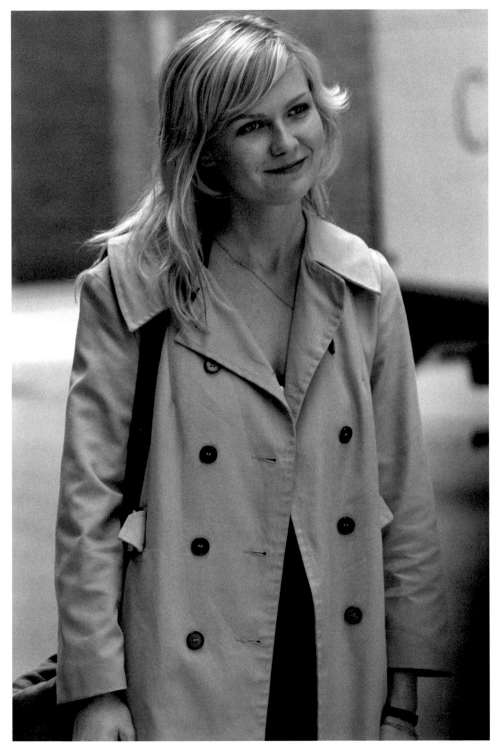

Kirsten Dunst, *Elizabethtown*, 2005

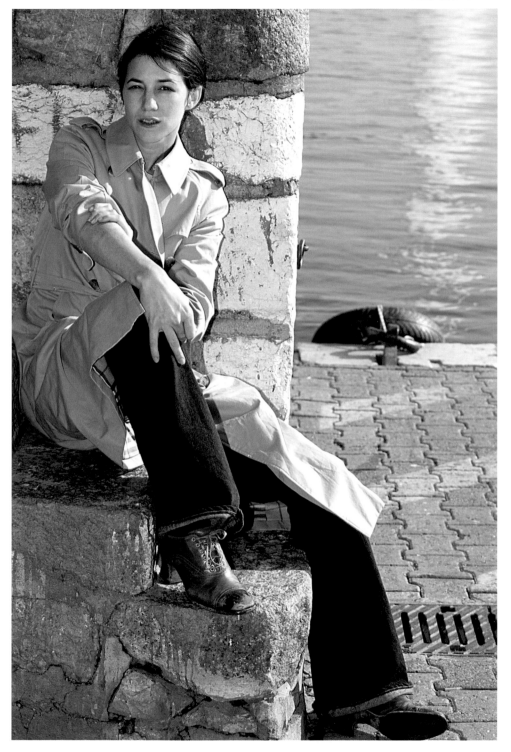

Charlotte Gainsbourg, 2002

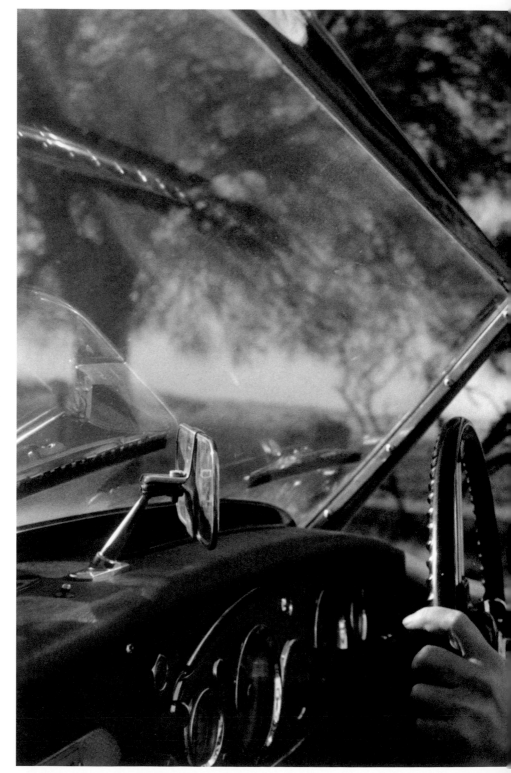

Ava Gardner,
On the Beach,
1959

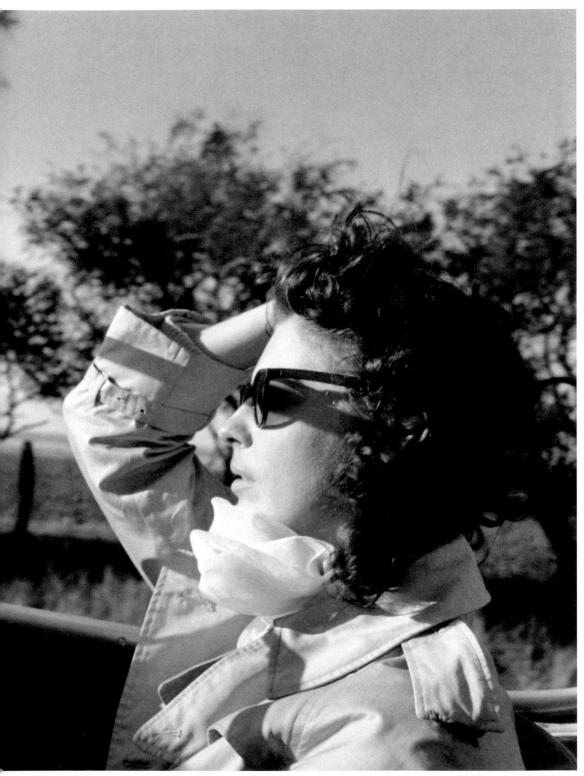

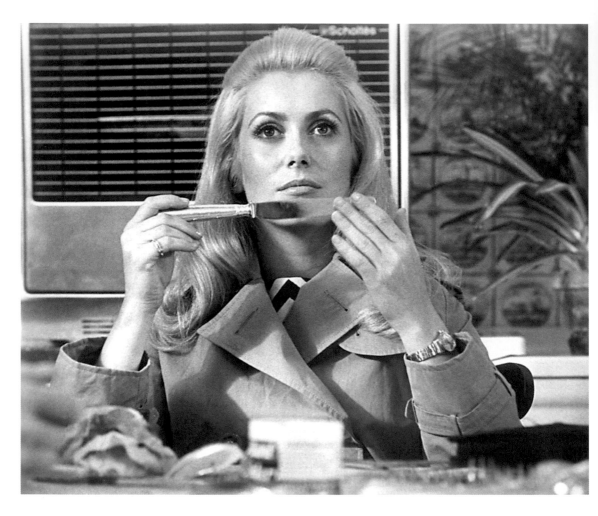

Catherine Deneuve, *Mississippi Mermaid*, 1969

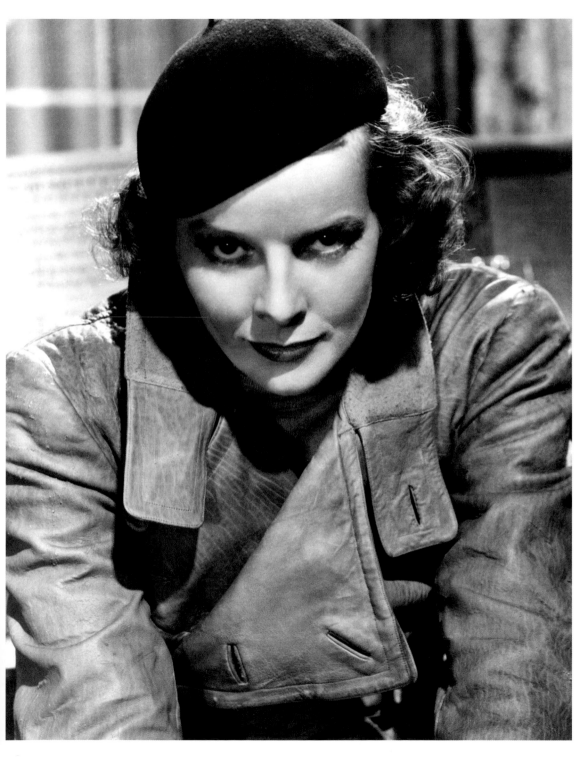

Katharine Hepburn, *Christopher Strong*, 1933

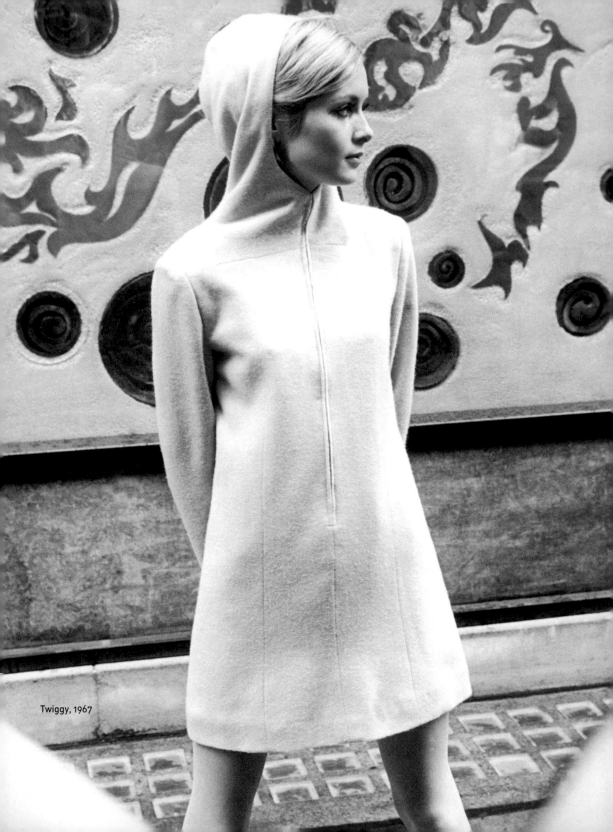

Twiggy, 1967

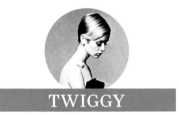

TWIGGY

The Miniskirt

The miniskirt enables young ladies to run faster,
and because of it, they may have to.

JOHN V. LINDSAY

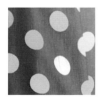

Icon **Twiggy**
Designer **Mary Quant**
Film ***Blow-Up***, Michelangelo Antonioni, 1966

Twiggy and her cat, London, 1966

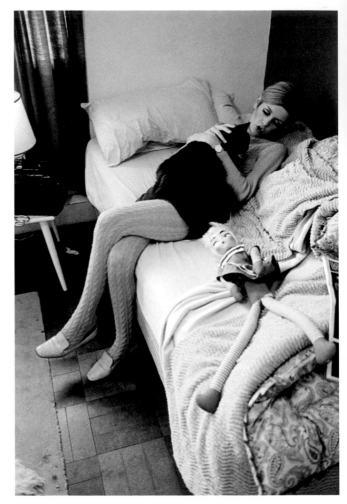

Her name was Leslie Hornby, but they called her 'Twiggy'. In 1966 she was hired as a model by Mary Quant, who is generally considered to have popularized the shocking skirt that ended above the knee – sometimes high above it. The invention of the miniskirt has long been the subject of dispute: in France the designer André Courrèges is credited as its true creator, while others attribute it to the costume designer Helen Rose, who designed various versions for the actress Anne Francis in the science-fiction film *Forbidden Planet* (Fred M. Wilcox, 1956).

Nonetheless, it was Twiggy who both supplied the face and modelled the new uniform for a generation that was striving for radical change, a culture in which being young was everything. The teenage Twiggy had no bust, hips or bottom: but such was her fame that young women around the globe cut their hair, applied their make-up and, of course, dressed just like her. The world was changing: the Vietnam War had begun, Pop art had exploded, Martin Luther King had received the Nobel Peace Prize, the Beatles ruled the world and women's liberation was growing.

Sabah, a famous Lebanese singer, was an icon of this struggle. Born in 1927 in Bdadoun, a small town not far from Beirut, she was the first public woman in the Arabic world to wear a miniskirt. She was seen as a feminist heroine and has been honoured both internationally and in her homeland.

The miniskirt is the best-loved garment of all time, at least according to 3,500 customers questioned in a survey for the British department store Harvey Nichols. Twiggy's 'rival', Veruschka von Lehndorff, wore it memorably in a famous scene from *Blow-Up* (Michelangelo Antonioni, 1966) in which she appeared as herself and was photographed by David Hemmings, playing a character inspired by David Bailey, in a tempestuous and mysterious portrayal of Swinging London. *The Mini-Skirt Mob* (Maury Dexter, 1968) even depicted a dangerous girl gang, led by blonde actress Diane McBain, that had a strict miniskirt dress code and rode motorbikes. But many thousands of legs had to be exposed to the fresh air by an army of persistent women, accompanied by lots of irreverent whistling and cheeky comments, before society's standards of decency came to terms with the idea of the miniskirt.

Ever since then, the miniskirt has ruled supreme: be it in the futuristic form

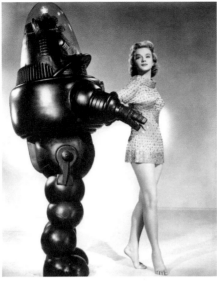

Anne Francis,
Forbidden Planet, 1956

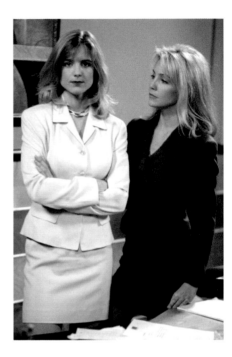

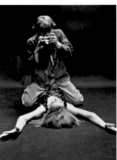

David Hemmings and
Verushka, *Blow-Up*, 1966

Courtney Thorne-Smith and Heather Locklear,
Melrose Place, 1995

modelled by Jane Fonda in *Barbarella* (Roger Vadim, 1968), the superficially innocent version worn by Sharon Stone in *Basic Instinct* (Paul Verhoeven, 1992), or the unforgettable Charlize Theron in a television commercial for Martini, wearing a tiny skirt that gradually unravelled its way up her hips. This sexy little piece of fabric embodies one of the most fascinating paradoxes of fashion: as Nigel Cawthorne notes in *Key Moments in Fashion*, it suggests strength and vulnerability, independence and a desire to please. It covers and reveals; it is grown-up but full of fun; it is both liberated and submissive. This paradoxical nature was happily resolved when the miniskirt became an acceptable

part of the power suit for working women, paired with masculine jackets with squared-off shoulders and double-breasted buttons. Television stars such as Sarah Jessica Parker in *Sex and The City* and Heather Locklear in *Melrose Place* have transformed it from a teenage fad into a powerful ally for sophisticated, beautiful, thirty-something women in complete control of their lives. And, as Valentino has often said: 'the miniskirt is a garment that no woman can do without, because the knees are the last part of the female figure to show their true age.'

Let's hear it for the miniskirt; and for all the women who wear it, every day and everywhere.

Twiggy during a shoot in London, 1966

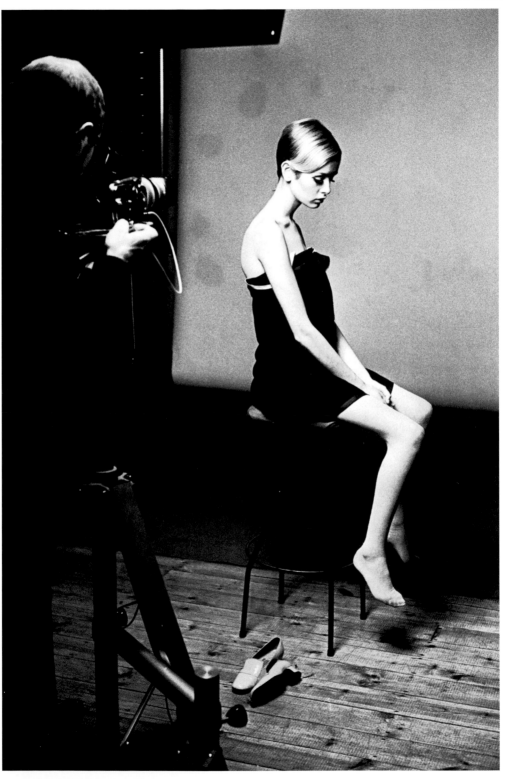

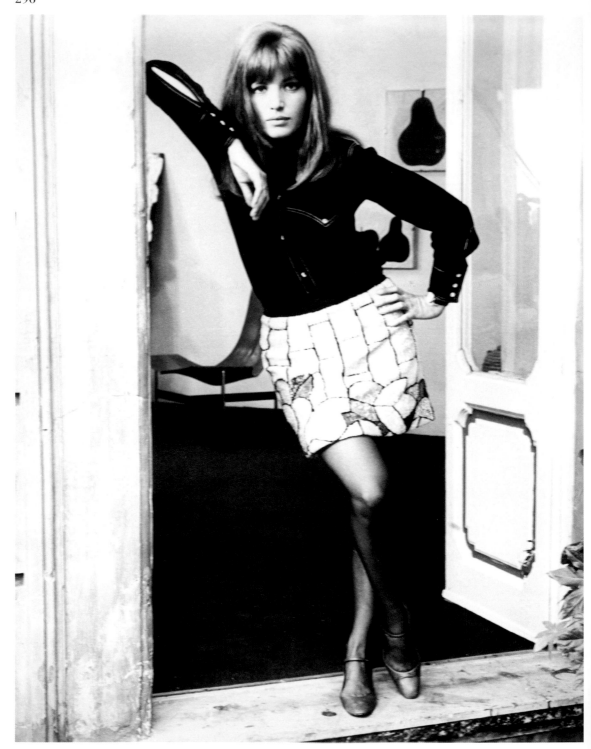

Monica Vitti, *I Married You For Fun*, 1967

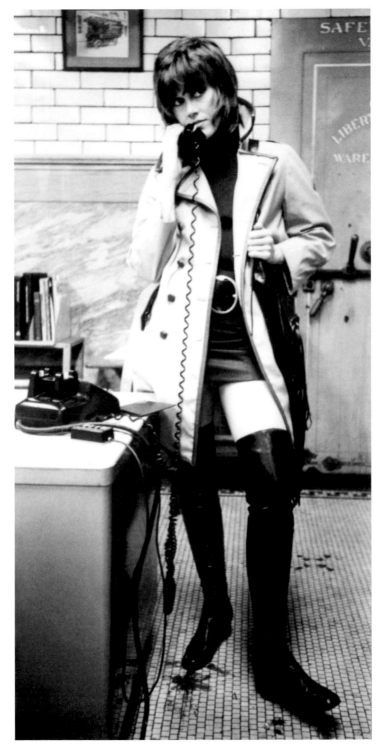

Jane Fonda, *Klute*, 1971

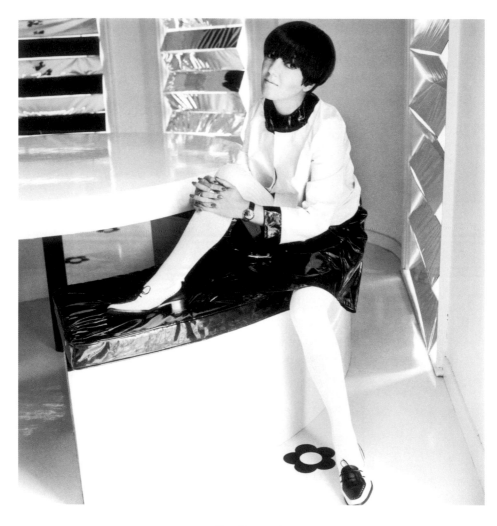

Mary Quant, 1965

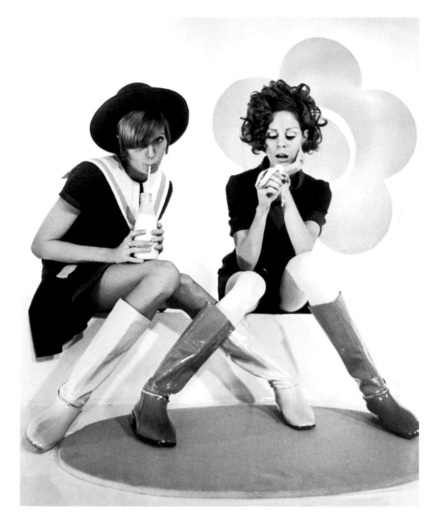

Murph and Jackie wearing designs by Mary Quant, London, 1967

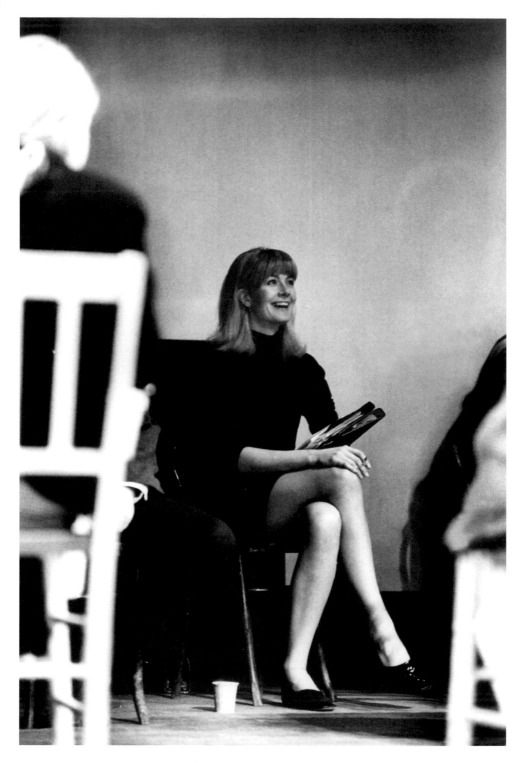

Vanessa Redgrave during rehearsals for *The Prime of Miss Jean Brodie*, 1966

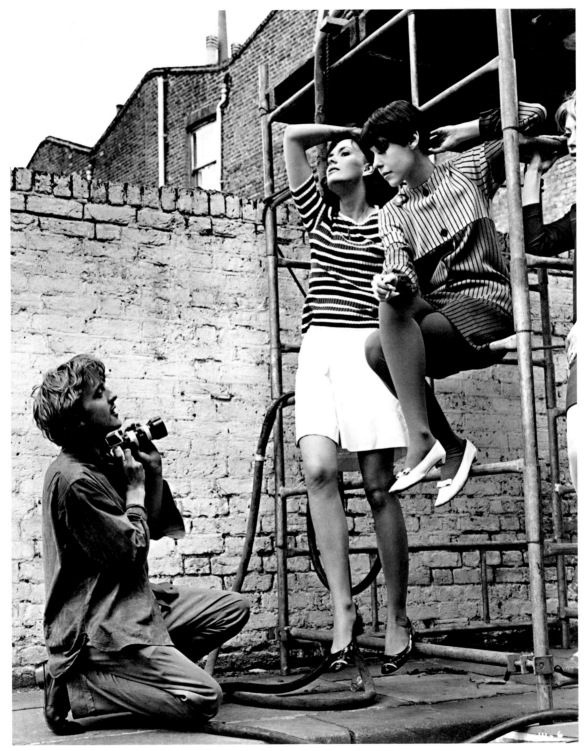

David Hemmings, Ann Norman and Peggy Moffitt, *Blow-Up*, 1966

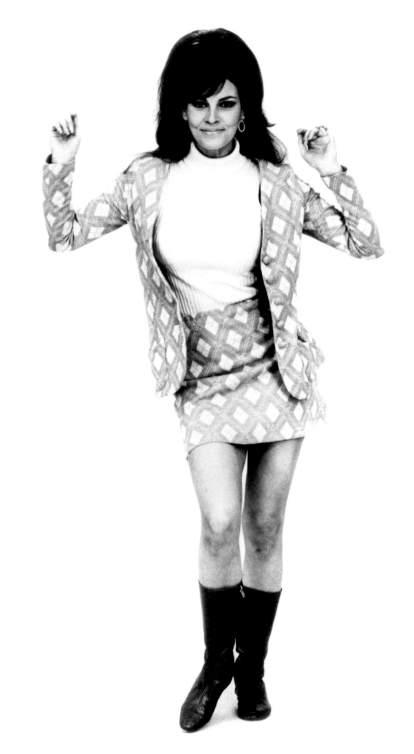

Raquel Welch, 1960s

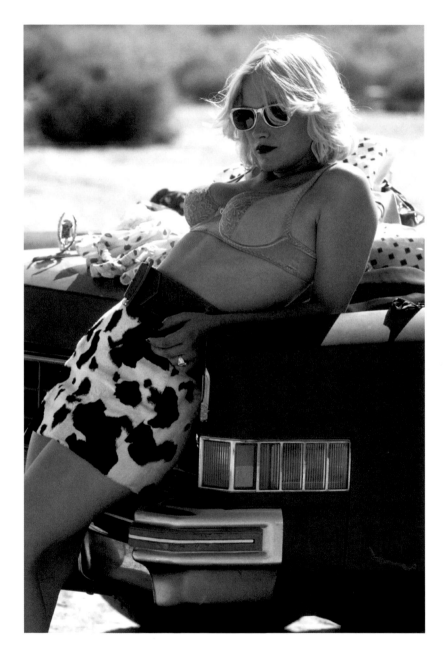

Patricia Arquette, *True Romance*, 1993

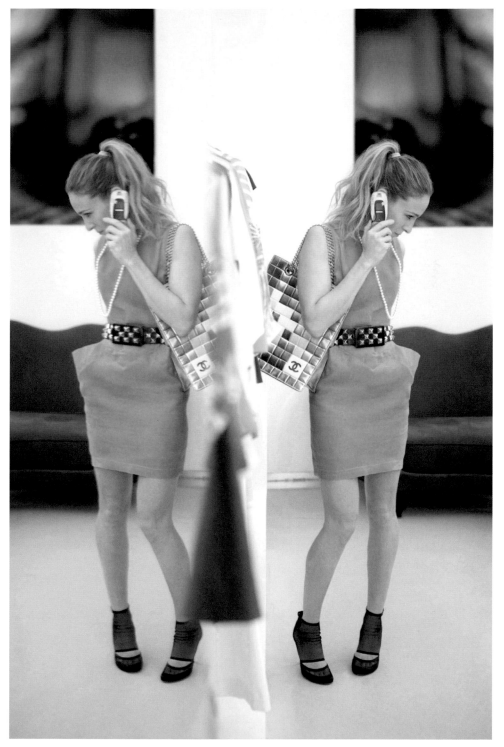

Sarah Jessica Parker, *Sex and the City*, 2008

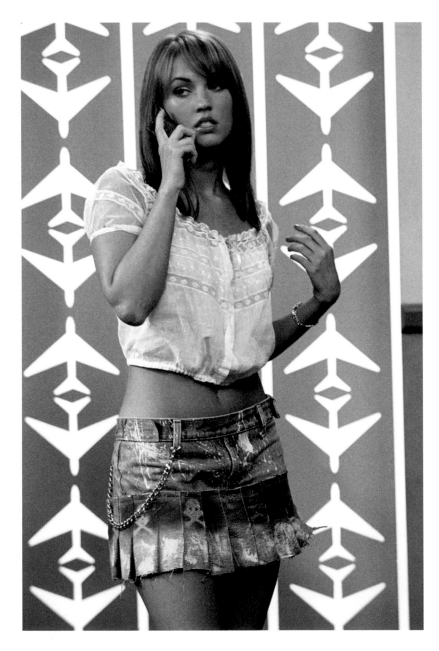

Megan Fox, *Hope & Faith*, 2003

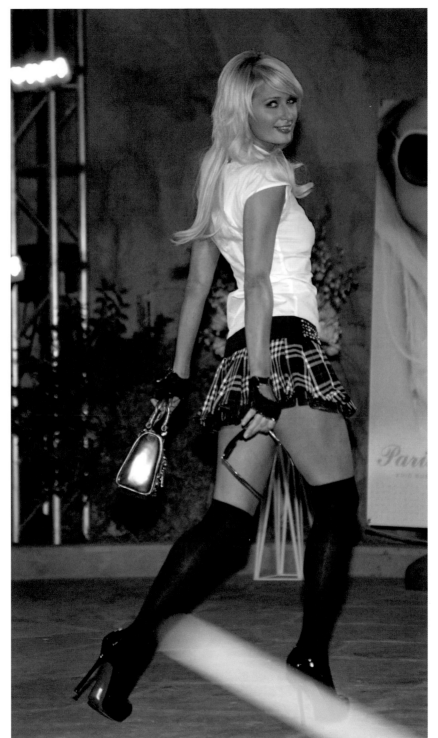

Paris Hilton, Las Vegas, 2009

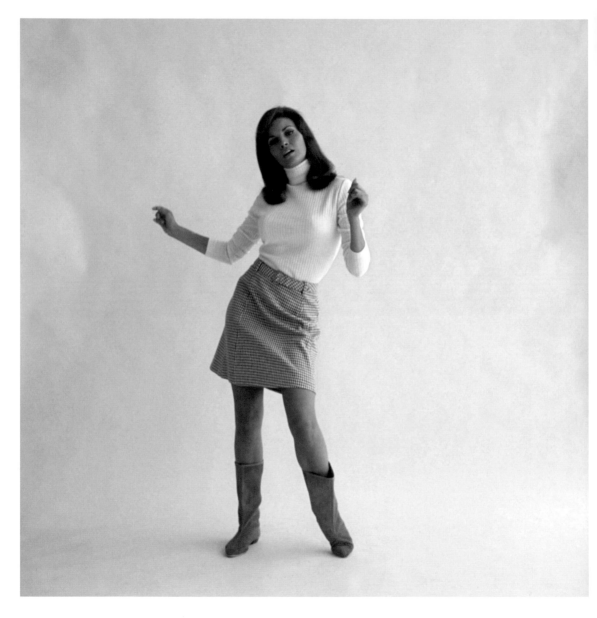

Raquel Welch, 1960s

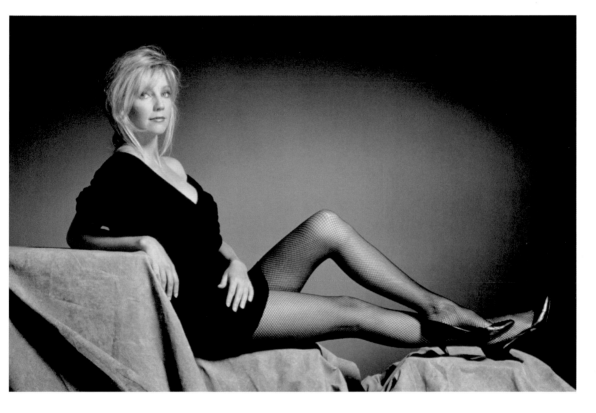

Heather Locklear, *Dynasty: The Reunion*, 1991

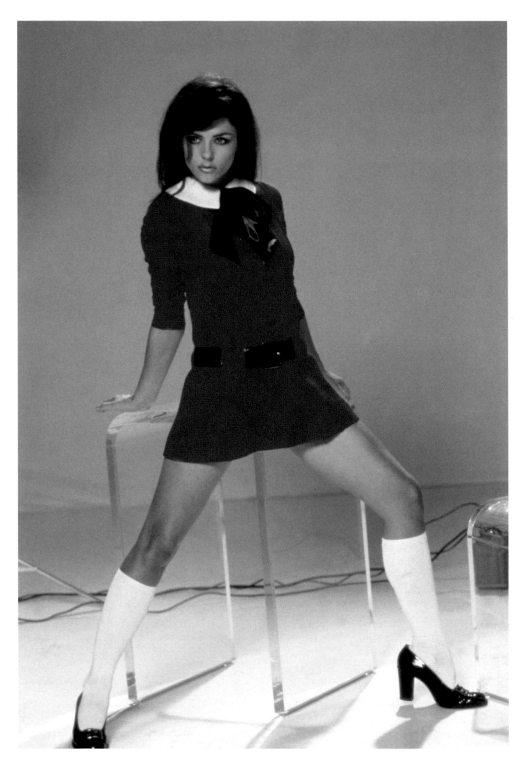

Elisabeth Hurley, *Austin Powers: International Man of Mystery*, 1997

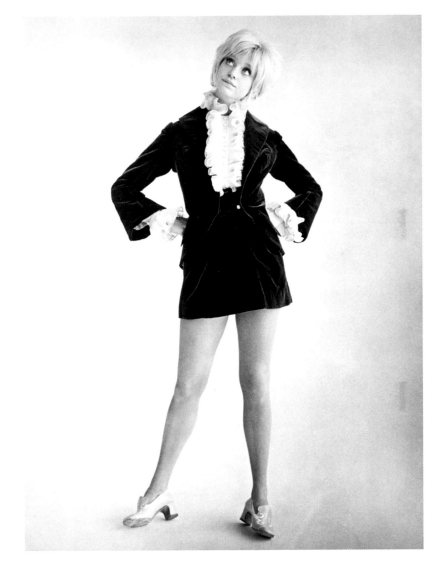

Goldie Hawn, *Cactus Flower*, 1969

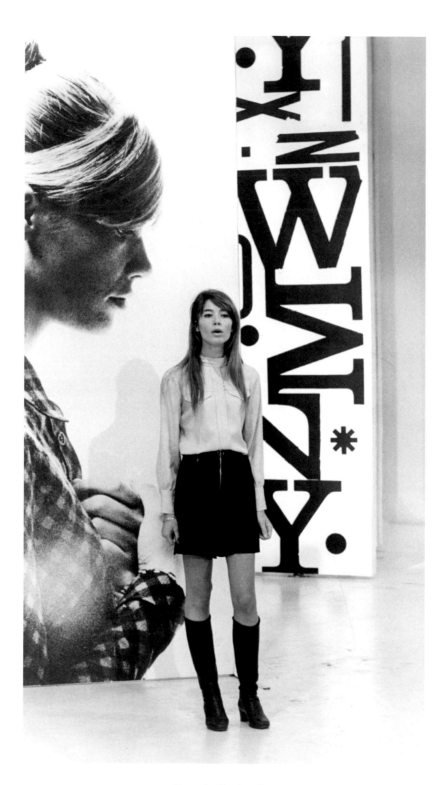

Françoise Hardy, 1960s

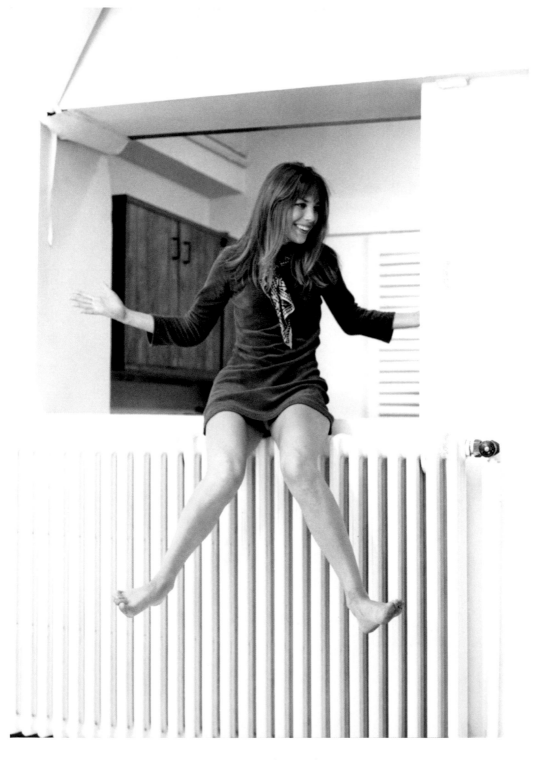

Jane Birkin, *Slogan*, 1969

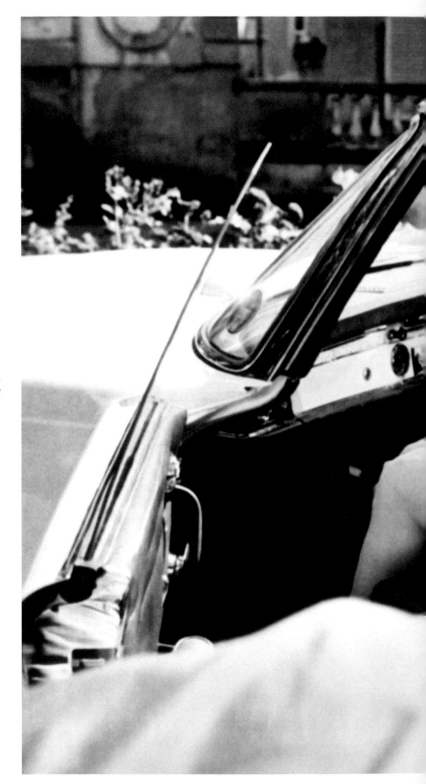

Audrey Hepburn, *Two for the Road*, 1967

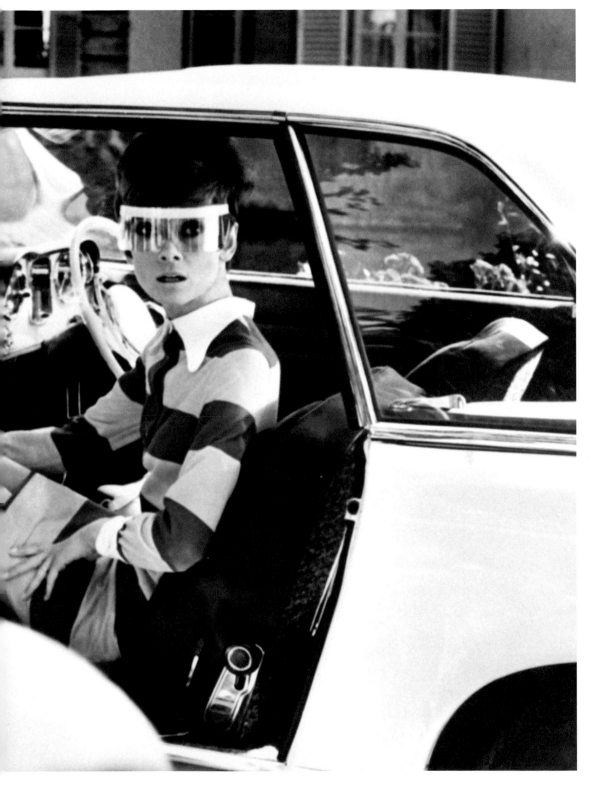

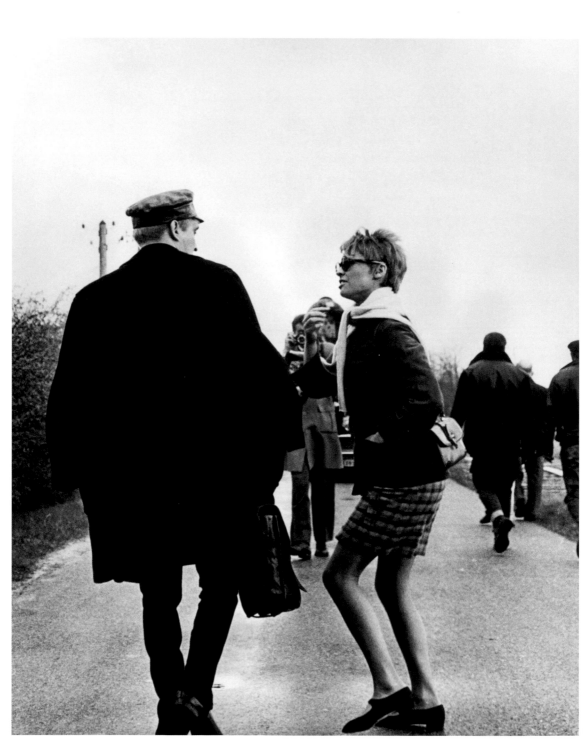

Julie Christie and Oskar Werner, France, 1966

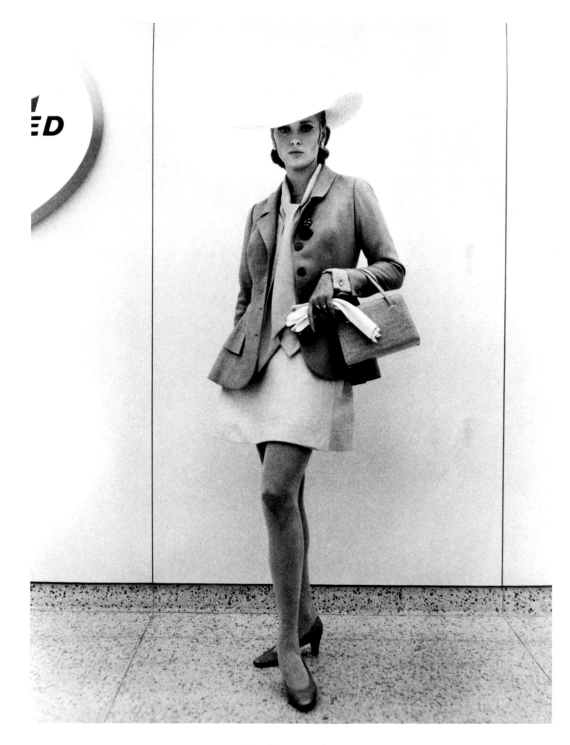

Faye Dunaway, 1960s

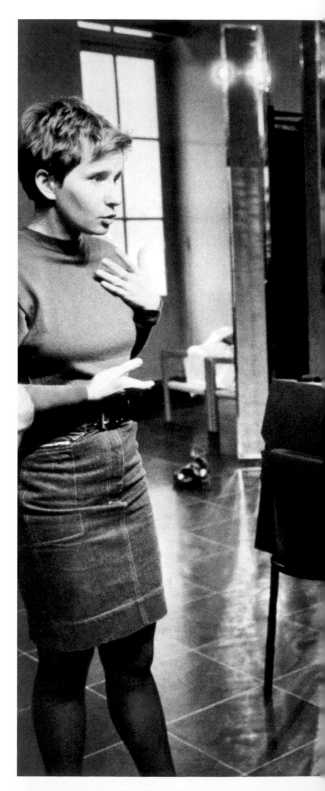

Tina Turner and her stylist Azzedine Alaia

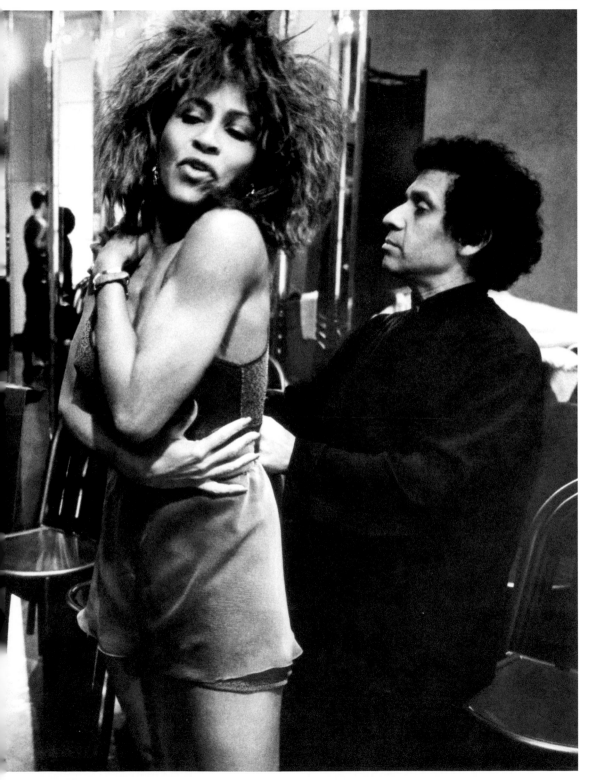

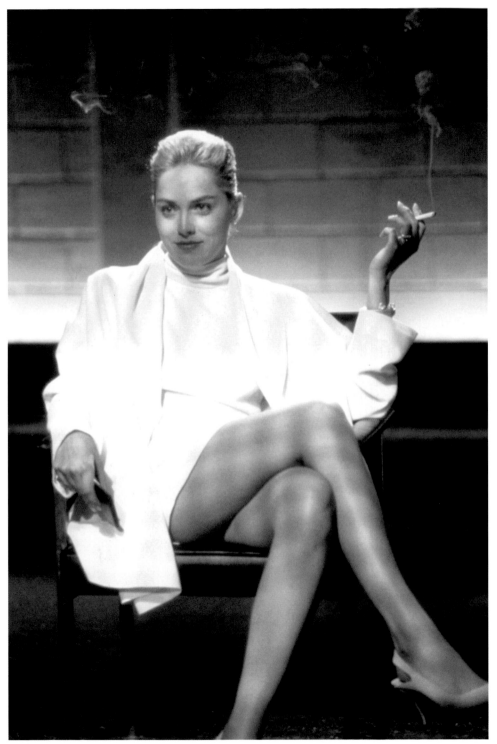

Sharon Stone, *Basic Instinct*, 1992

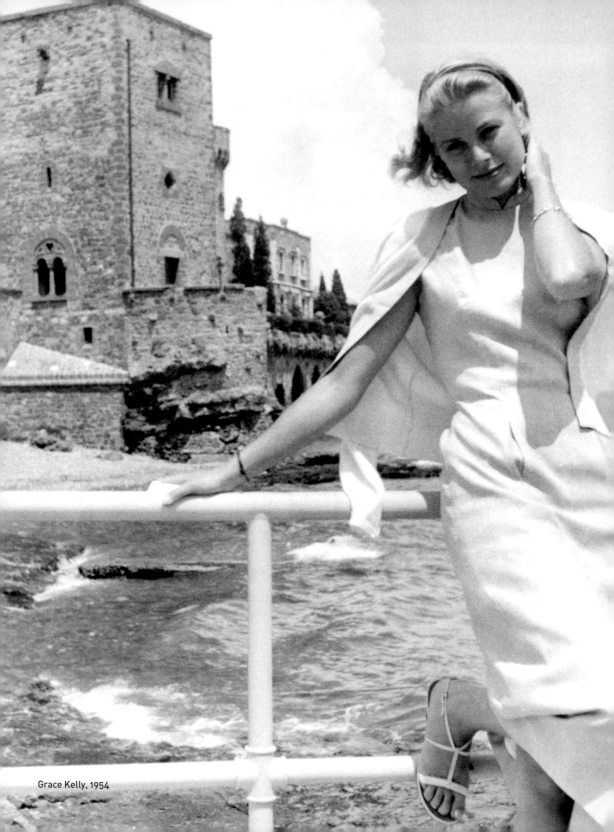
Grace Kelly, 1954

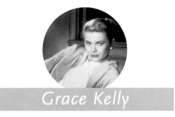

Grace Kelly

The Twinset

The cardigan ... is a signal that powerful women no longer
need to prove their strength by dressing shoulder to
padded shoulder with men.

SUZY MENKES, *INTERNATIONAL HERALD TRIBUNE*

Icon Grace Kelly
Designer Ballantyne
Film *Rear Window*, Alfred Hitchcock, 1954

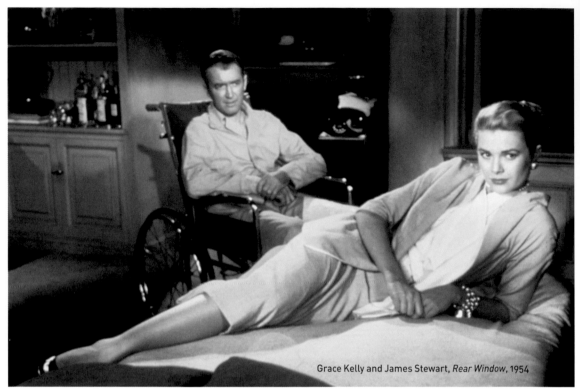

Grace Kelly and James Stewart, *Rear Window*, 1954

'May I ask you a personal question?', he says. 'I've been hoping you would,' she replies. He is John Robie, alias Cary Grant. She is Frances Stevens, alias Grace Kelly, in *To Catch a Thief* (Alfred Hitchcock, 1955). Both this film and Hitchcock's *Rear Window* (1954) allowed the director to present Kelly as his ideal of feminine beauty: a seemingly ice-cool blonde who is in reality a seething cauldron of emotion. The formal and sophisticated clothes she wears express the tension between her elegant appearance and her sparkling wit. 'Boiling ice' was how Hitchcock described her. It is said that when Grace Kelly gave up her career as an actress to become the Princess of Monaco, Hitchcock wept in secret. Her face, figure and style of performance embodied all his erotic obsessions, and she repaid him in inimitable style, with the three elements of dignity, naturalness and aristocratic mystery. This combination demanded extreme

elegance: she was regal and real, reassuring and voluptuous. Expensive accessories were a key part of her look – the 'Kelly Bag' made by Hermès acquired its name when the actress used it to hide her pregnancy from photographers – as was restrained but expensive jewelry, but the twinset was the definitive element.

The combination of a short-sleeved top and a matching buttoned cardigan in the same colour, both made from jersey knit, is still considered extremely modern. However, its origins are ancient, and humble: it simply evolved from the shawls and woollen jackets that women traditionally knitted to keep themselves warm on long winter nights. It was only after 1918 that cardigans were produced industrially and began to resemble the garments we know today. In the 1930s, Pringle designed a more elegant version suitable for afternoon wear. But it was not until the 1950s, when the twinset became associated with Grace Kelly's charming

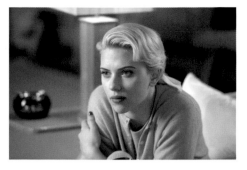

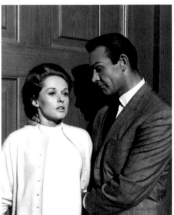

Scarlett Johansson,
Black Dahlia, 2006

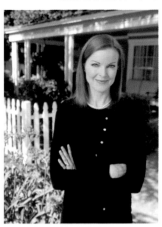

Marcia Cross,
Desperate Housewives, 2004

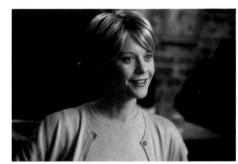

Tippi Hedren and
Sean Connery,
Marnie, 1964

Meg Ryan,
*You've Got
Mail*, 1998

beauty (and was also worn by Lauren Bacall, Deborah Kerr and Margot Fonteyn), that it became a fashion essential. By the 1960s, every lady needed several twinsets in different shades. Pure cashmere twinsets were famously worn by Tippi Hedren, another Hitchcock blonde, and by socialite Marella Agnelli.

Since then, the twinset has gone through several changes of fortune: it came back into fashion in the 1970s, with the cardigan now adorned by embroidery and jacquard designs. In the decade that followed, it fell foul of changing tastes and was considered suitable only for aunties, old maids and stern headmistress types. But it made a triumphant return in a sexy version worn by Scarlett Johansson in *The Black Dahlia* (Brian de Palma, 2006). It looked girlish on Reese Witherspoon in *Pleasantville* (Gary Ross, 1998), preppy on Meg Ryan in the sentimental *You've Got Mail* (Nora Ephron, 1998) and comfortable but gauche

on Gwyneth Paltrow in the role of the poet Sylvia Plath in *Sylvia* (Christine Jeffs, 2003). The present twinset revival is largely due to television series such as *Gossip Girl* and *Desperate Housewives* (where it is a signature look for the character Bree Van De Kamp, played by Marcia Cross).

Any frosty but fiery blonde actress will at some point be compared to Grace Kelly; indeed, many women would like to be her, right down to the twinset. In 2007 the pop singer Mika had a worldwide hit with his song about Grace Kelly: 'I try to be like Grace Kelly/But all her looks were too sad/So I try a little Freddie/I've gone identity mad!' Perhaps Alfred, wherever he may be, can now smile again.

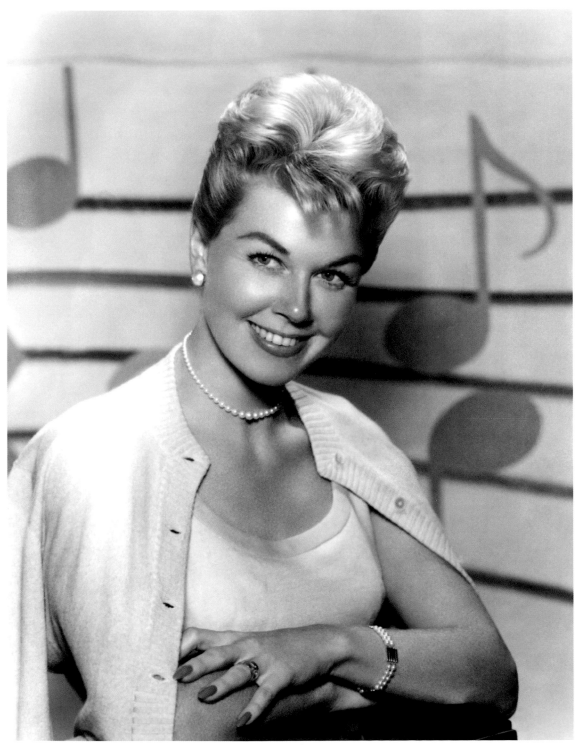

Doris Day, 1950s

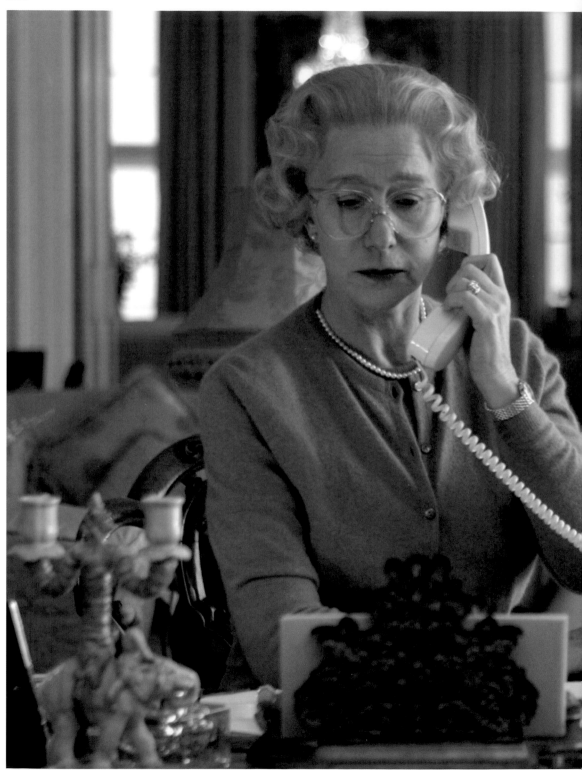

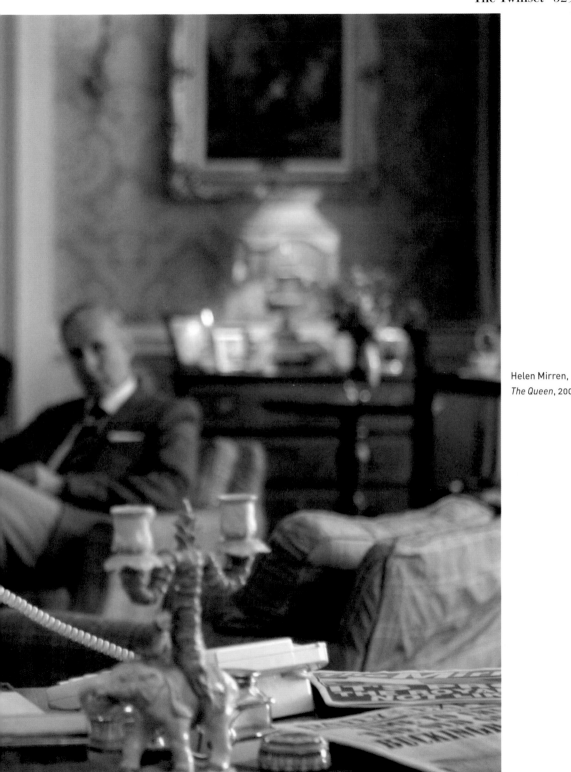

Helen Mirren,
The Queen, 2006

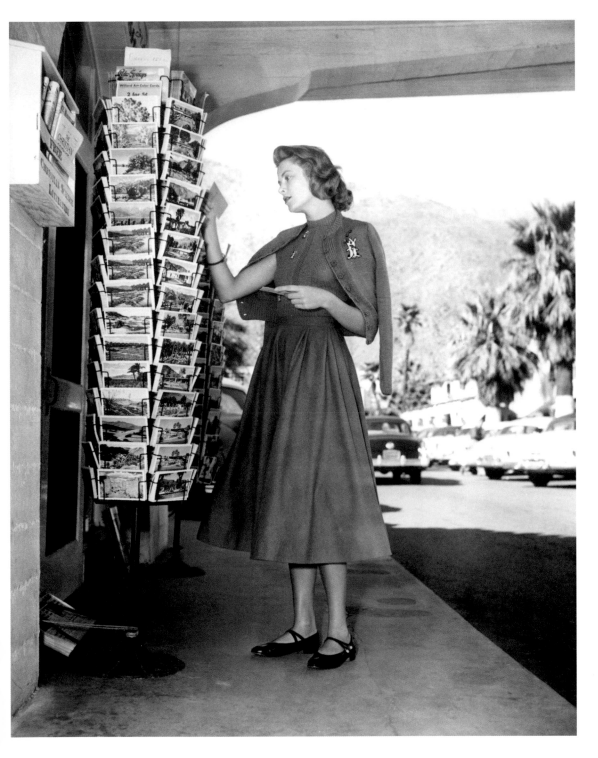

Grace Kelly, 1954

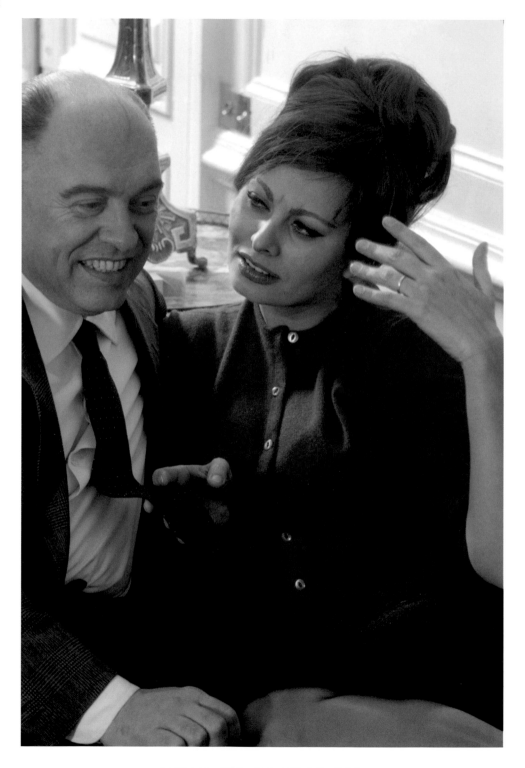

Sophia Loren with her husband Carlo Ponti, 1963

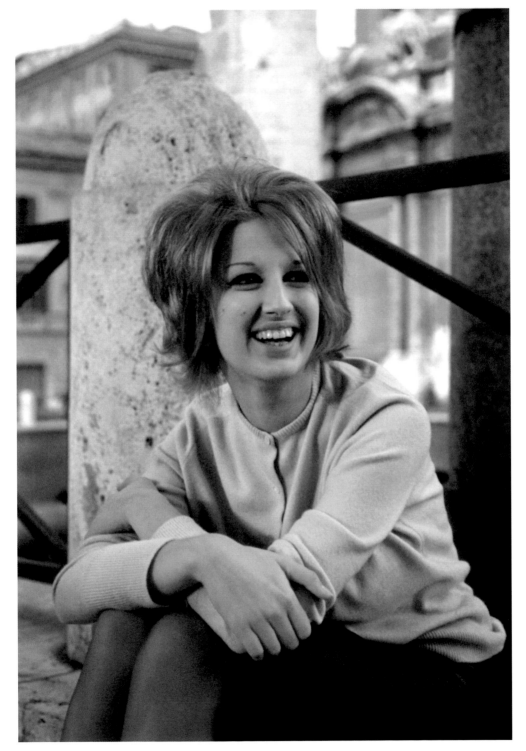

Mina, Rome, 1960

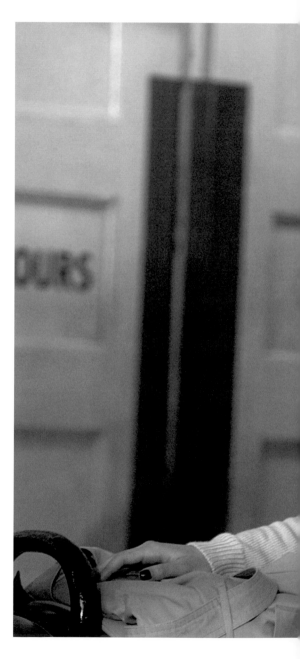

334

Scarlett Johansson, *Black Dahlia*, 2006

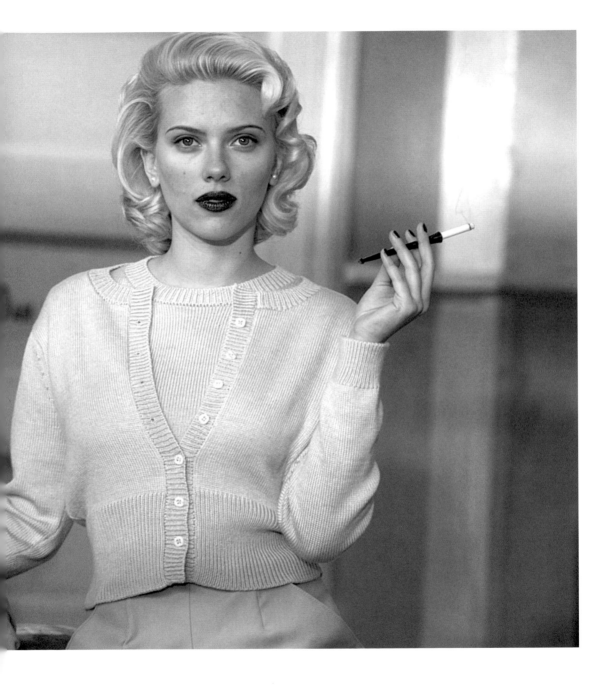

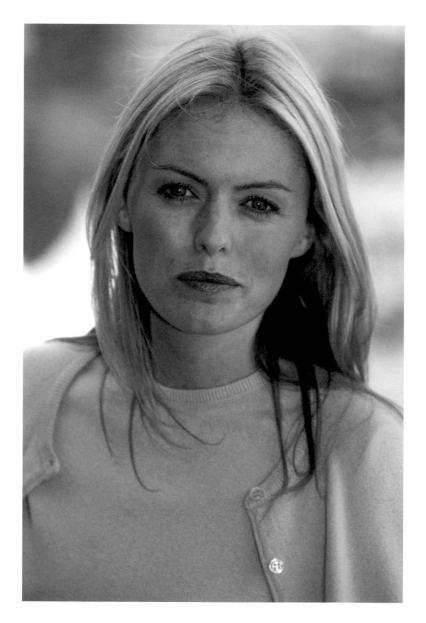

Patsy Kensit, Cannes, 1995

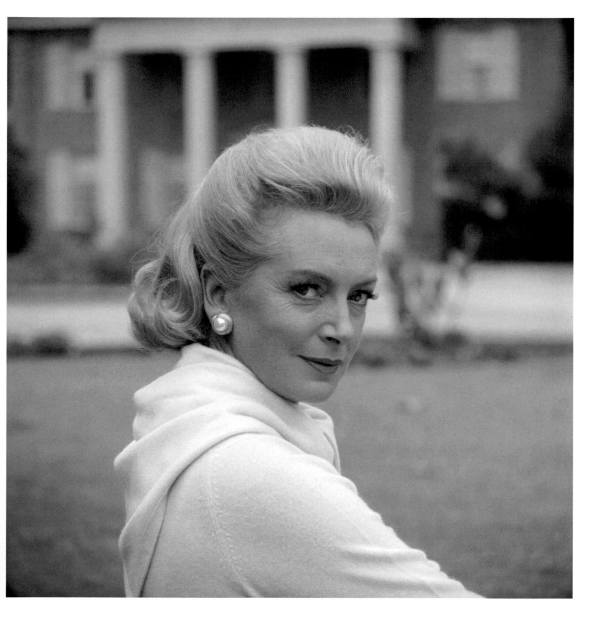

Deborah Kerr, *The Gypsy Moths*, 1969

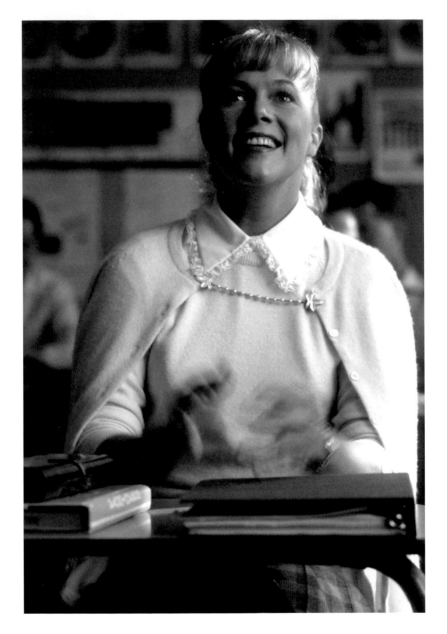

Kathleen Turner, *Peggy Sue Got Married*, 1986

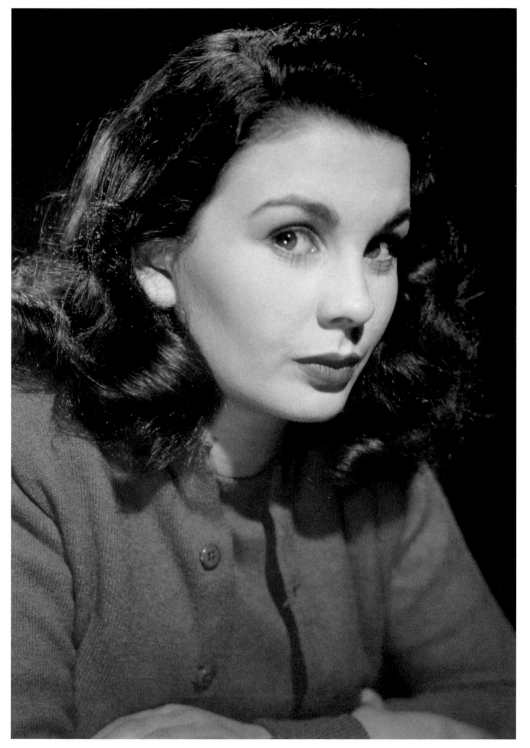

Jean Simmons, 1950s

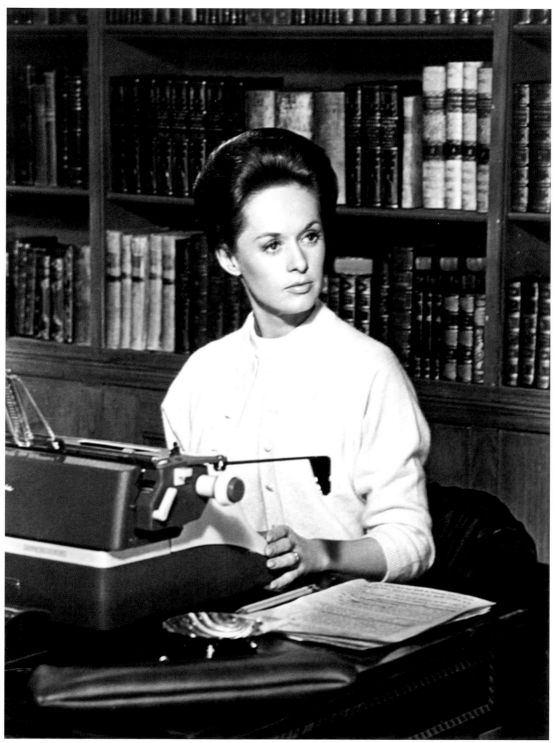

Tippi Hedren, *Marnie*, 1964

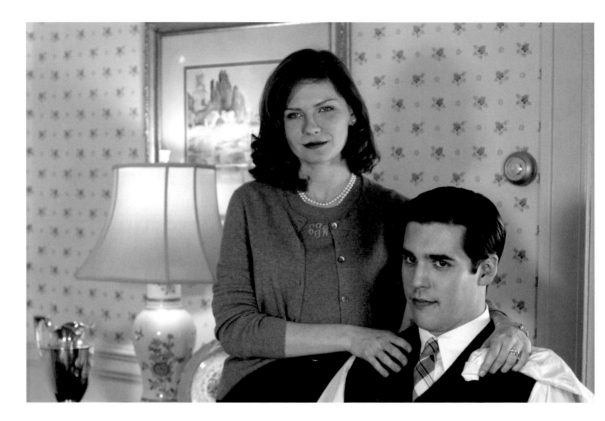

Kirsten Dunst and Jordan Bridges, *Mona Lisa Smile*, 2003

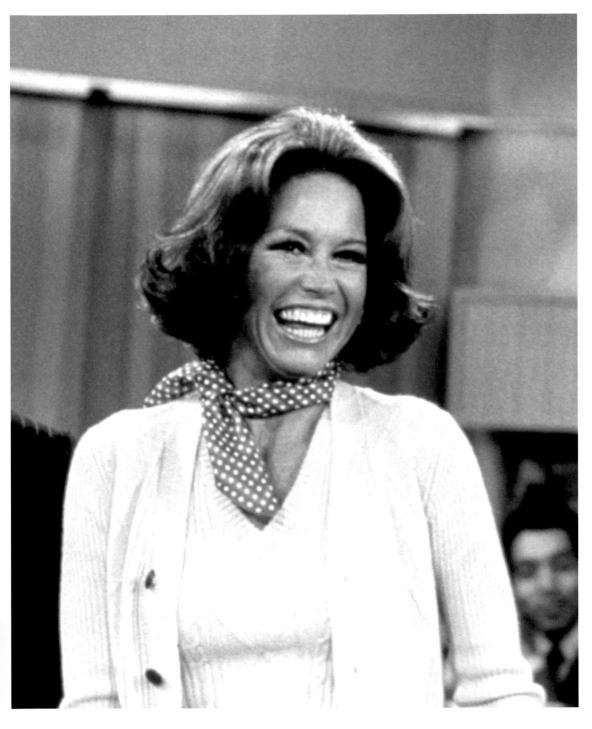

Mary Tyler Moore, *The Mary Tyler Moore Show*, 1970–77

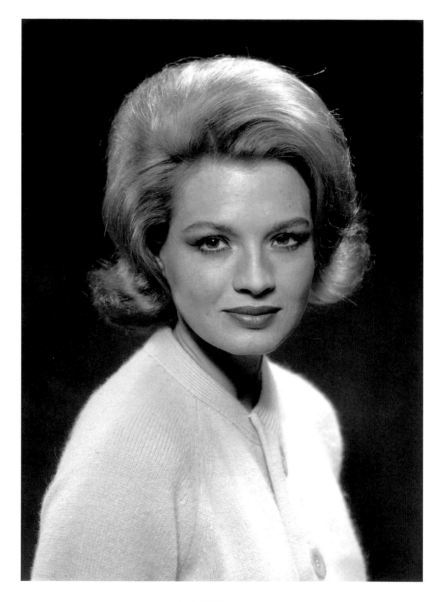

Angie Dickinson, 1963

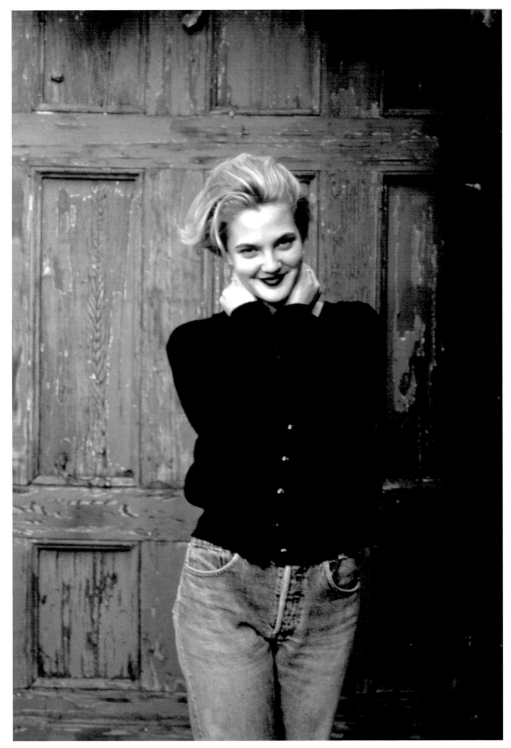

Drew Barrymore, 1990s

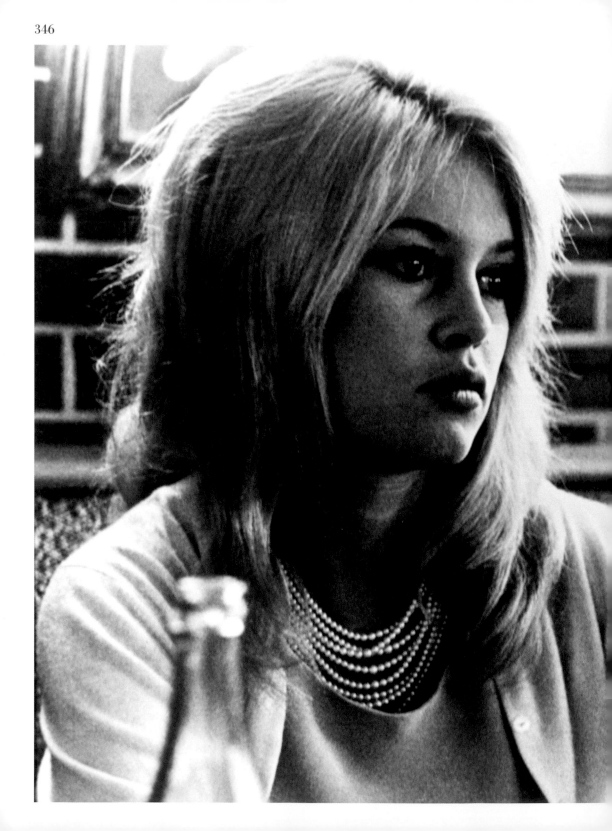

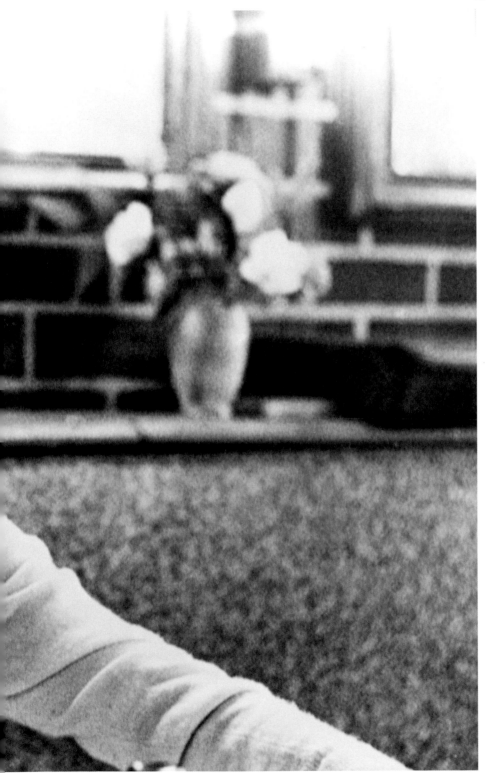

Brigitte Bardot,
1960s

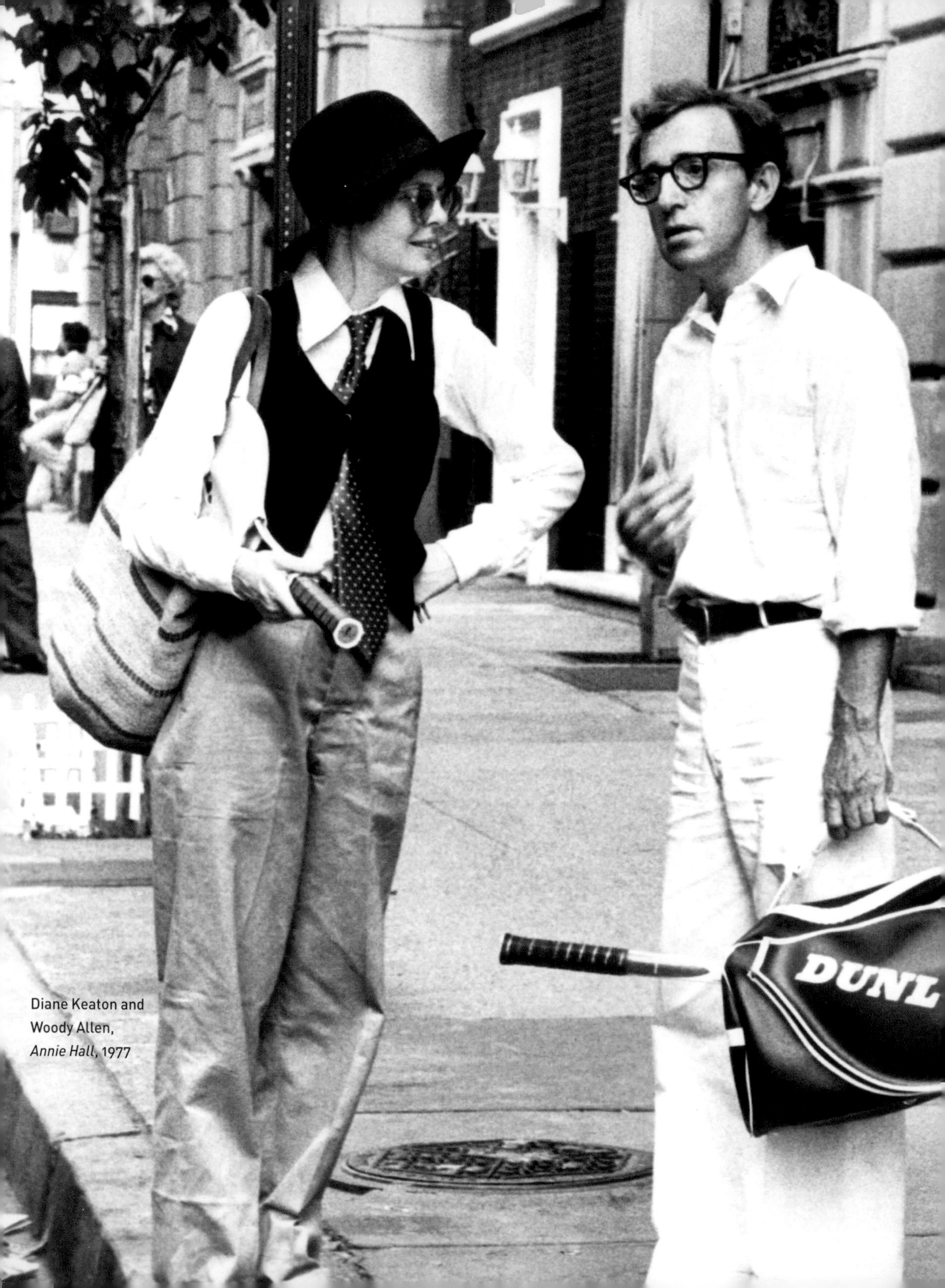

Diane Keaton and
Woody Allen,
Annie Hall, 1977

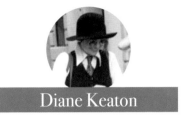

Diane Keaton

The Androgynous Look

Different though the sexes are, they intermix. In every human
being a vacillation from one sex to the other takes place, and
often it is only the clothes that keep the male or female likeness,
while underneath the sex is very opposite of what it is above.

VIRGINIA WOOLF

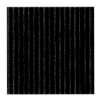

Icon **Diane Keaton**
Designer **Giorgio Armani**
Film ***Annie Hall*, Woody Allen, 1977**

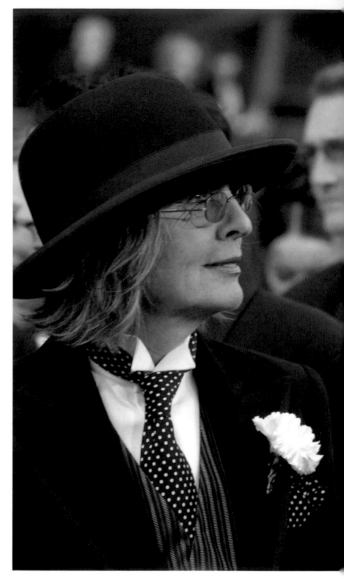

Diane Keaton at the
Academy Awards, 2004

Baggy trousers, men's jackets, ties worn like necklaces, white shirts with rolled-up sleeves, men's waistcoats, wide-brimmed felt hats and glasses with heavy frames: they are all essential accessories for the lead character in *Annie Hall* (Woody Allen, 1977), played by Diane Keaton.

The androgynous look had already had famous exponents in cinema, but it was with Diane Keaton that it acquired its most expressive form. It demonstrated that not only had women's consciousness been raised definitively since the advent of feminism, as clinging clothes and visible lingerie were no longer necessary tools of seduction, but also that the rules of attraction between the sexes had definitely changed. This look was so astonishingly successful that even Giorgio Armani, a rising star at the time, declared that Keaton's character had influenced him and that he believed that 'a woman wearing a man's overcoat as she walks along the street is much more sensual than one wearing an evening dress'.

In the 1980s, this way of living and dressing became a uniform for the successful woman who could demonstrate that she was equal to men by literally wearing their clothes. This clash of the masculine and the feminine also had a darkly seductive side, as a female body hidden beneath clothes stolen from a man's wardrobe can be a powerful source of sexual fantasies.

Initially, crossdressing on film was an intriguing game for actresses. Among the first to take the plunge was silent star Louise Brooks; she was famously followed by Greta Garbo, whose character dressed in men's clothes to increase her authority in *Queen Christina* (Rouben Mamoulian, 1933). The costume designer Howard Shoup recalled that off-screen, Marlene Dietrich had outfits made to match those of her male accompanists. In *Seven Sinners* (Tay Garnett, 1940) we see Dietrich seducing that embodiment of testosterone, John Wayne, while wearing a naval uniform identical to his own. Even Katharine Hepburn used men's clothes to create a powerful image in *Christopher Strong* (Dorothy Arzner, 1933), in which she played a pilot in love with a married man. In 1950, the grown-up Judy

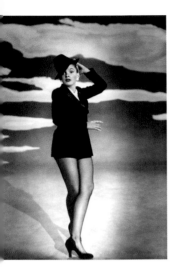

Judy Garland,
Summer Stock, 1950

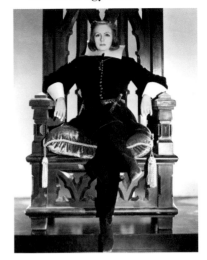

Greta Garbo,
Queen Cristina, 1933

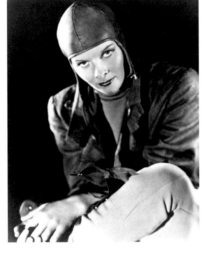

Katharine Hepburn,
Christopher Strong, 1933

Garland made a triumphant return wearing a tuxedo jacket and a black fedora for her dance routine in *Summer Stock*; an ensemble that was revisited by her daughter, Liza Minnelli, many years later. In *Victor Victoria* (Blake Edwards, 1982) Julie Andrews plays 'a woman who pretends to be a man who pretends to be a woman' and fools everyone, until an underworld boss, played by James Garner, falls in love with her. Barbra Streisand both directed and starred in *Yentl*, the story of a Jewish girl in Poland who disguises herself as a boy in order to attend a religious school and falls in love with a man, who in turn is in love with another girl whose parents are determined that she should marry Yentl. Female androgyny, as opposed to transvestism, is embodied by the lithe figure of Tilda Swinton, who as the hero–heroine of *Orlando* (Sally Potter, 1992) is perfectly at ease and equally seductive in both the crinoline dress of a 19th-century lady and the clinging breeches of an Elizabethan nobleman. The androgynous look implies that sexuality is primarily in the mind, and that apart from a few biological details the differences between men and women are a cultural construct that we can overturn simply by changing our clothes. When Dustin Hoffmann dresses as a woman in *Tootsie* (Sydney Pollack, 1982) he discovers a sensitivity that he didn't know he possessed. Such is the power of androgyny.

Tilda Swinton, Venice, 2002

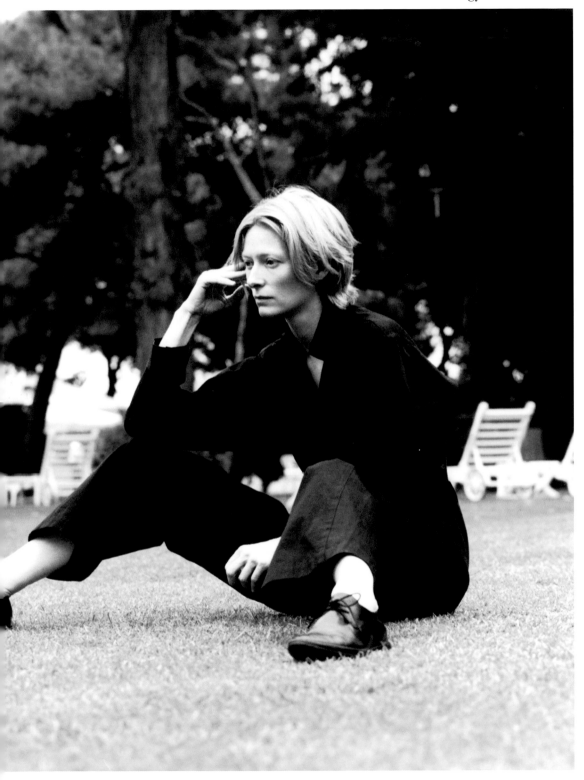

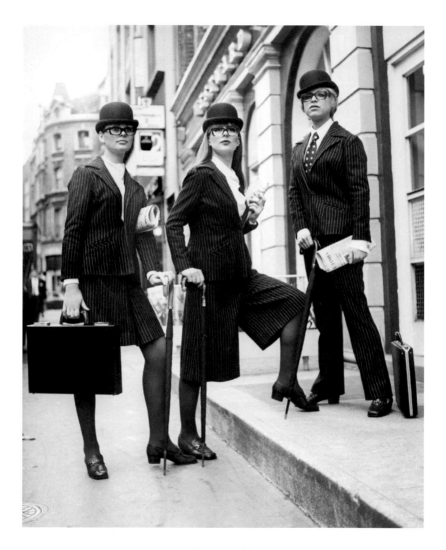

London, 1968

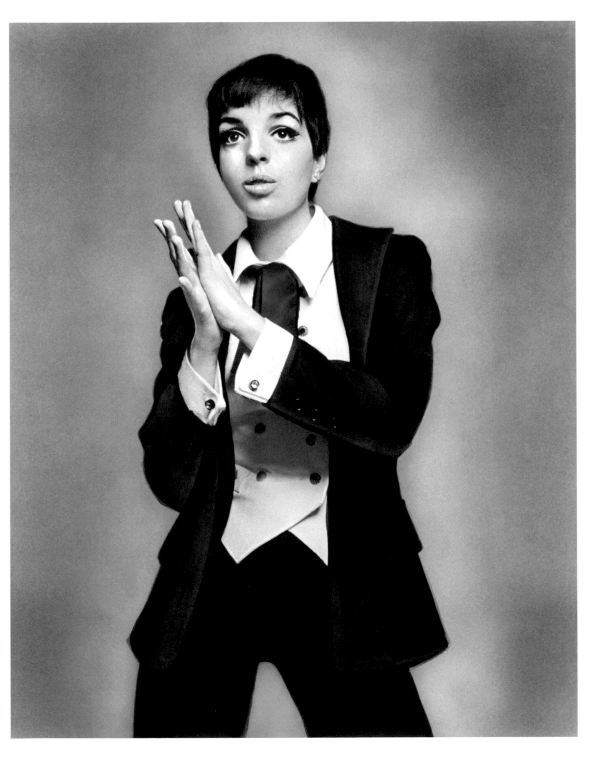

Liza Minnelli, 1967

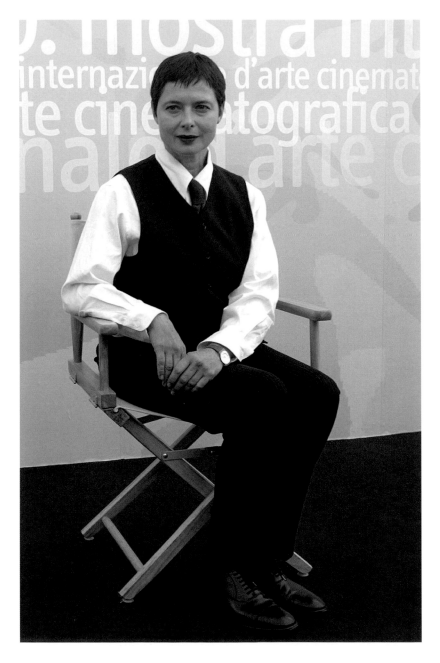

Isabella Rossellini, Venice, 2003

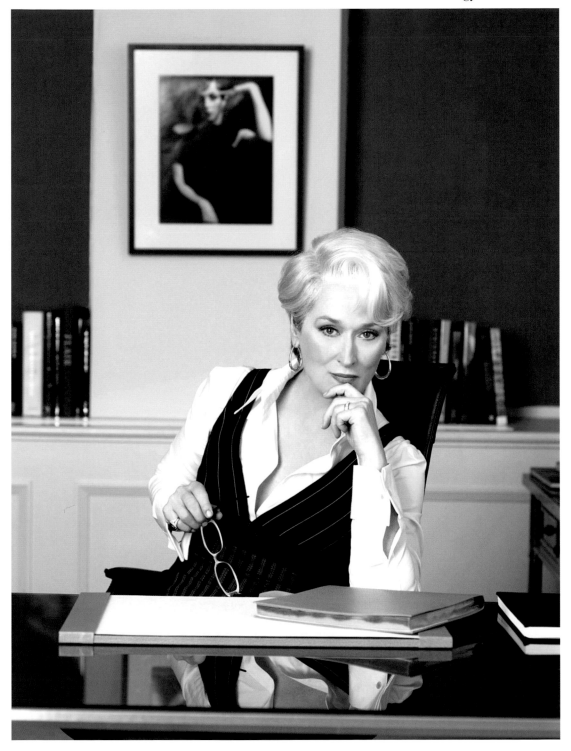

Meryl Streep, *The Devil Wears Prada*, 2006

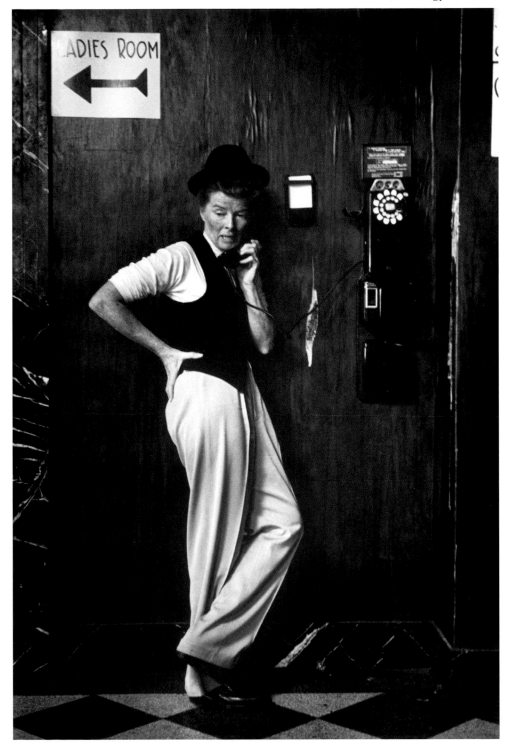

Katharine Hepburn, *Long Day's Journey into Night*, 1961

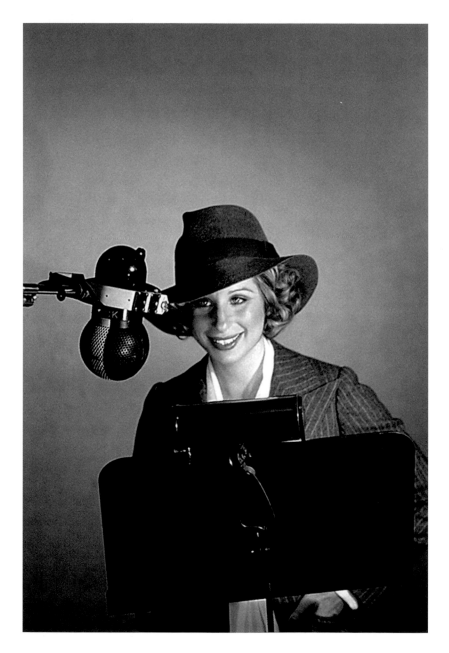

Barbra Streisand, *Funny Lady*, 1975

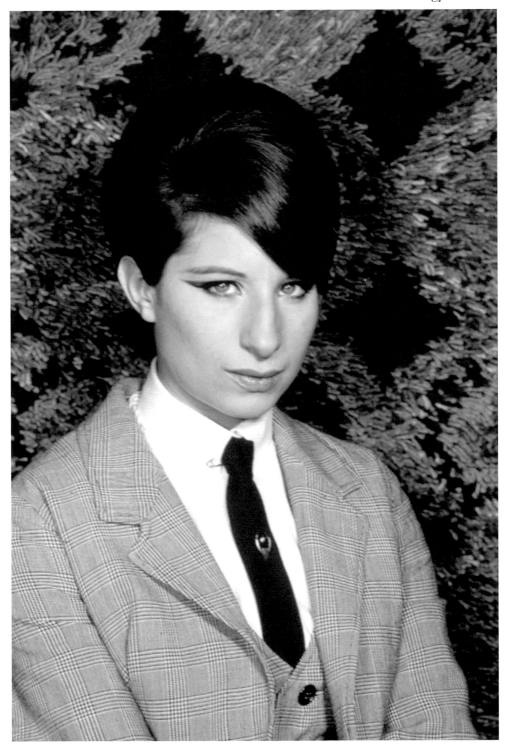

Barbra Streisand, 1960s

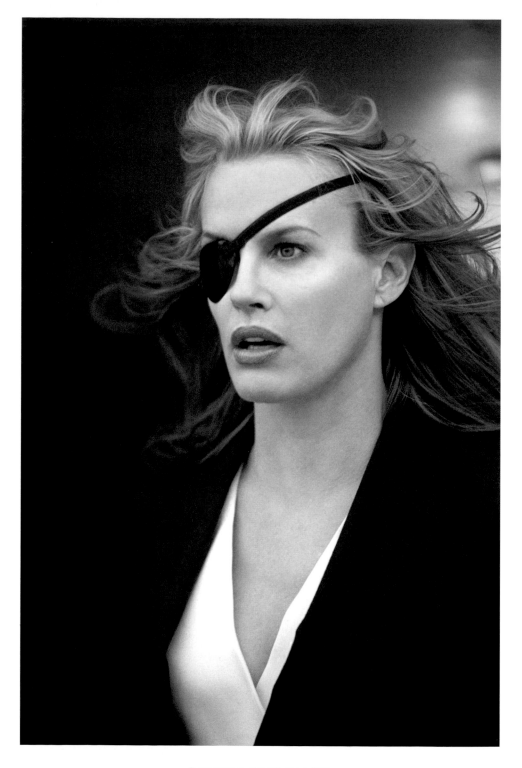

Daryl Hannah, *Kill Bill: Vol. 1*, 2003

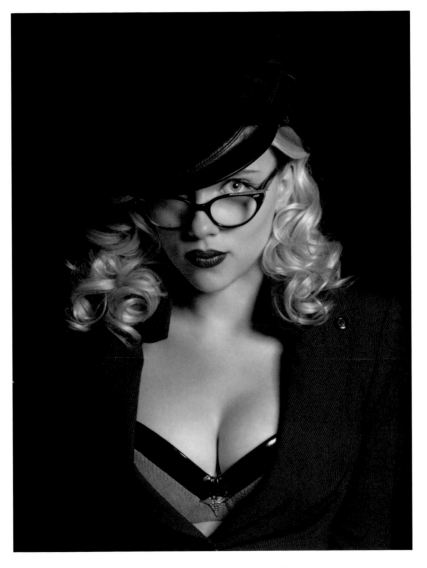

Scarlett Johansson, *The Spirit*, 2008

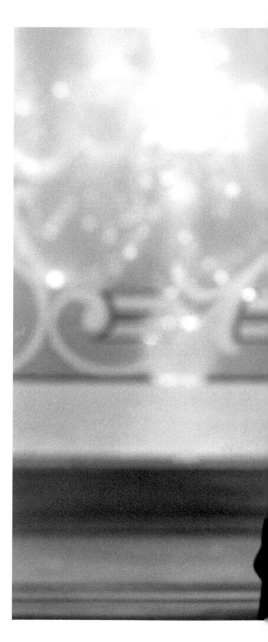

Julie Andrews, *Victor Victoria*, 1982

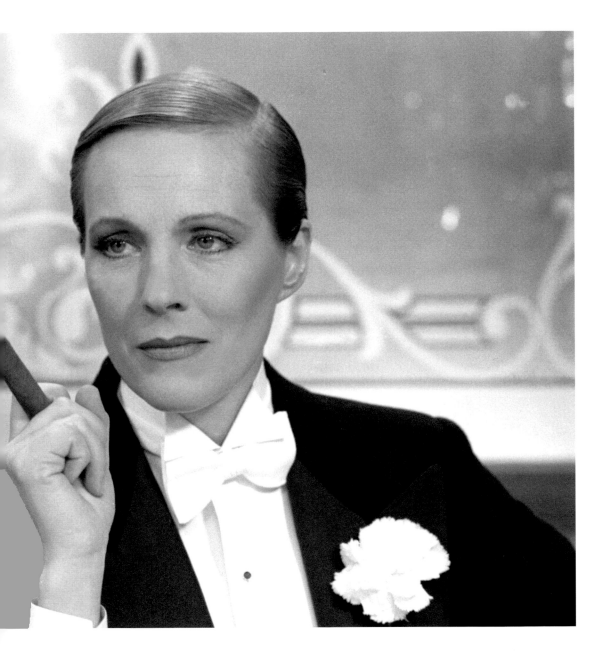

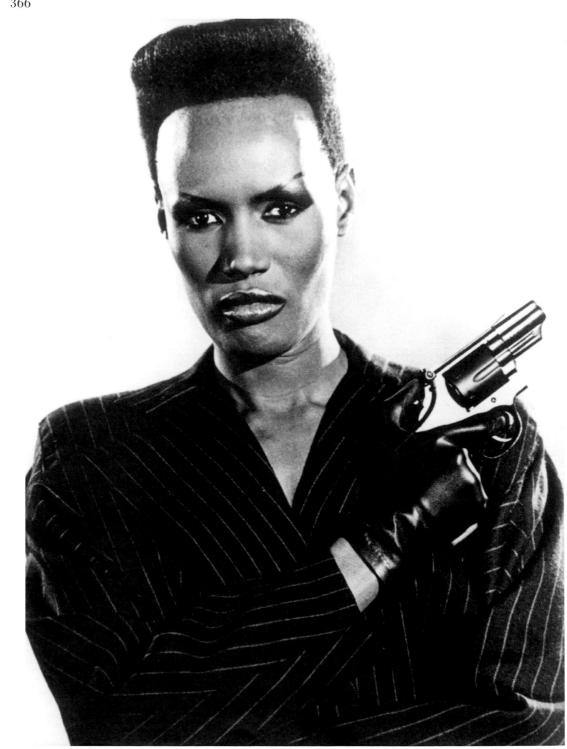

Grace Jones, *A View to a Kill*, 1985

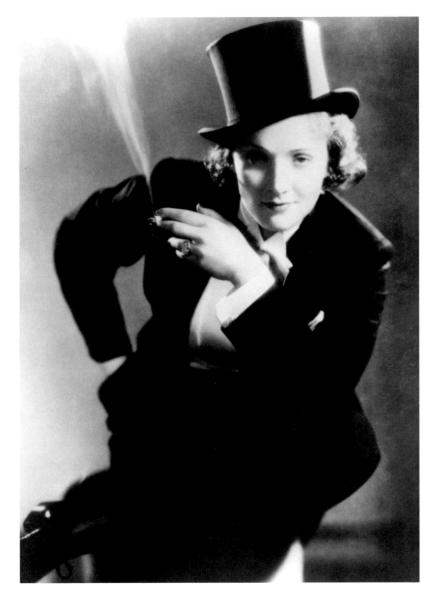

Marlene Dietrich, *Morocco*, 1930

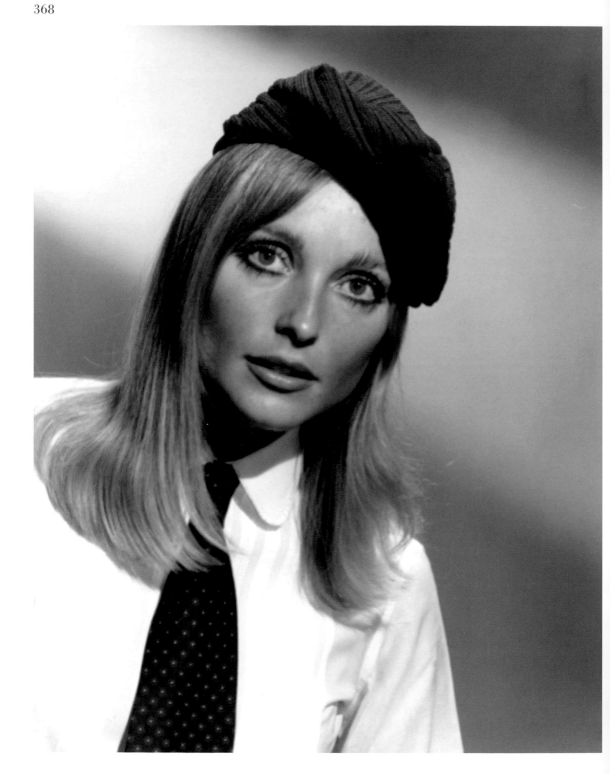

Sharon Tate, 1960s

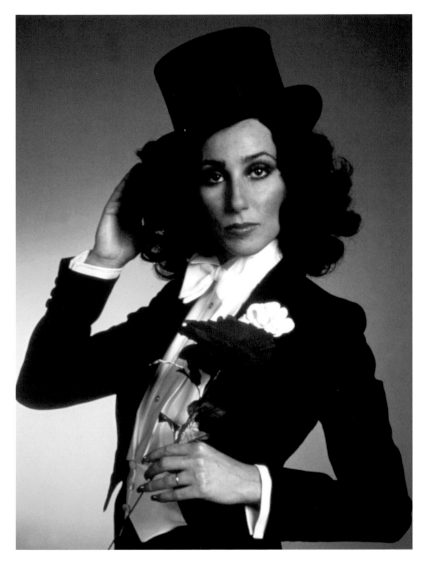

Cher, *Cher*, 1975

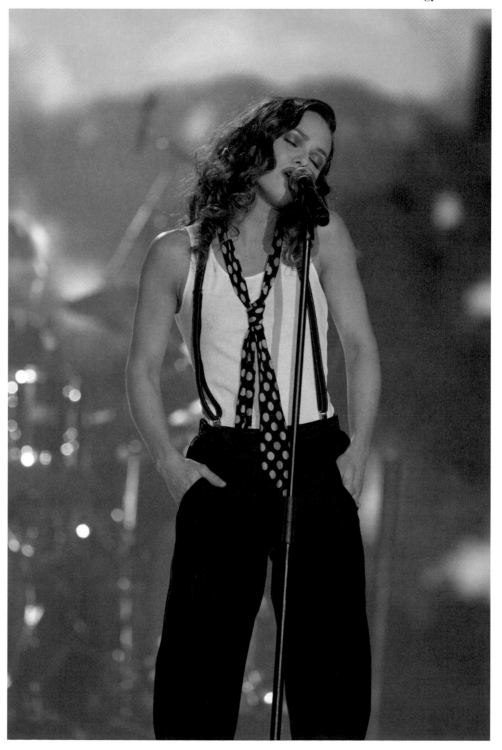

Vanessa Paradis, Paris, 2008

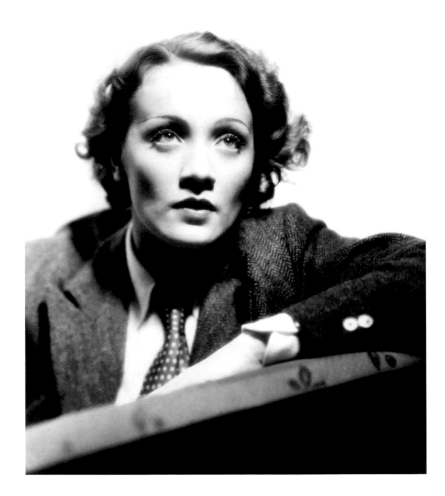

Marlene Dietrich, 1930s

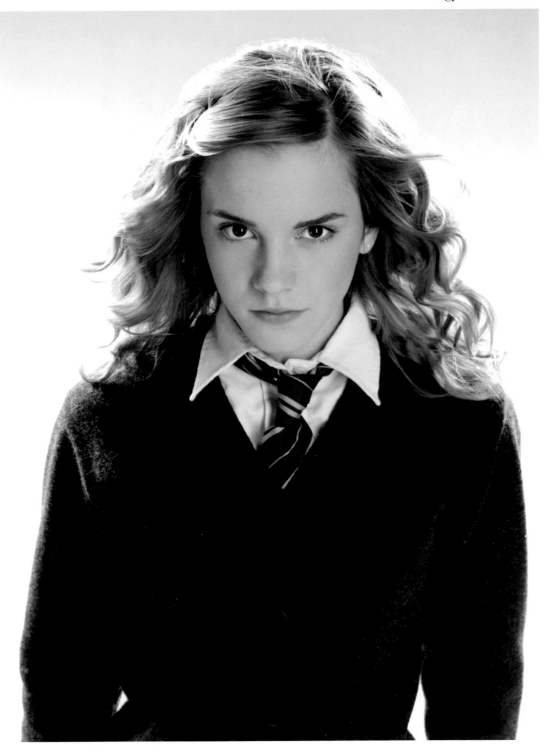

Emma Watson, *Harry Potter and the Order of the Phoenix*, 2007

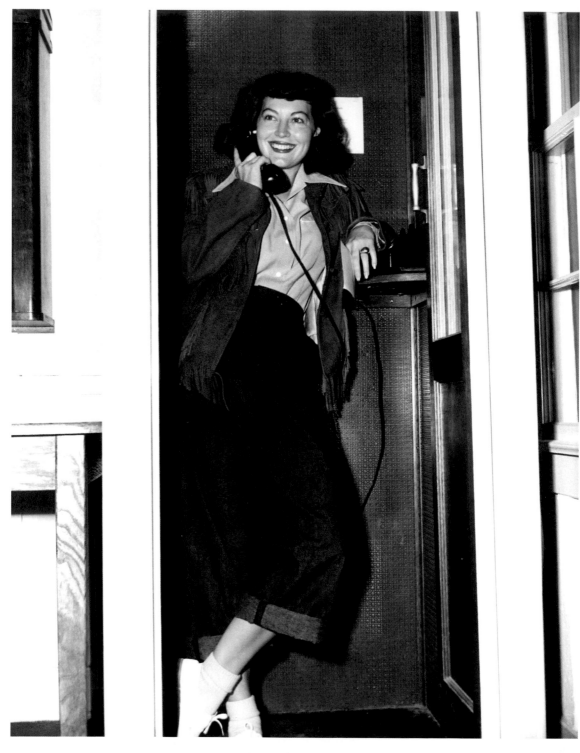

Ava Gardner, Santa Barbara, California, 1944

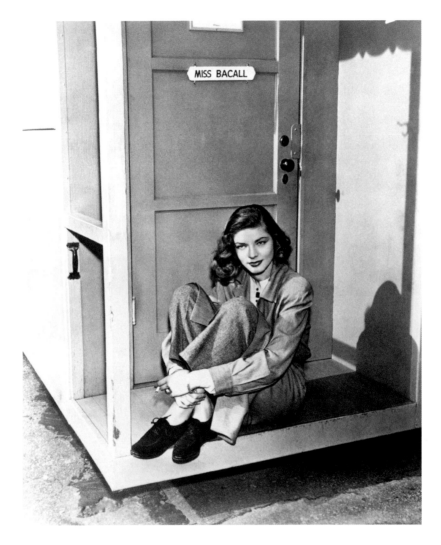

Lauren Bacall, 1950s

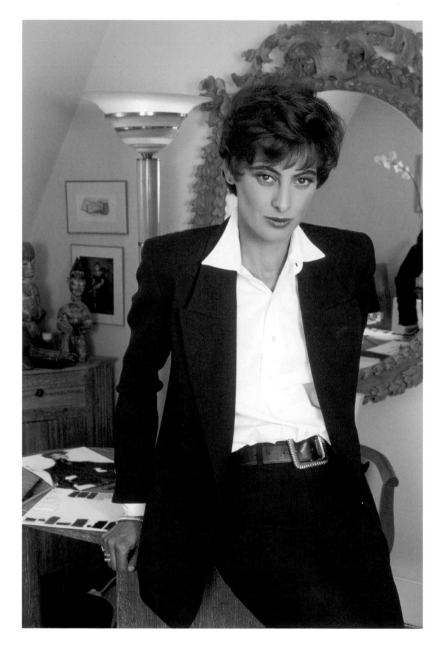

Inès de la Fressange, 1991

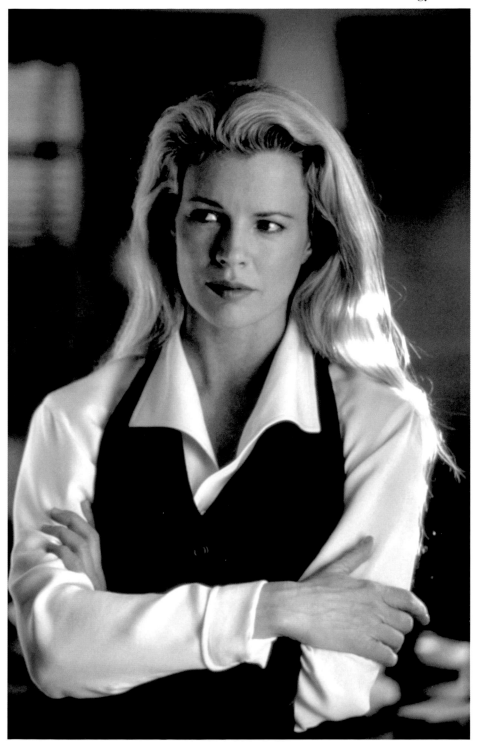

Kim Basinger, *Final Analysis*, 1992

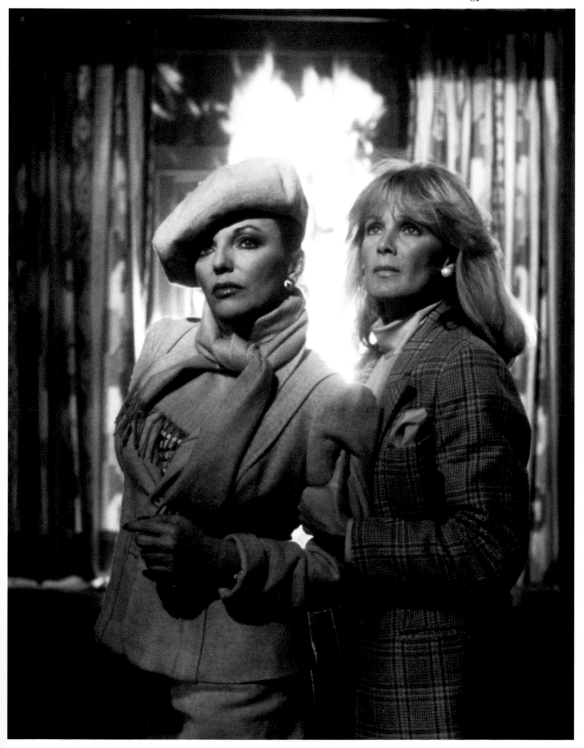

Joan Collins and Linda Evans, *Dynasty*, 1981–89

Madonna,
Blond Ambition tour, 1990

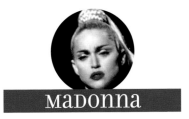

MADONNA

The Corset

A woman in a corset is a lie, a falsehood, a fiction, but for us,
this fiction is better than reality.

EUGÈNE CHAPUS

Icon Madonna
Designer Jean-Paul Gaultier

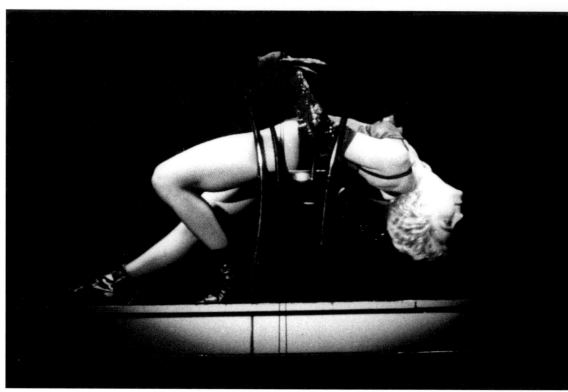

With her *Blond Ambition* tour Madonna Louise Veronica Ciccone, better known simply as 'Madonna', broke all records for sales and was awarded *Rolling Stone*'s prize for the best tour of the year with her 'elaborately choreographed, sexually provocative extravaganza', which depicted all the infinite variations of sexuality in an apparently transgressive but carefully staged orgy of pleasure.

At the centre of it all was Madonna and her infamous boned bustier with its exaggerated cone-shaped breasts, an extreme vision of a dominant female that took a playful view of fetishistic stereotypes. Its influence has reached the street, where one can glimpse women with suspiciously artificial points beneath their sweaters. Jean-Paul Gaultier's little perfume bottles, which sit proudly on the shelves of perfume shops, are shamelessly modelled on Madonna's stagewear. The French designer also styled Madonna for her *Confessions Tour* in 2006 and for the cover of

her album *Hard Candy* (2008), when she again wore her regulation bustier, with the added defence of a wrestling belt.

Modern bustiers evolved from the traditional corsets that hugged a woman's hips to create a classic 'wasp waist' figure. Although the modern 'waspie' was actually invented by Marcel Rochas in 1945, it was Christian Dior who revived it from the courtly dress of the 18th century and made it a key component of his collections in the period immediately after the Second World War. As a means of body modification, corsets long pre-date modern plastic surgery, tattoos and piercings; they have their roots in the stiffly boned undergarments that were banned by the French Revolution in a symbolic gesture supporting the liberation of women.

In the 1970s, women all around the world loudly proclaimed their liberation from this form of bodily constriction in which hips and breasts were either squashed down or pushed up into teasing curves. But in the 1980s,

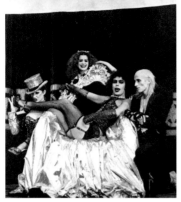

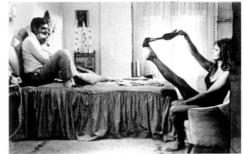

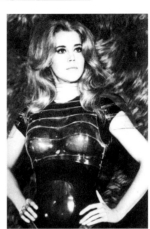

Sophia Loren and Marcello Mastroianni, *Yesterday, Today and Tomorrow*, 1963

Tim Curry, *The Rocky Horror Picture Show*, 1975

Madonna singing 'Open Your Heart', Tokyo, 1987

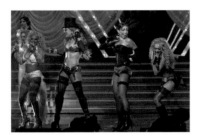

Lil'Kim, Pink, Mya and Christina Aguilera performing 'Lady Marmalade', 2001

Jane Fonda, *Barbarella*, 1967

corsets and basques reappeared as essential garments in the fetish counterculture.

The corset has gone through an infinite number of transformations. It has been both a weapon of seduction and an instrument of social control over the female body. Nonetheless, it has given us lasting images that have remained indelibly impressed on our collective memory. It was worn by Brigitte Bardot, Gina Lollobrigida and even Jane Fonda before she embraced feminism, but it was Sophia Loren who made it truly iconic. Her striptease scene in *Yesterday, Today and Tomorrow* (Vittorio De Sica, 1963) was so legendary that she repeated it more than thirty years later in *Prêt-à-Porter* (Robert Altman, 1994). While Sophia herself looked as alluring as ever, on this occasion Marcello Mastroianni simply fell asleep. In *Malena* (Giuseppe Tornatore, 2000), Monica Bellucci wore underwear specially designed for her by Dolce & Gabbana, which brought the corset out into the open as a visible and powerful

tool of seduction for modern women. Pop stars such as Pink, Lil'Kim and Christina Aguilera wear it in their videos and concerts, as does Kylie Minogue, who has even sold one of her corsets at a charity auction.

It can also look amazing on a man: think of Tim Curry in the role of Dr Frank N. Furter, a transvestite scientist with alien origins and a colourful sex life in *The Rocky Horror Picture Show* (Jim Sharman, 1975). This movie manifesto on sexual roles goes beyond heterosexuality, bisexuality and homosexuality, taking a festival of sensuality and turning it into hypothetical normality. The corset has completed its journey from the constrictive garment hated by Coco Chanel because it 'humiliated women' to a symbol of the subversion of established gender roles. Although it may have come full circle, the corset forever remains both revolutionary and rebellious.

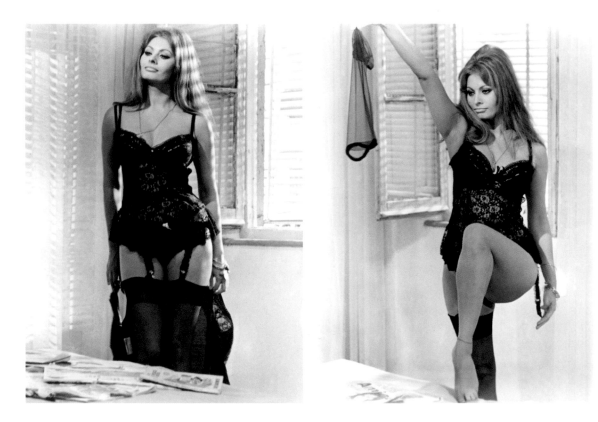

Sophia Loren, *Yesterday, Today and Tomorrow*, 1963

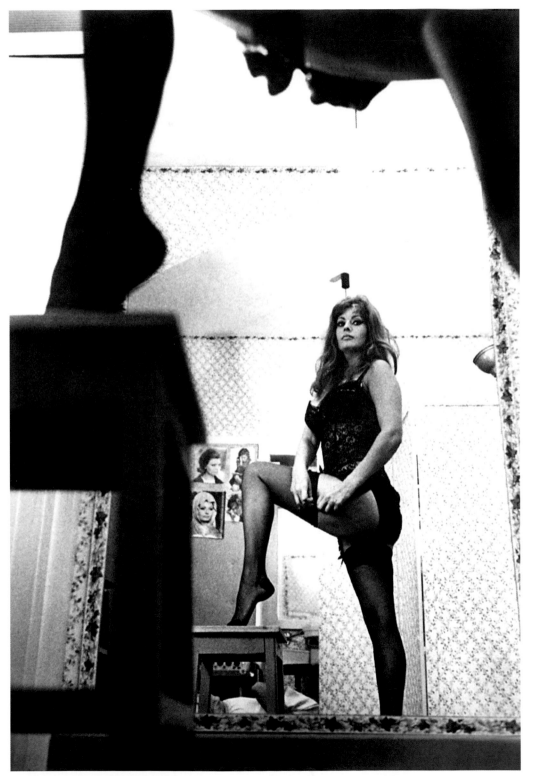

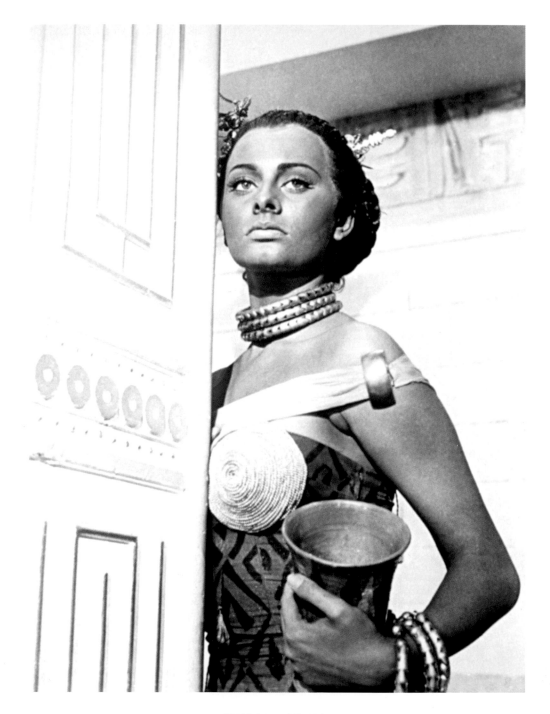

Sophia Loren, *Aida*, 1953

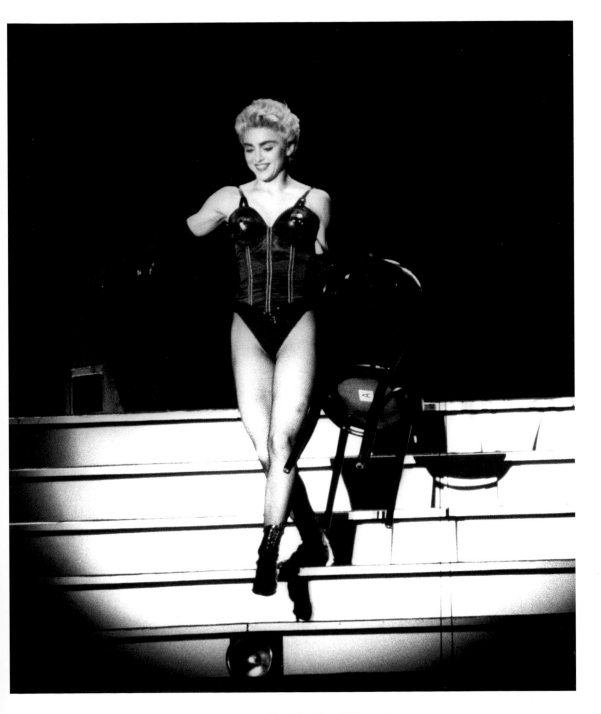

Madonna singing 'Open Your Heart', Tokyo, 1987

Jane Fonda, 1960s

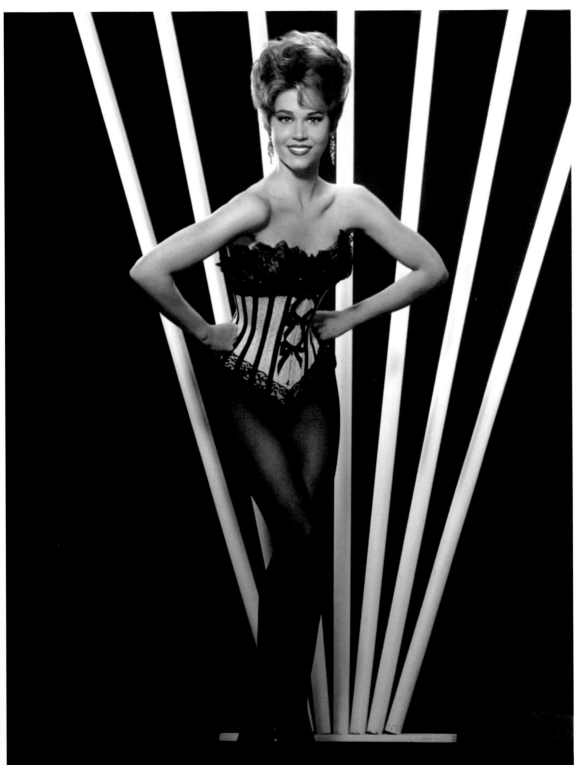

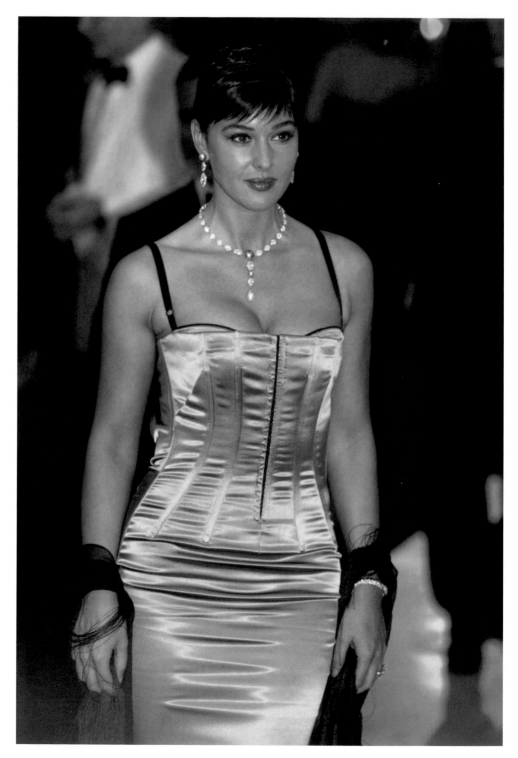

Monica Bellucci, 2002

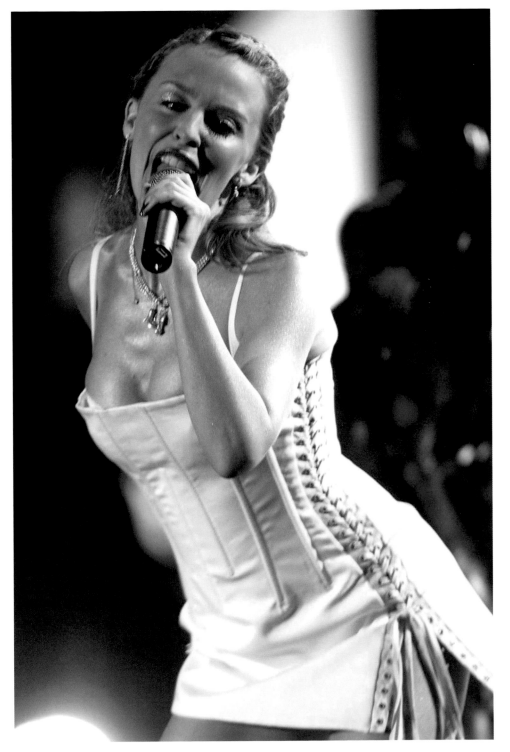

Kylie Minogue, London, 2002

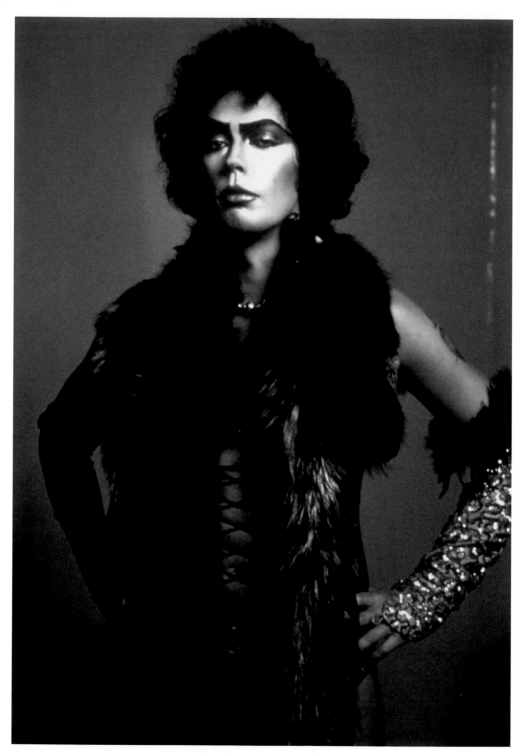

Tim Curry, *The Rocky Horror Picture Show*, 1975

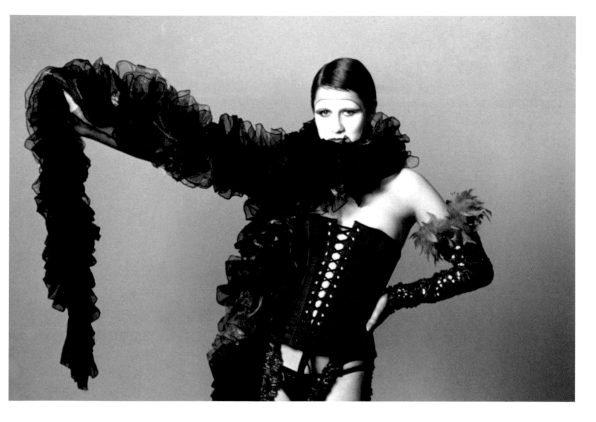

Nell Campbell, *The Rocky Horror Picture Show*, 1975

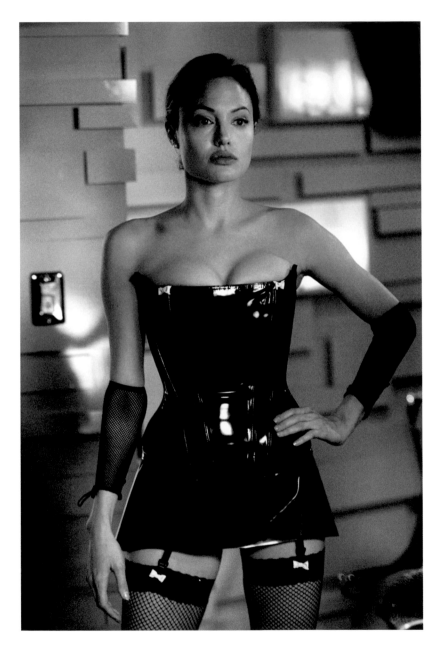

Angelina Jolie, *Mr & Mrs Smith*, 2005

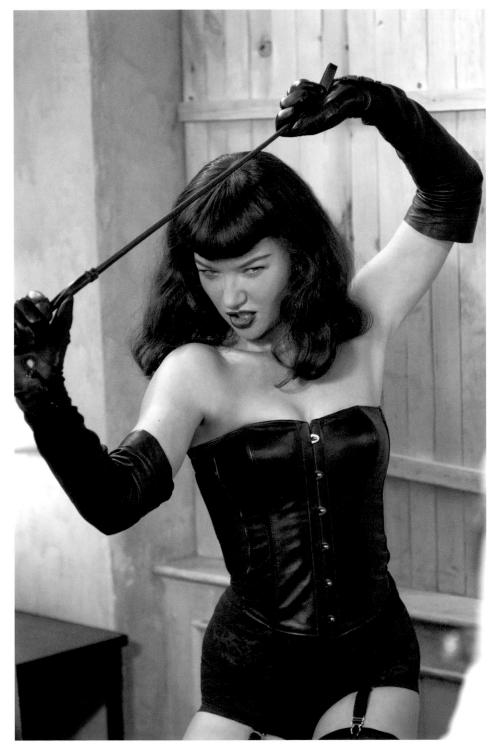

Gretchen Mol, *The Notorious Bettie Page*, 2005

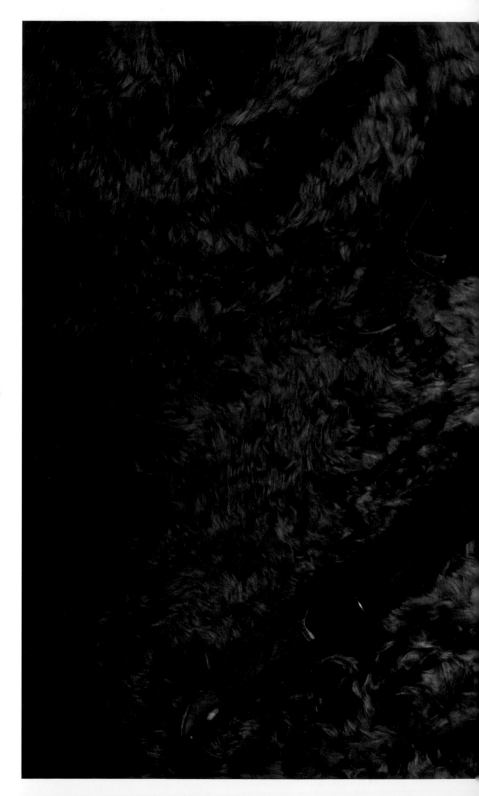

Jane Fonda, *Barbarella*,
1967

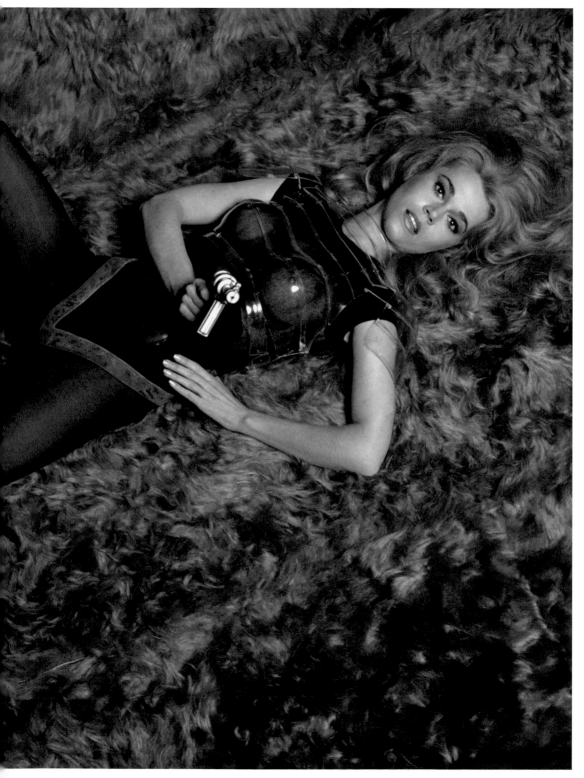

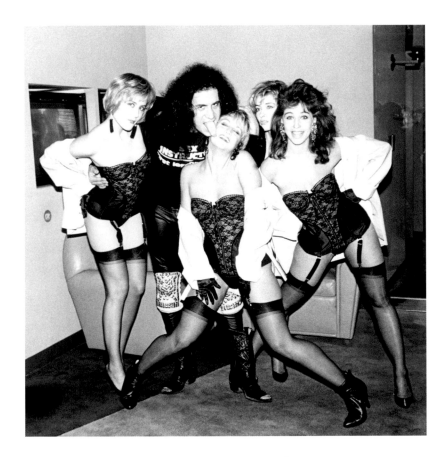

Gene Simmons with his fans, 1980s

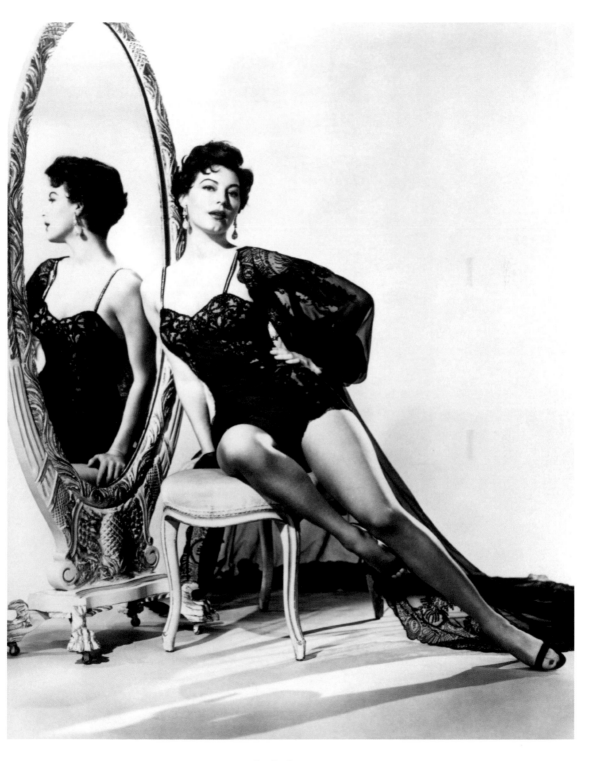

Ava Gardner, 1952

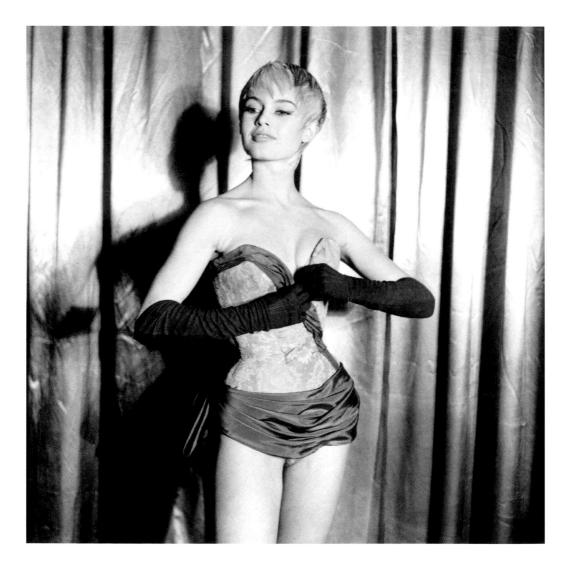

Brigitte Bardot, *Plucking the Daisy*, 1956

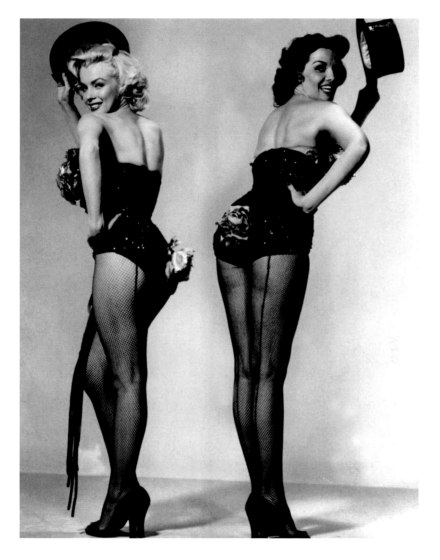

Marilyn Monroe and Jane Russell, *Gentlemen Prefer Blondes*, 1953

Penélope Cruz, *Nine*, 2009

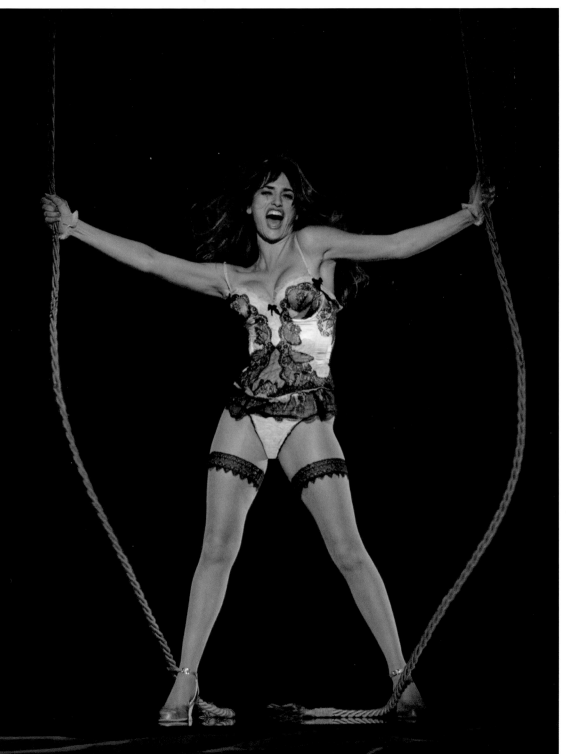

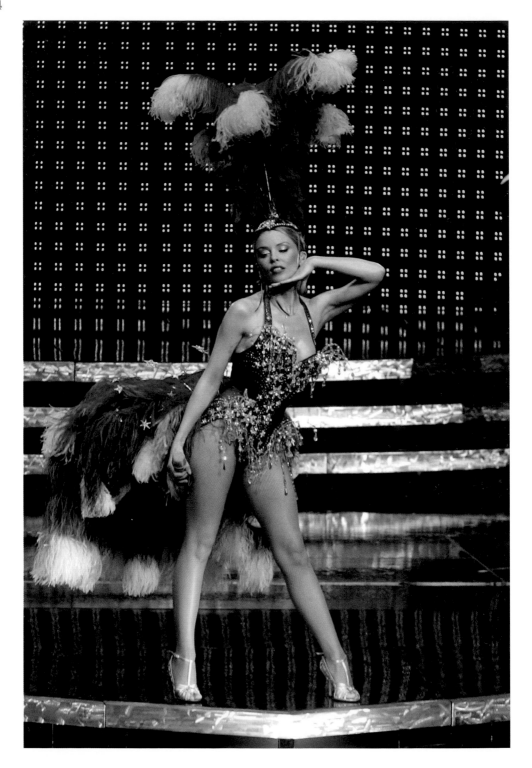

Kylie Minogue, *Showgirl* tour, 2005

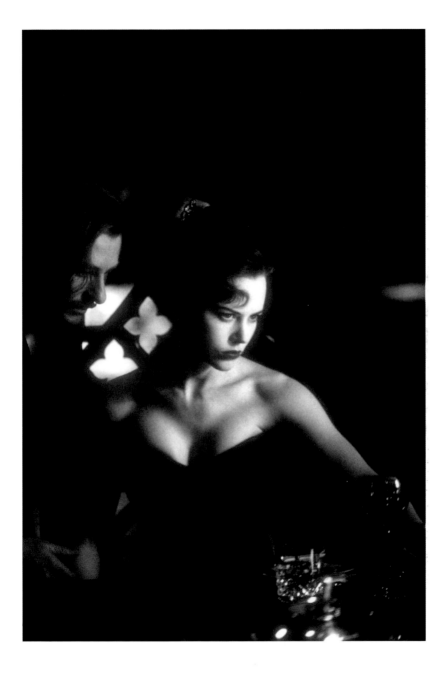

Nicole Kidman and Richard Roxburgh, *Moulin Rouge!*, 2001

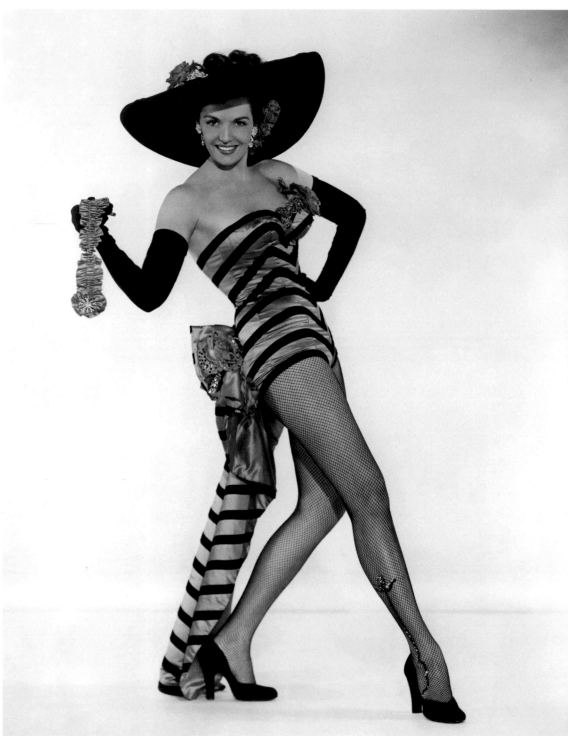

Jane Russell, *Son of Paleface*, 1952

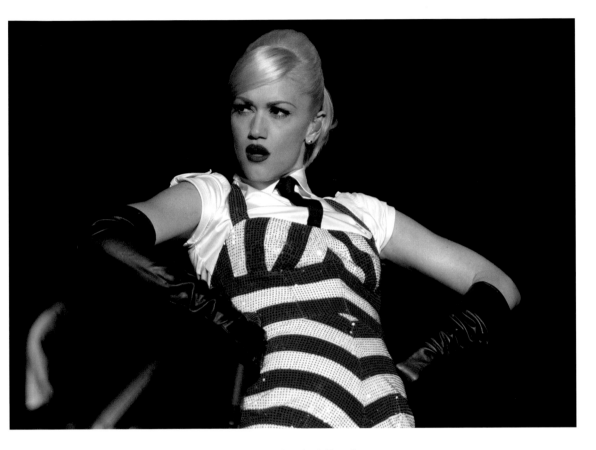

Gwen Stefani, performing in Bogotà, 2007

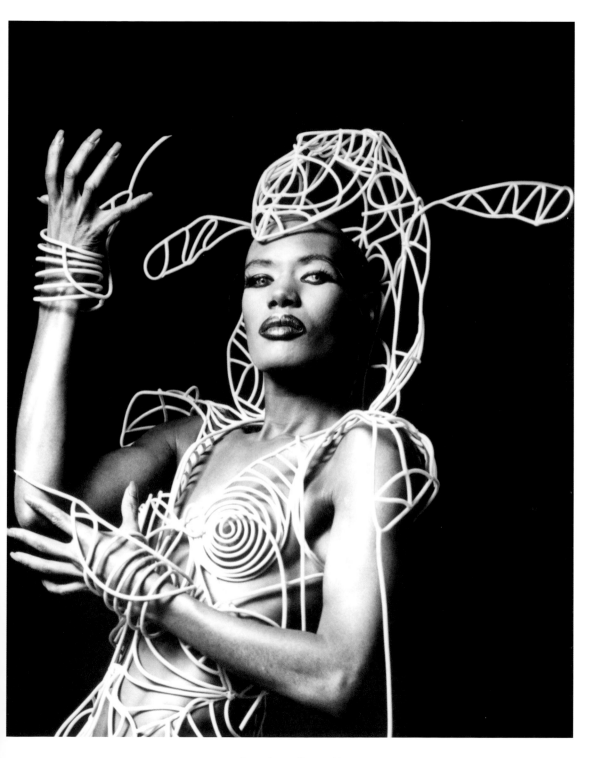

Grace Jones, *Vamp*, 1986

Sandra Dee, 1963

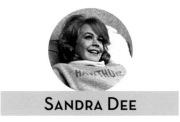

SANDRA DEE

Capri Pants

I suggested to the producer that when I vacuum the rug, I wear pants. I couldn't imagine putting on a little dress for that.

MARY TYLER MOORE

Icon Sandra Dee
Designers Sonja de Lennart, Sorelle Fontana
Film *A Summer Place*, Delmer Daves, 1959

Sandra Dee, 1960s

Sandra Dee was the prototype blonde, the eternal ingénue, the good girl. She was the figurehead of a generation of American teenagers in the 1950s and 60s who were caught in a struggle between their hormones and the views of a narrow-minded society in which premarital sex was forbidden. Think of her in films such as *Gidget* (Paul Wendkos, 1959), or *A Summer Place* (Delmer Daves, 1959), in which her innocent love for Troy Donahue is unreasonably opposed by her severe parents. She was the archetypal young and innocent California girl, and capri pants were the ideal costume for both her on- and off-screen personas. Sadly she fell out of favour with Hollywood's dream factory all too quickly.

Nevertheless, Sandra Dee had a moment of revival in 1978 thanks to the film *Grease*, directed by Randal Kleiser, in which the naive Sandy Olsson (Olivia Newton-John) is teased by the more provocative and glamorous Betty Rizzo (Stockard Channing). The lyrics of the song 'Look at Me, I'm Sandra Dee' encapsulated the innocence of the 1950s star: 'Look at me, I'm Sandra Dee/Lousy with virginity/Won't go to bed 'til I'm legally wed/ I can't, I'm Sandra Dee!' Younger audiences assumed that Sandra was an imaginary figure, a symbol of virginity to torment would-be male seducers; this misunderstanding was apparently great source of amusement for the real-life Sandra Dee, now very much grown up.

Capri pants were designed by the Prussian-born Sonja de Lennart in 1948, and popularized by the television series *The Dick Van Dyke Show* where they were worn by the lead character's wife, Laura Petrie, a young and attractive homemaker played by Mary Tyler Moore. In 1953, the great costumier Edith Head had Audrey Hepburn's costumes for *Roman Holiday* made by the Sorelle Fontana atelier in a 'Capri' style; and a year later Hubert de Givenchy designed his own version for Hepburn to wear in the film *Sabrina* (Billy Wilder, 1954). Edith Head also introduced the Capri skirt, the Capri blouse and the wide Capri belt, but it was the Capri pants that became a classic, and were worn by style

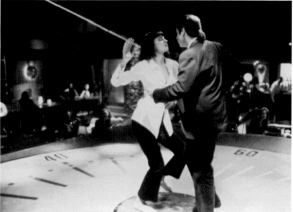

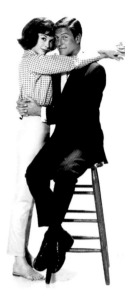

Uma Thurman
and John Travolta,
Pulp Fiction, 1994

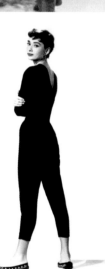

Mary Tyler Moore
and Dick Van Dyke,
*The Dick Van Dyke
Show*, 1961–66

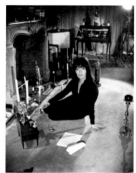

Audrey Hepburn,
Sabrina, 1954

Juliette Greco,
1966

icons such as Doris Day, Jane Russell, Katharine Hepburn, Gina Lollobrigida, Ava Gardner, Elizabeth Taylor, Jacqueline Kennedy, Marilyn Monroe, Kim Novak and Anita Ekberg. Capri pants were one of the first leisurewear garments to be adopted rather than rebuffed by the international intellectual set. The costume historian Gundula Wolter wrote that in the bars of Saint-Germain-des-Prés in existentialist Paris: 'all the girls loved themselves in black roll-necks, tight capri pants, flat sandals, along with straight long hair and black painted eyes à la Juliette Gréco.' Capri pants were also favoured by aristocrats such as the Countess von Stauffenberg and Queen Soraya Esfandiary, the first wife of the

Shah of Iran, who always included a pair of capri pants in her suitcase for their journeys to Europe. They are now back in style once again after having been seen on Uma Thurman's long legs in *Pulp Fiction* (Quentin Tarantino, 1994). The highly successful tennis player Rafael Nadal has worn them in nearly all of his matches – and won. Perhaps the spirit of Sandra Dee is laughing to herself as she wiggles her way through paradise alongside cheeky muscle-bound surfers. Capri pants are no longer a guilty pleasure.

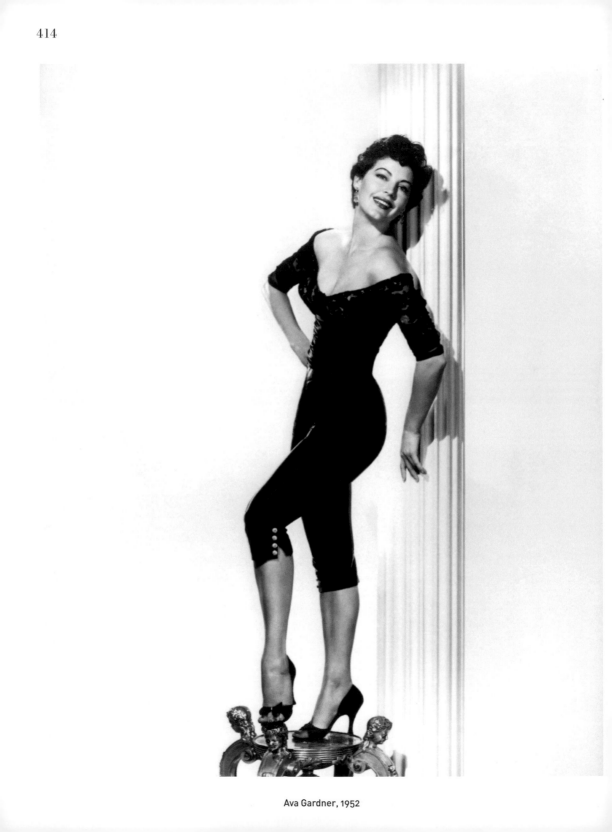

Ava Gardner, 1952

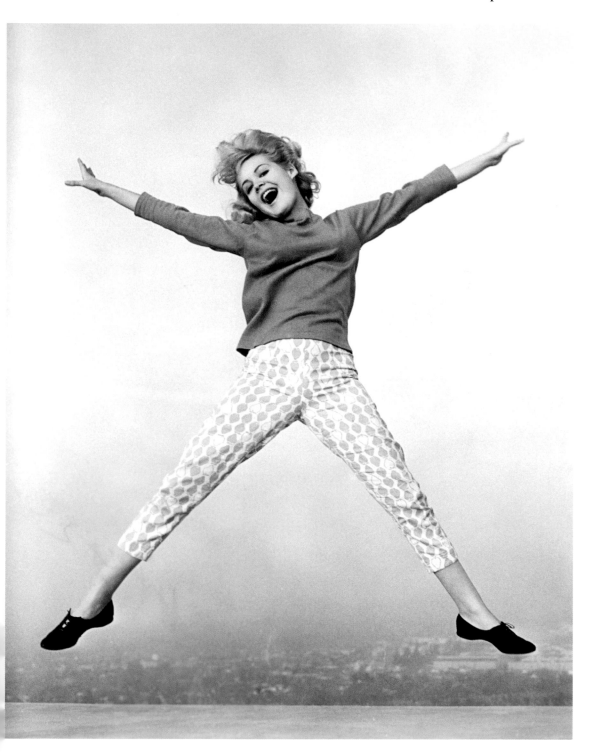

Sandra Dee, *The Restless Years*, 1958

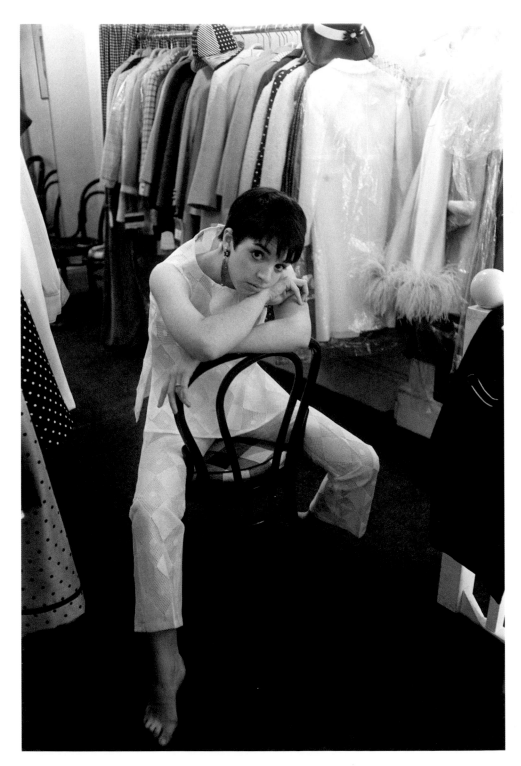

Liza Minnelli, London, 1966

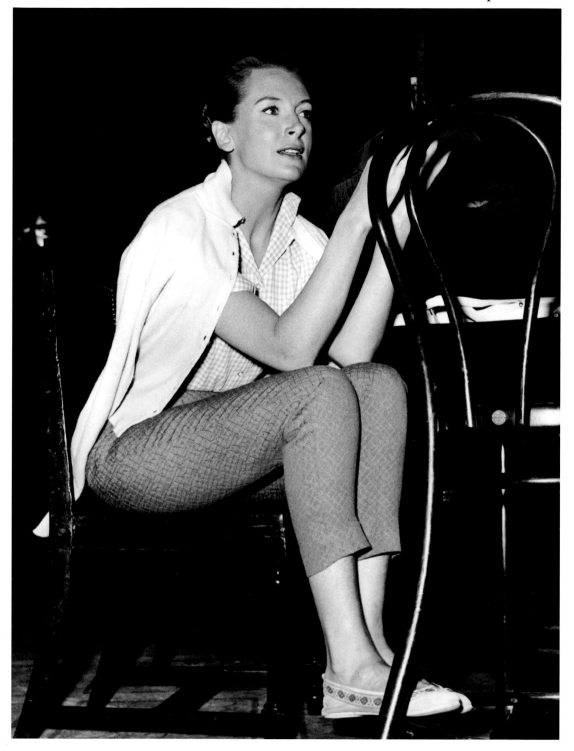

Deborah Kerr during rehearsals for *Bonjour Tristesse*, 1957

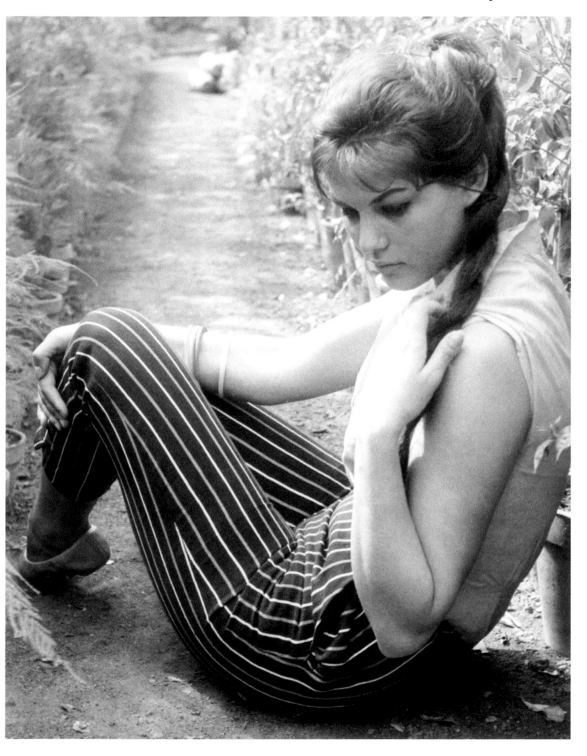

Claudia Cardinale in a glasshouse on the Via Aurelia, Rome, 1958

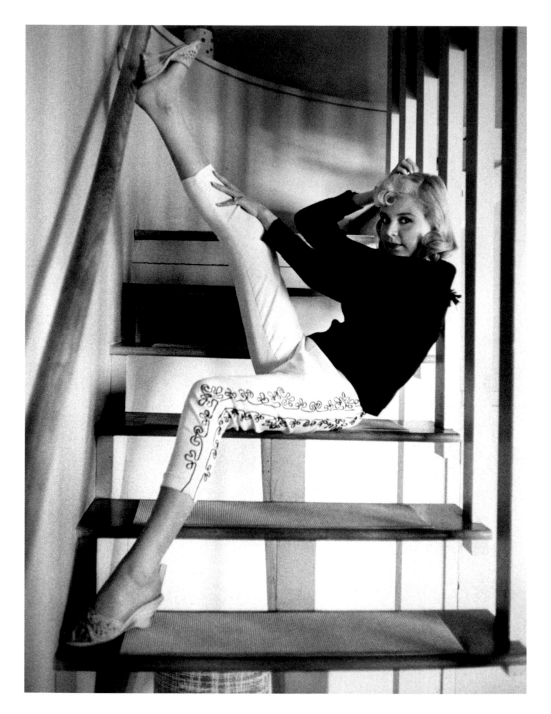

Sandra Dee, 1960s

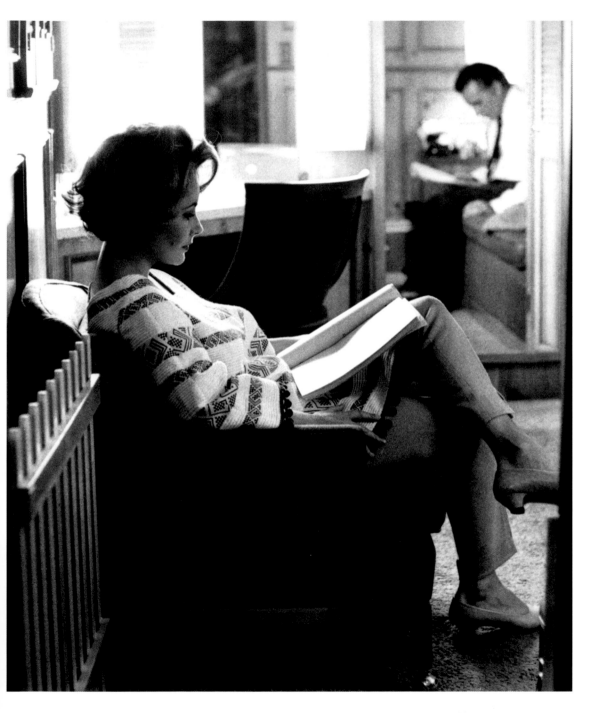

Elizabeth Taylor and Richard Burton on the set of *Who's Afraid of Virginia Woolf?*, 1966

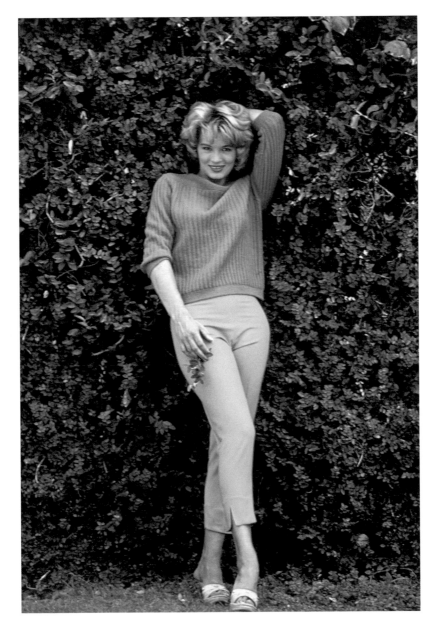

Angie Dickinson, 1960s

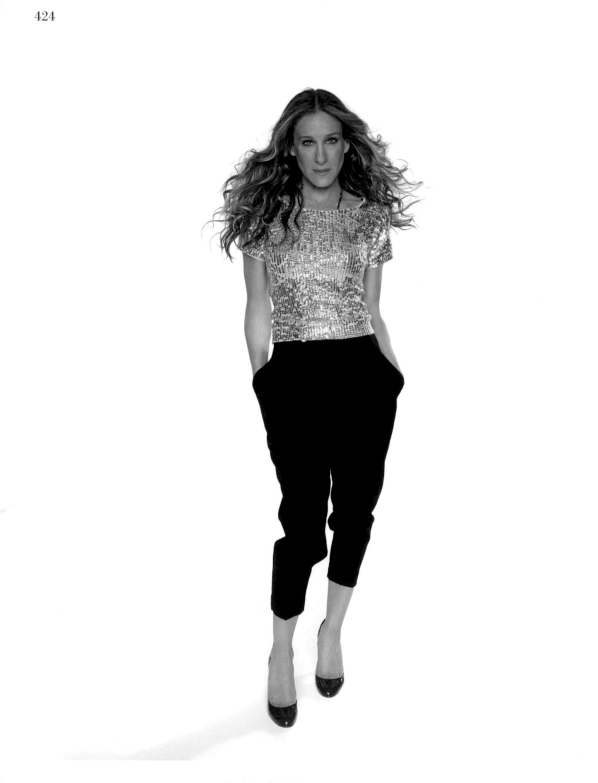

Sarah Jessica Parker, *Sex and the City*, 2008

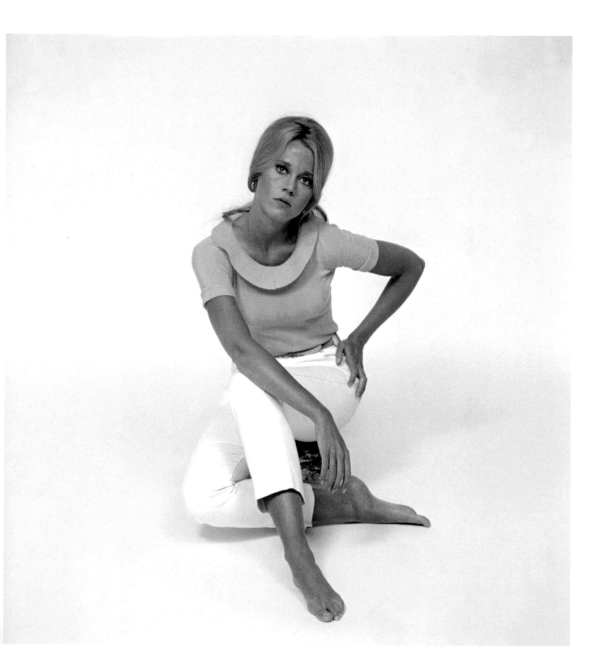

Jane Fonda, 1960s

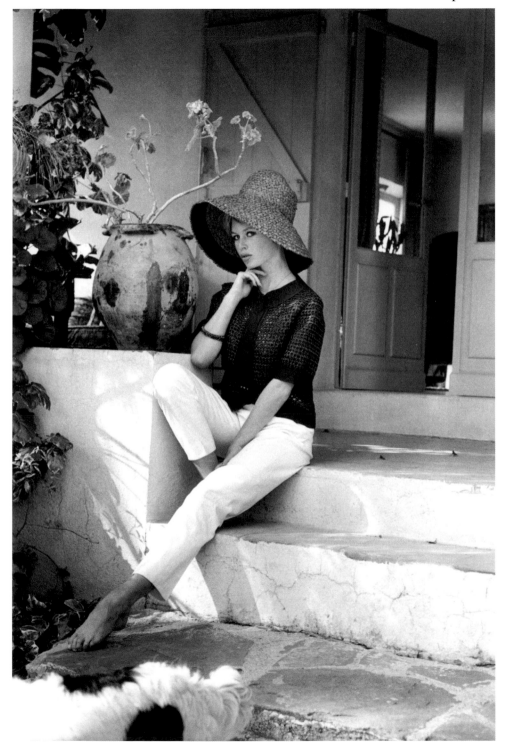

Brigitte Bardot, Saint-Tropez, 1960

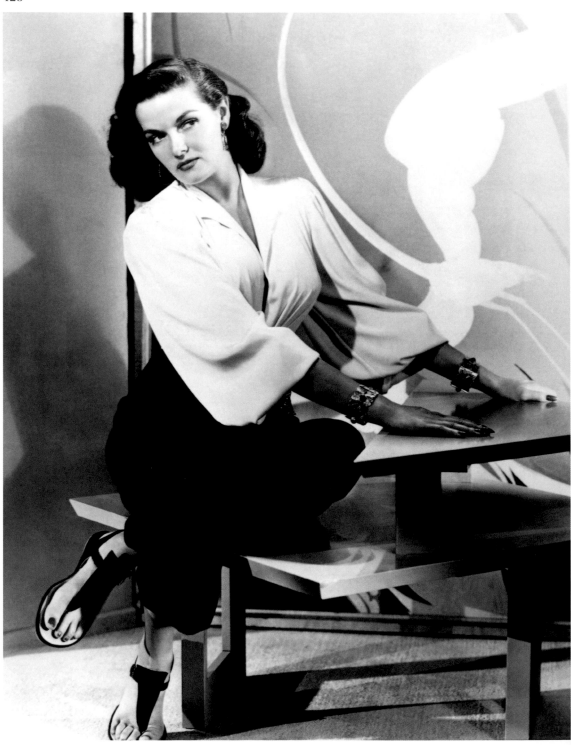

Jane Russell, 1960s

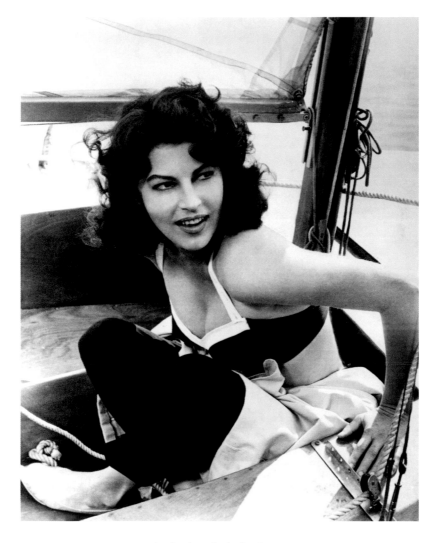

Ava Gardner, *On the Beach*, 1959

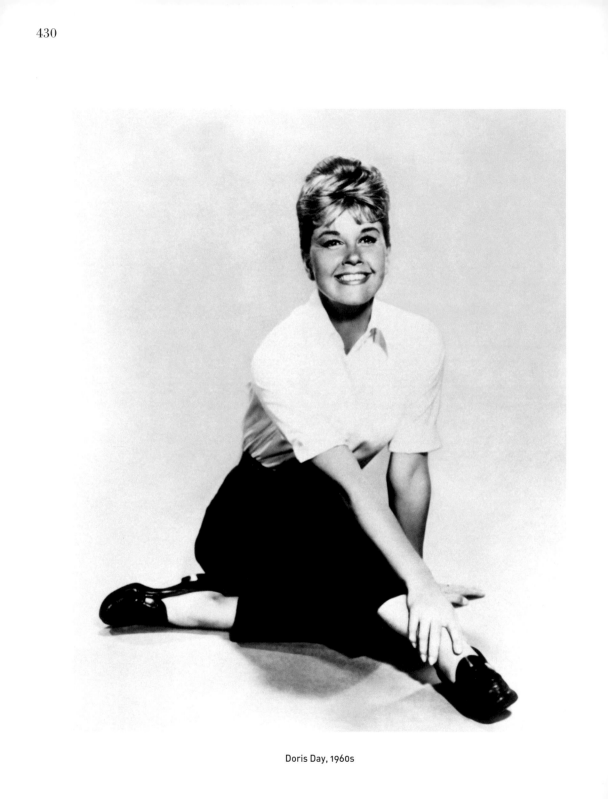

Doris Day, 1960s

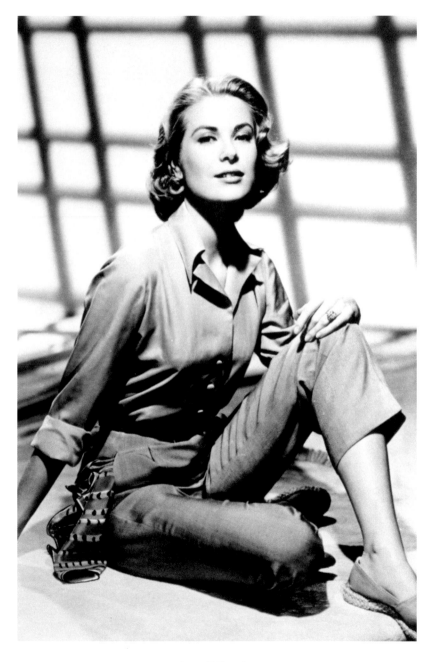

Grace Kelly, 1960s

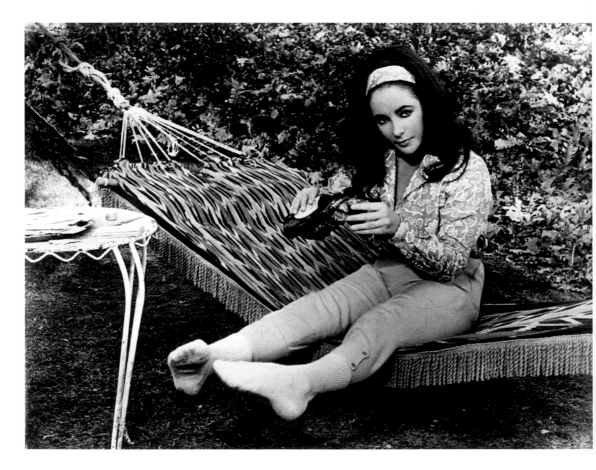

Elizabeth Taylor, *Reflections in a Golden Eye*, 1967

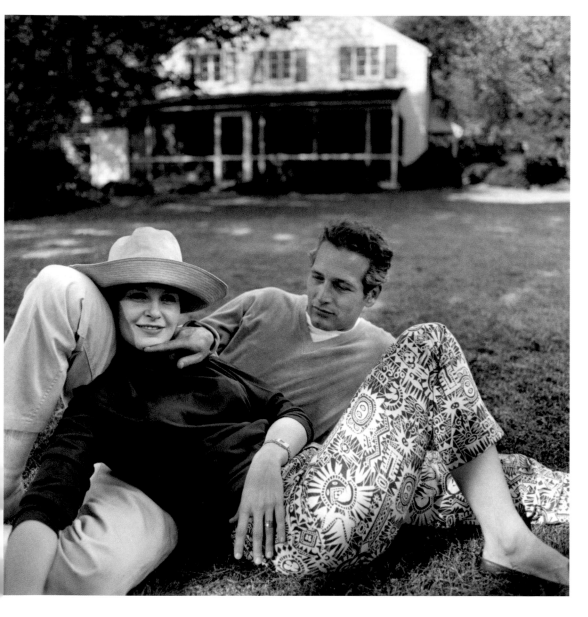

Paul Newman and Joanne Woodward, Westport, Connecticut, 1965

Ava Gardner, *On the Beach*, 1959

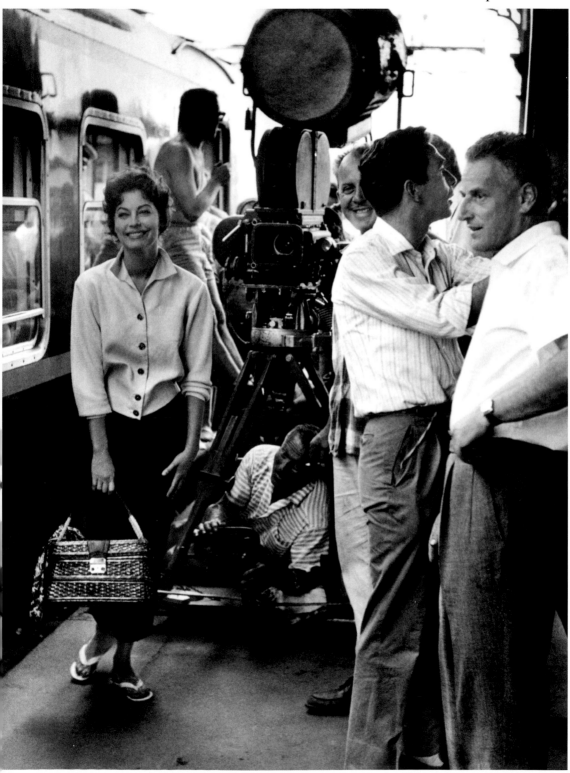

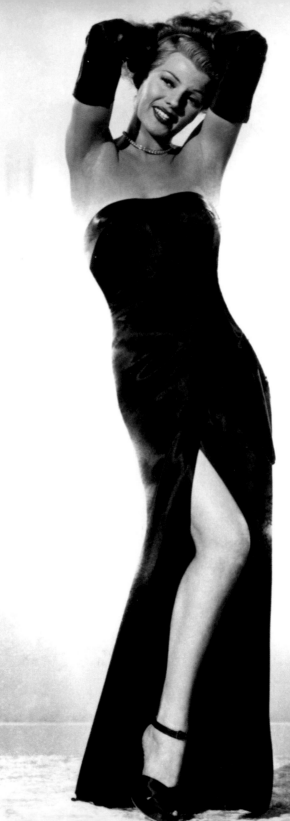

Rita Hayworth,
Gilda, 1946

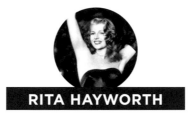

RITA HAYWORTH

The Sheath Dress

But I can still paint the town
All the colours of your evening gown
While I'm waiting for your blonde hair
To turn grey.
MICK JAGGER, 'EVENING GOWN'

Icon Rita Hayworth
Designer Valentino
Film *Gilda*, Charles Vidor, 1946

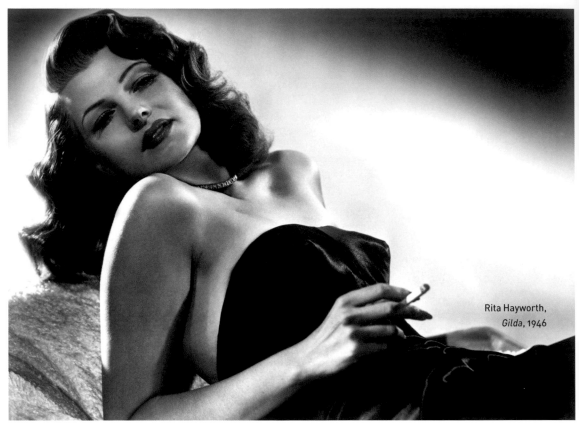

Rita Hayworth,
Gilda, 1946

'Men go to bed with Gilda, but wake
up with me.' This frank declaration
by Rita Hayworth, also known as
the 'Love Goddess', would never have been
made if Jean Louis, her friend, collaborator
and stylist, had not designed the legendary
black satin dress for her to wear in *Gilda*,
the 1946 film directed by Charles Vidor in
which she performed a one-glove striptease
that shot her straight into the femme fatale
hall of fame. It is hard to believe that the
draped tube of fabric that rippled over her
hips had been created to hide her incipient
pregnancy. That black sheath dress turned
her into an elegant and sensual siren; the
gown itself became famous and was later
sold at auction in California.

The brilliant Jean Louis was well
accustomed to creating memorable clothes:
he also designed the dress worn by Marilyn
Monroe when she sang 'Happy Birthday

Mr President'. As the dress clung to her
tightly and was made from flesh-coloured
fabric, it made her appear to be virtually
nude; it was also encrusted with thousands
of rhinestones.

Like other iconic divas of the 1940s,
such as Ava Gardner, Marlene Dietrich
and Greta Garbo, Rita Hayworth was the
embodiment of sensual femininity, and is
the movie star most often associated with the
sheath dress. The gown enhances the body,
restraining some parts and lifting up others.
By leaving strategic zones uncovered,
especially the arms, it emphasizes the curves
of the bust and neck, the posture of the head
and the sweep of the hair. The style is still
popular with actresses today who need all
the star quality they can muster when they
walk the red carpet on Oscar night. Angelina
Jolie, Scarlett Johansson, Halle Berry and
Charlize Theron, for example, are dedicated

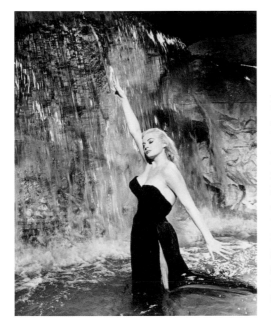

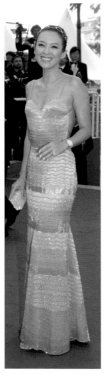

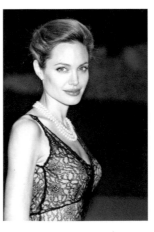

Anita Ekberg,
La dolce vita, 1960

Zhang Ziyi,
Cannes, 2009

Angelina Jolie,
Venice, 2007

fans of the best gown designers, including Valentino, Giorgio Armani, Yves Saint Laurent and John Galliano for Dior.

A new wave of actresses from the Far East has also embraced the glamour of long, fabulous evening gowns. Chinese actress Zhang Ziyi looked sublime on the red carpet at the Cannes Film Festival in 2009 in her ultra-clingy sequin-embroidered dress, reminding the world that old-style Hollywood glamour can cross the boundaries of geography and history. It is as if we had returned to the days when Coco Chanel was summoned to Hollywood by Gloria Swanson, who often travelled to Paris to visit her.

Chanel was given a royal welcome when she arrived to design the clothes for *Tonight or Never*, directed by Mervyn LeRoy, in 1931. The designer was determined to remove all the frills that swamped the female stars of the cinema at the time, and created a clinging dress in black velvet with crossed shoulder straps and draping sleeves worn low on the arms. Unfortunately, cinema demands that its actresses appear both elegant and larger than life, and Chanel's design was too considered too understated for the big screen.

There have been other, more successful, onscreen partnerships between designers and actresses, including Hubert de Givenchy and Audrey Hepburn, Yves Saint Laurent and Catherine Deneuve, and Fernanda Gattinoni and Anita Ekberg (a union that produced the black siren dress worn in the Trevi Fountain scene in *La dolce vita*), but the pairing of couturiers and stars is often better demonstrated off-screen.

The golden age of the cinema created timeless ideals of elegance. Great costumiers such as Adrian, Edith Head, Travis Banton, Walter Plunkett and Jean Louis attempted to enhance the actors' physiques while illuminating the psychology of their characters, amd were crucial in creating a bridge between fashion and cinema.

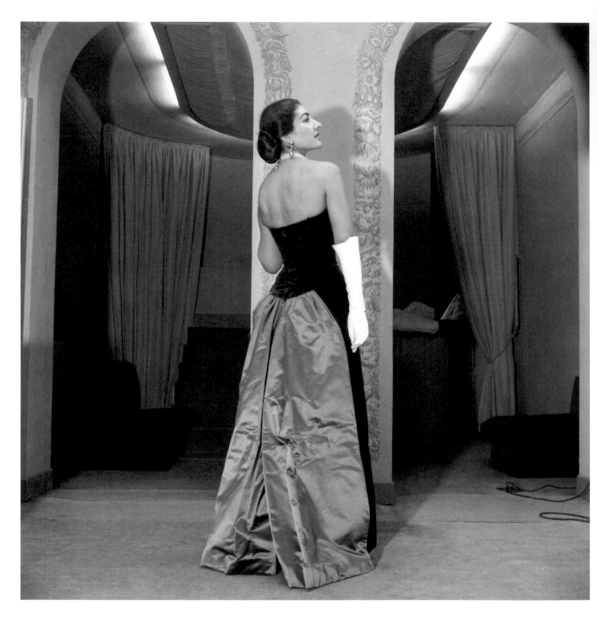

Maria Callas, Milan, 1956

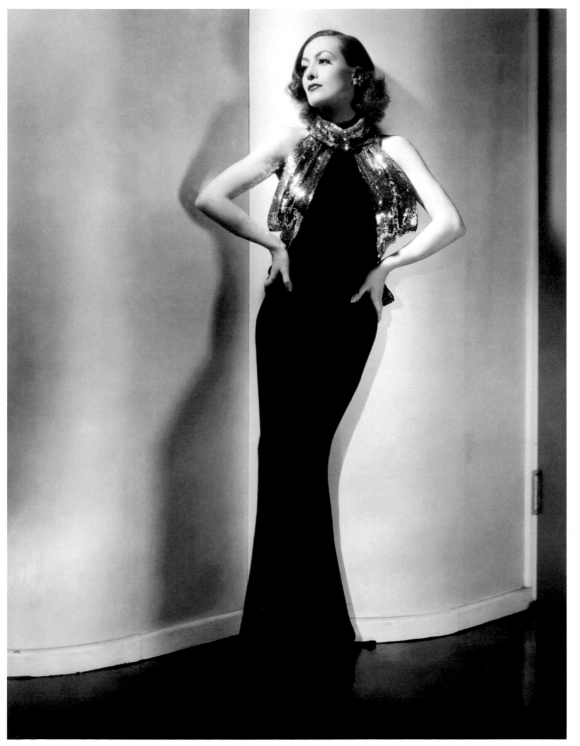

Joan Crawford, *Sadie McKee*, 1934

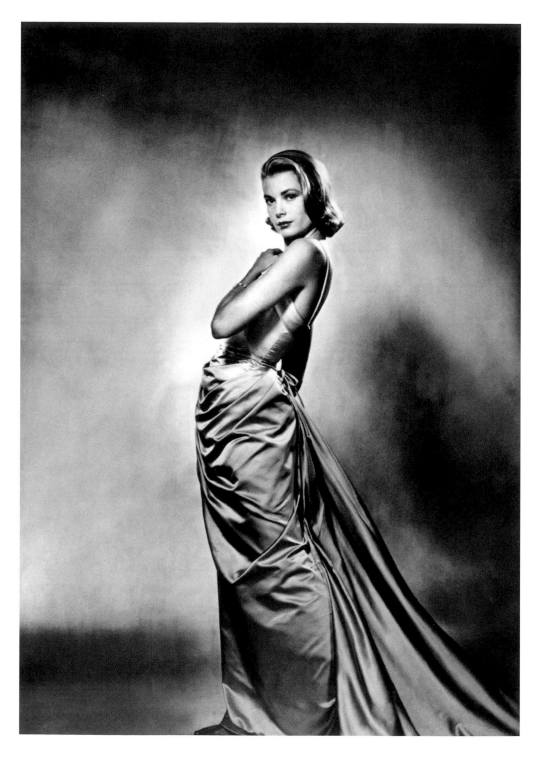

Grace Kelly, Los Angeles, 1955

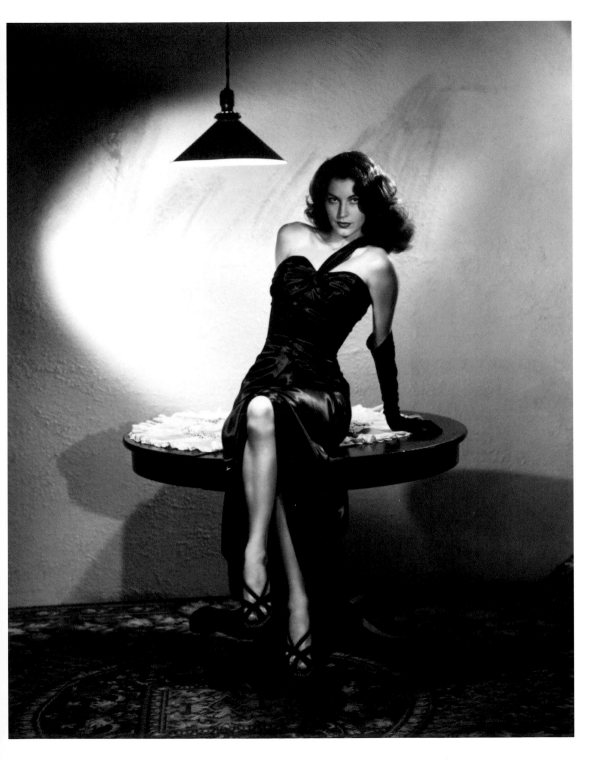

Ava Gardner, *The Killers*, 1946

Elsa Pataky, Cannes, 2009

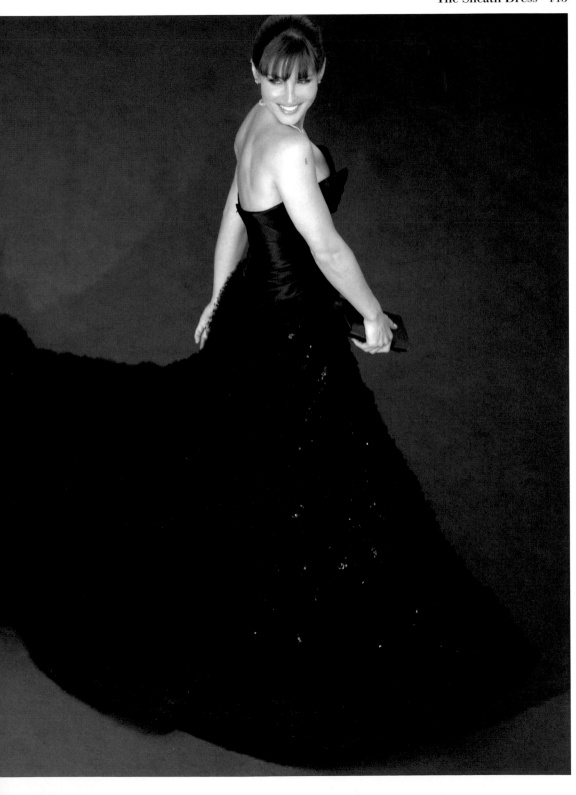

Audrey Hepburn, *Sabrina*, 1954

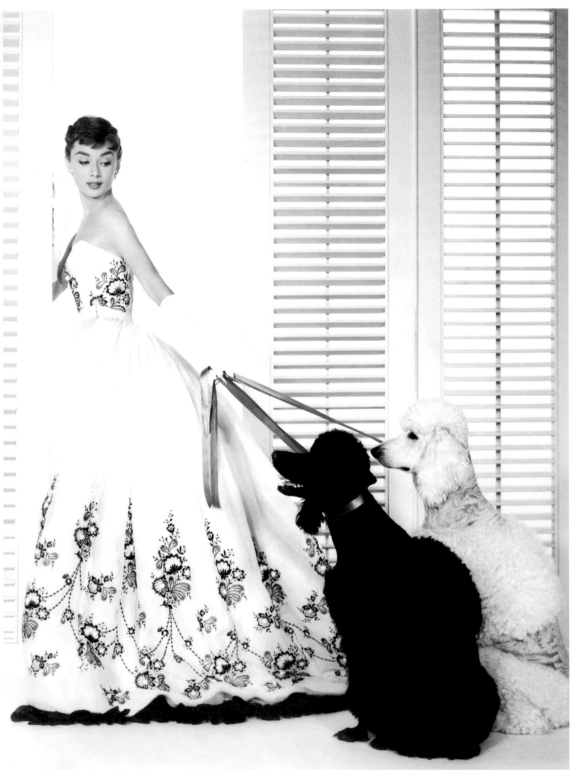

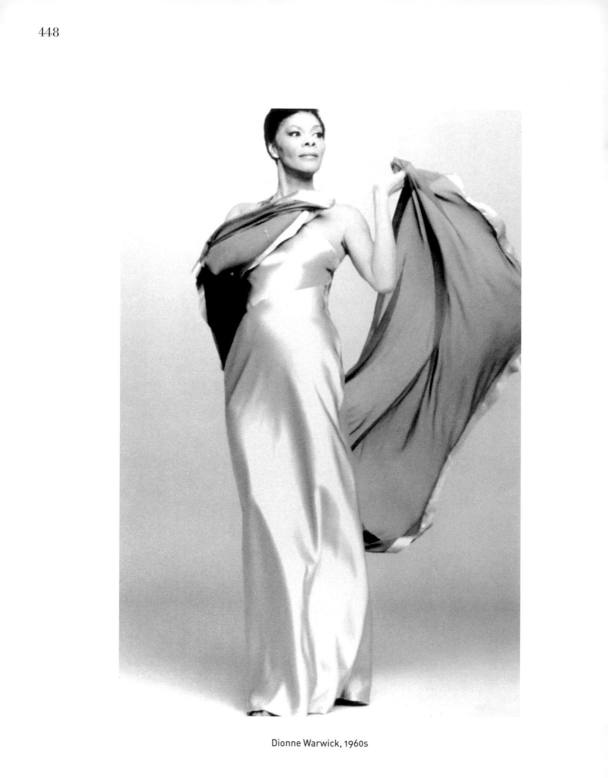

Dionne Warwick, 1960s

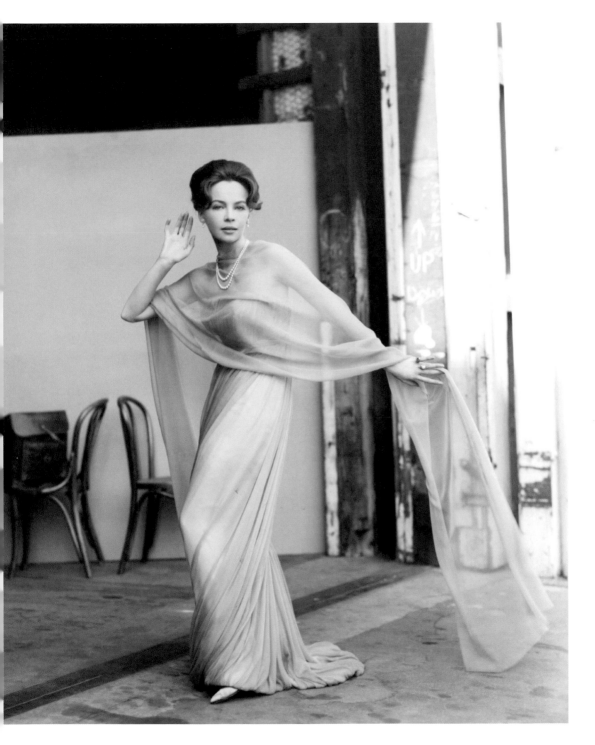

Leslie Caron, *The Man Who Understood Women*, 1959

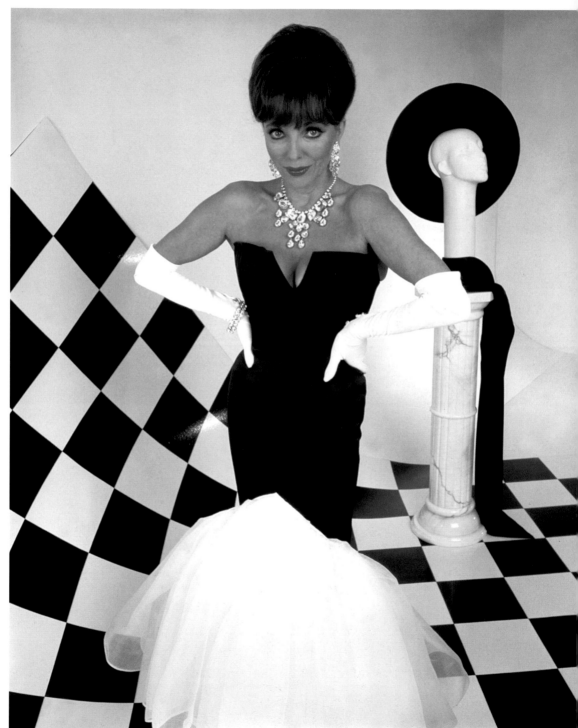

Joan Collins, 1980s

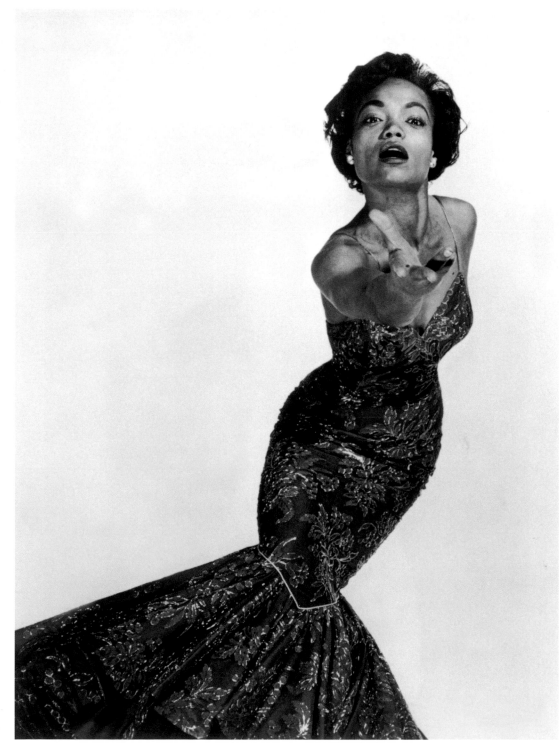

Eartha Kitt, 1954

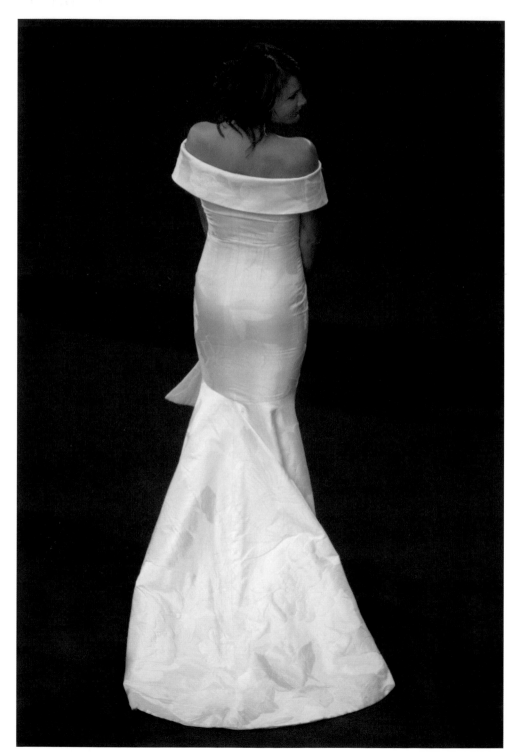

Cameron Diaz, Los Angeles, 2007

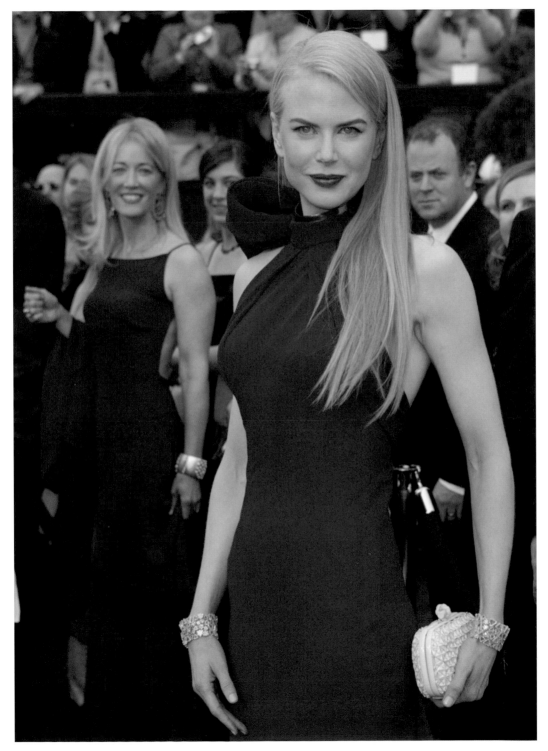

Nicole Kidman, Hollywood, 2007

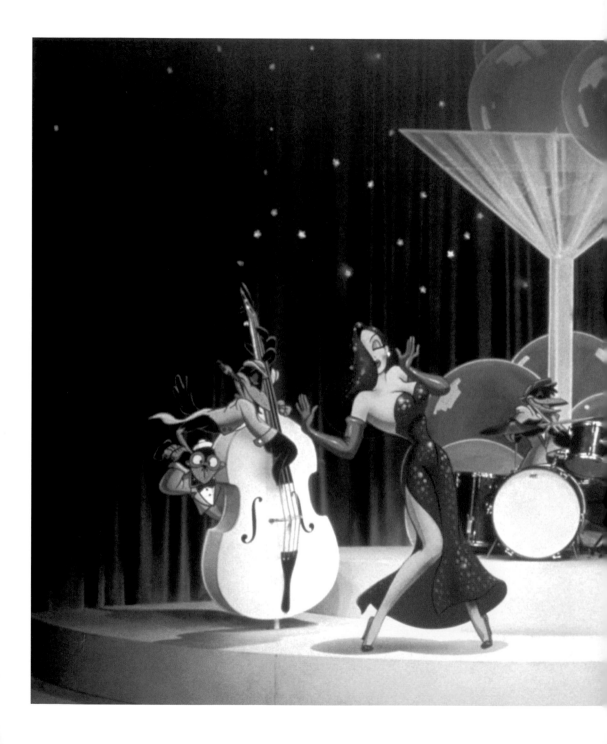

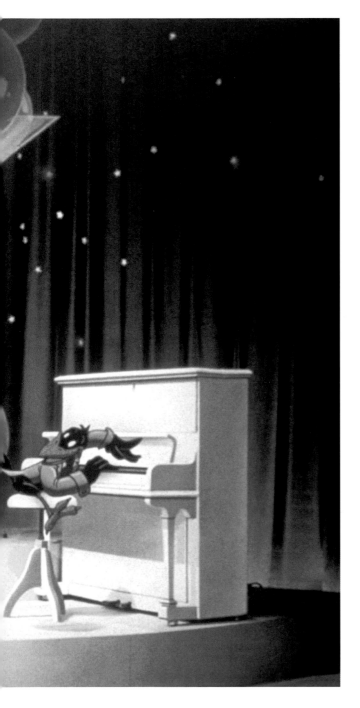

Jessica Rabbit,
Who Framed Roger Rabbit?, 1988

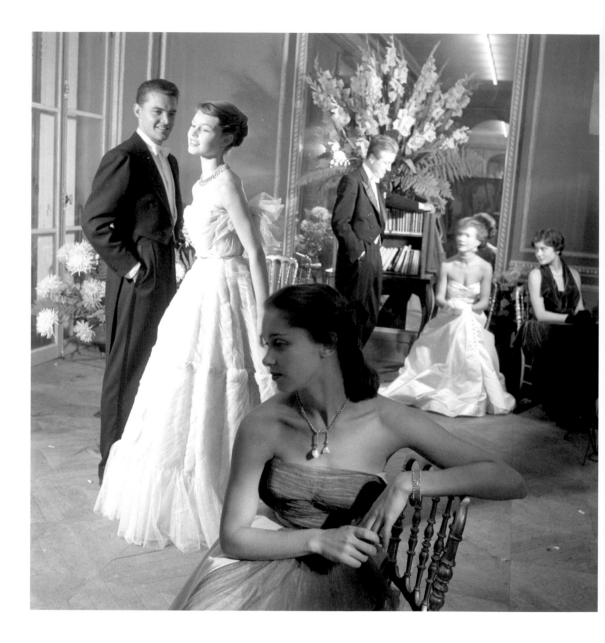

Brigitte Bardot, 1950

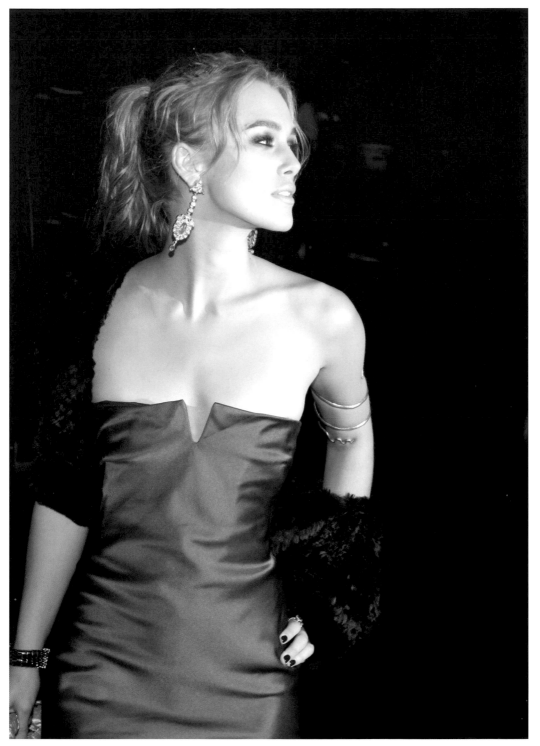

Keira Knightley, New York, 2005

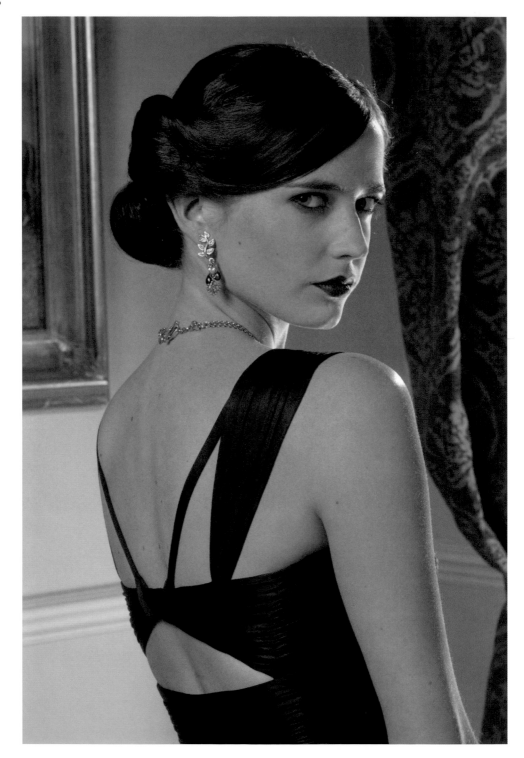

Eva Green, *Casino Royale*, 2006

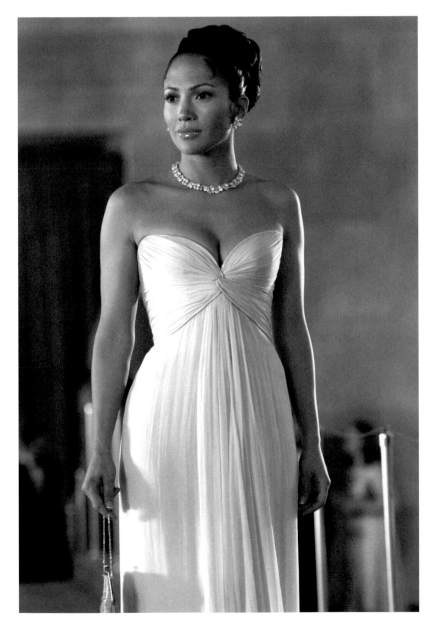

Jennifer Lopez, *Maid in Manhattan*, 2002

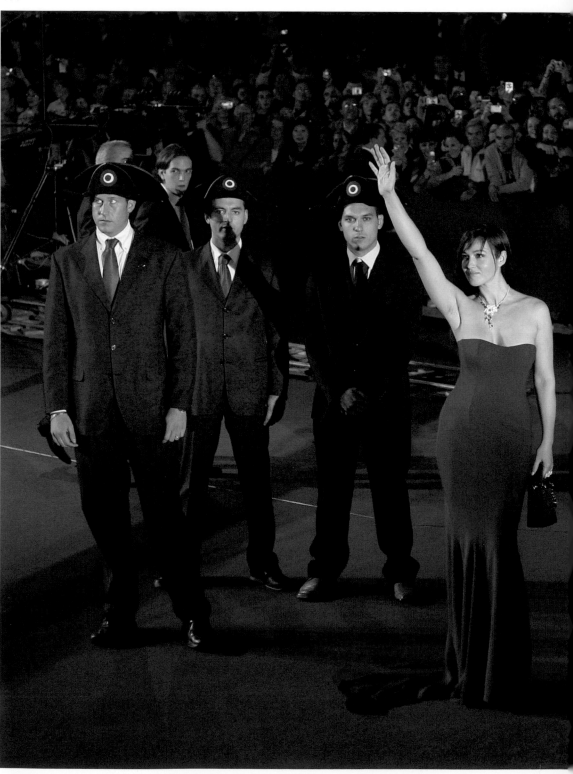

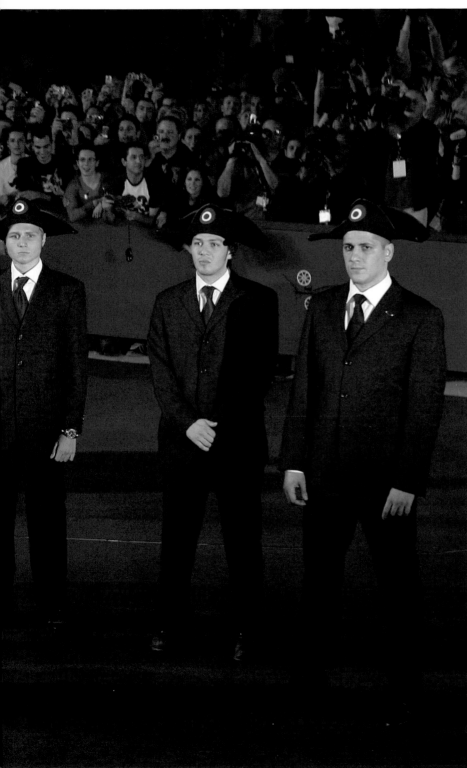

Monica Bellucci,
Rome, 2006

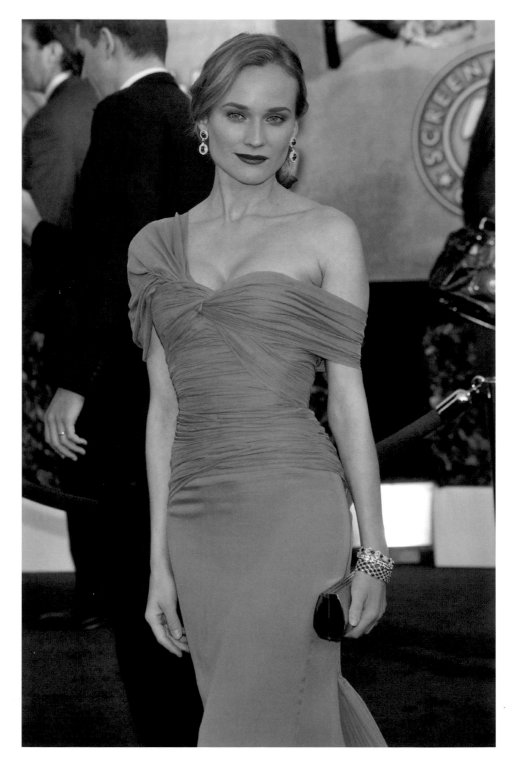

Diane Kruger, Los Angeles, 2010

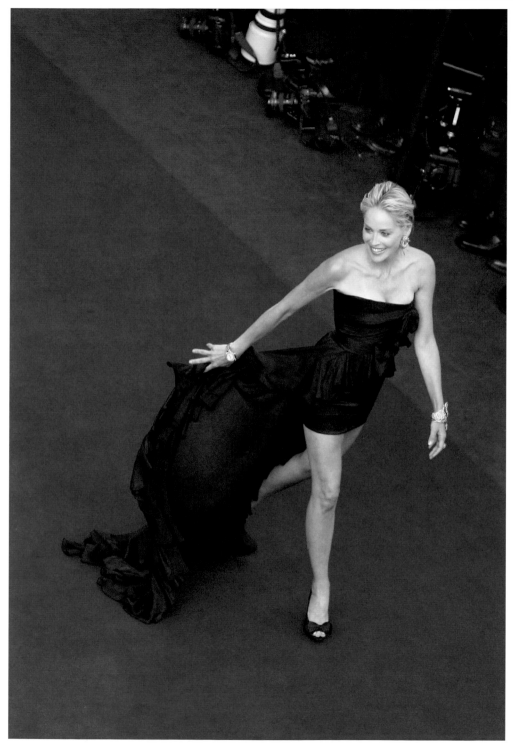

Sharon Stone, Cannes, 2009

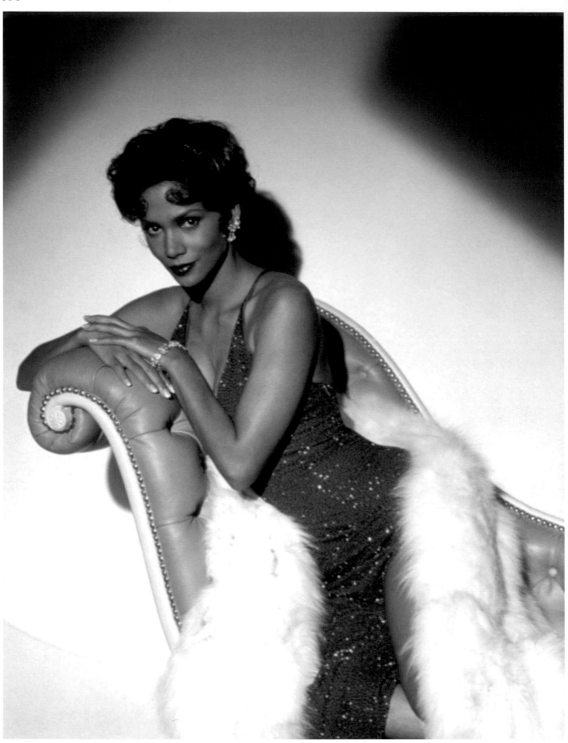

Halle Berry, *Introducing Dorothy Dandridge*, 1999

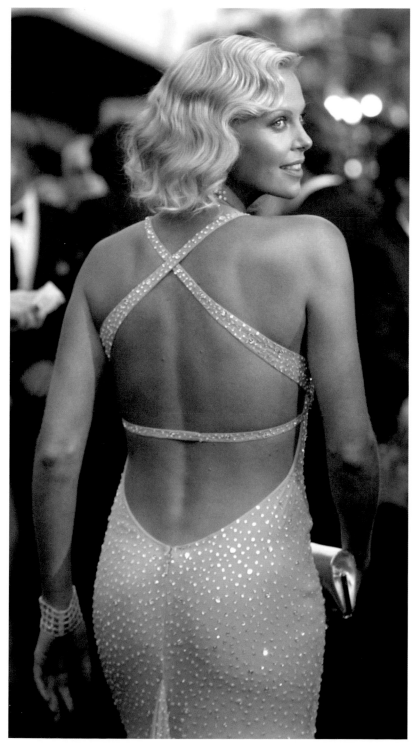

Charlize Theron, Los Angeles, 2004

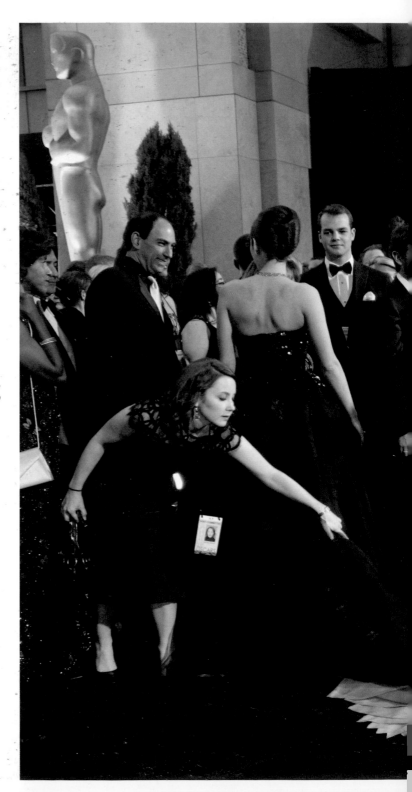

Marion Cotillard and Marisa Tomei,
Hollywood, 2009

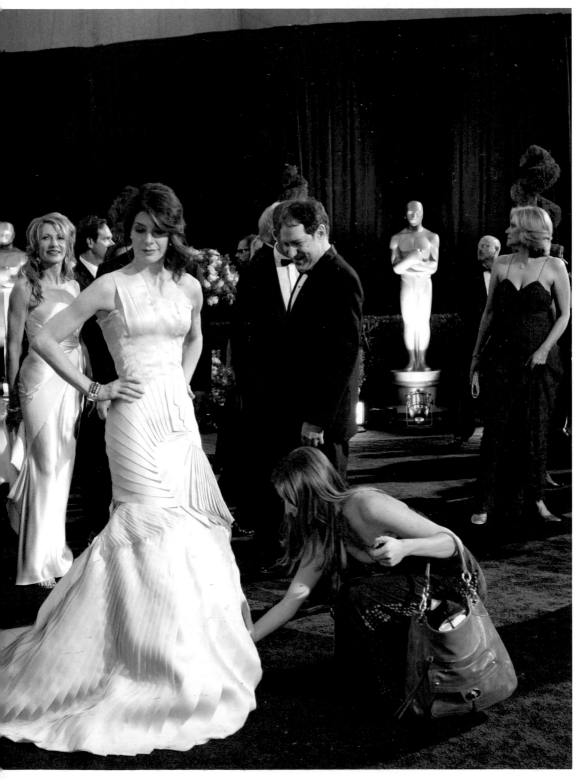

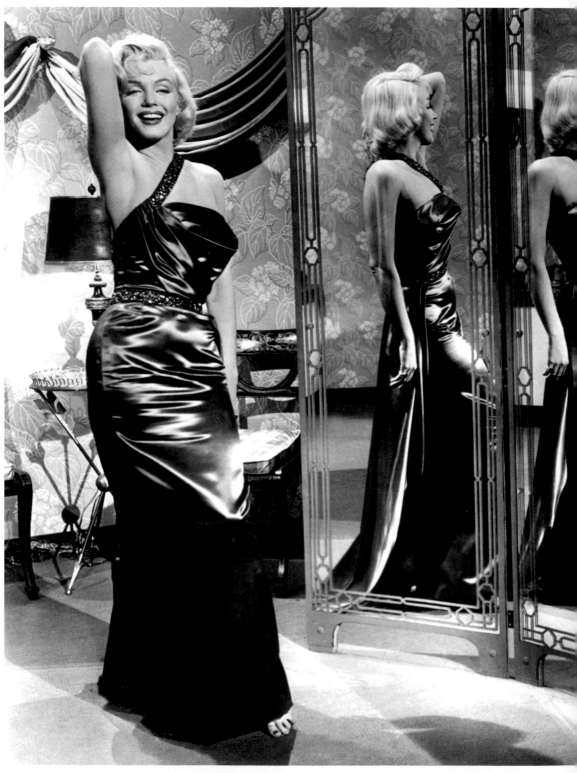

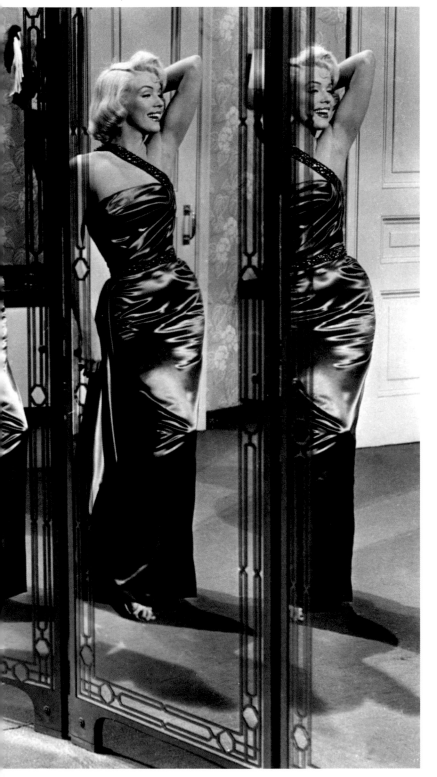

Marilyn Monroe,
How to Marry a Millionaire, 1953

Photography Credits

10 Everett Collection
11 Paramount Pictures / Album
12 Everett Collection
13 (*top left*) Everett Collection
13 (*top right*) Inge Morath / The Inge
    Morath Foundation / Magnum Photos
13 (*botton left*) Everett Collection
14 (*top*) Pele Coll / Gamma / Eyedea
14 (*bottom*) Paramount Pictures / Album
15 Everett Collection
16 Keystone / Eyedea Presse
17 Philippe Halsman / Magnum Photos
18 Emanuele Scorcelletti / Gamma / Eyedea
19 Emanuele Scorcelletti / Gamma / Eyedea
20 Peter Morgan / Reuters
21 Martine Franck / Magnum Photos
23 Botti / Stills / Gamma
24 Everett Collection
25 Gamma / Eyedea
26 Warner Bros. / Album
27 Everett Collection
28 New Line Cinema / Everett Collection
29 Emanuele Scorcelletti / Gamma / Eyedea
30 George Taylor / Everett Collection
31 20th Century Fox / Everett Collection
32 Emanuele Scorcelletti / Gamma / Eyedea
33 Emanuele Scorcelletti, Eric Vandeville /
    Gamma / Eyedea
34 Patrick Kovarik / Reuters
35 Nicolas Tikhomiroff / Magnum Photos
36 Weinstein Company / Everett Collection
37 Sony Pictures / Everett Collection
38–39 David W. Cerny / Reuters
40 Bob Henriques / Magnum Photos
41 Bob Henriques / Magnum Photos
42 Everett Collection

43 (*top*) MEGA / Gamma / Eyedea
43 (*bottom left*) Paramount Pictures /
    Album
43 (*bottom centre*) Everett Collection
43 (*bottom right*) Rysher Entertainment /
    Everett Collection
44 Everett Collection
45 Pele Coll / Gamma / Eyedea
46 Miramax / Album
47 Warner Bros. / Everett Collection
48 Eve Arnold / Magnum Photos
49 Everett Collection
50 Wayne Miller / Magnum Photos
51 Inge Morath / The Inge Morath
    Foundation / Magnum Photos
52 Eve Arnold / Magnum Photos
53 Eve Arnold / Magnum Photos
54 Strand Releasing / Everett Collection
55 Warner Bros. / Courtesy Everett
    Collection
56 Dani Cardona / Reuters
57 Emanuele Scorcelletti / Gamma / Eyedea
58 Emanuele Scorcelletti / Gamma / Eyedea
59 Emanuele Scorcelletti / Gamma / Eyedea
60 Everett Collection
61 Dimension Films / Album
62 Everett Collection
63 Fotoblitz / Gamma / Eyedea
64 Dee Cercone / Everett Collection
65 Kristin Callahan/Everett Collection
66 Everett Collection
67 20th Century Fox / Everett Collection
69 Dennis Stock / Magnum Photos
70 Eve Arnold / Magnum Photos
71 Dennis Stock / Magnum Photos
72 Philippe Halsman / Magnum Photos

73 (*left*) Paramount / Everett Collection
73 (*top right*) Everett Collection
73 (*bottom right*) Everett Collection
74 Martí E. Berenguer / Album
75 Album
76 20th Century Fox / Courtesy Everett Collection
77 Paramount Pictures / Album
78 Everett Collection
79 Marc Serata / Reuters
81 Bonfanti Marcello / Contrasto
82 Emanuele Scorcelletti / Gamma / Eyedea
83 20th Century Fox Licensing / Merchandising / Everett Collection
84 Miramax / Everett Collection
85 Warner Bros. / Everett Collection
86 Giancolombo / Contrasto
87 United Artists / Everett Collection
88 Everett Collection
89 Warner Bros. / Everett Collection
90–91 Emanuele Scorcelletti / Gamma / Eyedea
92 Universal / Courtesy Everett Collection
93 Album
94 New Line Cinema / Everett Collection
95 20th Century Fox / Everett Collection
97 Chris Botti / Gamma / Eyedea
98 Everett Collection
99 Eve Arnold / Magnum Photos
100 Eve Arnold / Magnum Photos
101 (*left*) Pele / 20th Century Fox / Everett Collection
101 (*top right*) Pele / Stills / Gamma / Eyedea
101 (*bottom right*) Warner Bros. /Everett Collection
103 CBS / Everett Collection
105 Kammerman / Rapho / Eyedea
106 D'Elia V. / Gamma / Eyedea
107 Europa Press / Gamma / Eyedea
108 Philippe Wojazer / Reuters
109 Alain Benainous, Emanuele Scorcelletti / Gamma / Eyedea
110 Davide Lanzilao / Contrasto
111 Davide Lanzilao / Contrasto
112 Everett Collection
113 Giancolombo / Contrasto

115 Robert Capa / Cornell Capa / Magnum Photos
116 Everett Collection
117 20th Century Fox / Everett Collection
119 Jerry Tavin / Fox / Everett Collection
120 Federico Garolla / Contrasto
121 Everett Collection
122 Pele coll / Gamma / Eyedea
123 20th Century Fox / Everett Collection
124–25 Jerry Tavin / Everett Collection
126 Everett Collection
127 David Hurn / Magnum Photos
128 Everett Collection
129 (*top left*) Everett Collection
129 (*bottom left*) MGM / Everett Collection
129 (*top right*) Eve Arnold / Magnum Photos
129 (*bottom right*) Universal / Everett Collection
130 Elliott Erwitt / Magnum Photos
131 Everett Collection
132 Everett Collection
133 Everett Collection
134 Peter Buckingham / Redux
135 Everett Collection
136 Giancolombo / Contrasto
137 Everett Collection
138 Fabio Lovino / Contrasto
139 20th Century Fox / Everett Collection
140 Everett Collection
141 MGM / Everett Collection
143 Burt Glinn/Magnum Photos
144 20th Century Fox / Everett Collection
145 Roadside Attractions / Everett Collection
146 Bruce Gilden / Magnum Photos
147 Everett Collection
148 Everett Collection
149 20th Century Fox / Everett Collection
150 Fabio Lovino / Contrasto
151 Warner Bros. / Everett Collection
152 Quinio / Gamma / Eyedea
153 Everett Collection
154 Botti / Stills / Gamma / Eyedea
155 Botti / Stills / Gamma / Eyedea
156 Everett Collection

157 (*top left*) Everett Collection
157 (*top right*) 20th Century Fox /
     Everett Collection
157 (*bottom*) Everett Collection
158 Europapress / Gamma / Eyedea
159 Everett Collection
160 Everett Collection
161 Walt Disney Co. / Everett Collection
162 CSU Archives / Everett Collection
163 David Seymour / Magnum Photos
164 Everett Collection
165 Everett Collection
166–67 Picot / Gamma / Eyedea
169 Album
170 Everett Collection
171 Everett Collection
172 Everett Collection
173 Warner Bros. / Album
174 Album
175 Everett Collection
176 Columbia Pictures / Everett Collection
177 Columbia Pictures / Everett Collection
178 Everett Collection
179 Everett Collection
181 Dennis Stock/Magnum Photos
182 Everett Collection
183 Everett Collection
184 Everett Collection
185 (*top left*) Everett Collection
185 (*bottom left*) Everyman Pictures /
     Four by Two / Media Rights Capital /
     Frank Okenfels / Album
185 (*right*) Paramount Pictures / Album
187 Everett Collection
188 Guild / Album
189 Everett Collection
190 20th Century Fox / Merrick Morton /
     Album
191 Miramax / Everett Collection
192–93 Paramount Classics / Album
194 Everett Collection
195 Everett Collection
197 Botti / Gamma / Eyedea
198 Warner Bros. / Everett Collection
199 Reuters
200 Warner Bros. / Everett Collection
201 Warner Bros. / Sam Emerson / Album

202 Shobha / Contrasto
203 Everett Collection
204 Eric Gaillard / Reuters
205 Michael Desmond / The CW / Everett
     Collection
206 Everett Collection
207 Everett Collection
208 Kristin Callahan / Everett Collection
209 HBO / Courtesy Everett Collection
210–11 Everett Collection
212 Paramount / Perlberg-Seaton Prod /
     Album
213 Everett Collection
214 Everett Collection
215 (*top left*) James Veysey / CAMERA
     PRESS
215 (*centre right*) Everett Collection
215 (*bottom*) Everett Collection
216 Focus Films / Everett Collection
217 Touchstone Pictures / Everett
     Collection
219 Everett Collection
220–21 Federico Garolla / Contrasto
222 Everett Collection
223 Warner Bros. / Album
224 Keystone-France / Keystone
225 United Artists / Everett Collection
226 Europapress / Gamma / Eyedea
227 Kristin Callahan / Everett Collection
228 Everett Collection
229 Everett Collection
230 Everett Collection
231 Everett Collection
232 Paramount / Everett Collection
233 Everett Collection
235 Everett Collection
236 R.A. / Gamma / Eyedea
237 R.A. / Gamma / Eyedea
238 R.A. / Gamma / Eyedea
239 (*top left*) Warner Bros. / John
     Engstead / Album
239 (*top right*) Warner Bros. / Album
239 (*bottom*) MCA / Everett Collection
240 Kristin Callahan / Everett Collection
241 Jeff Knight / Everett Collection
242 Paramount Pictures / Mark Fellman /
     Album

243 Scope Features / Gamma / Eyedea
245 20th Century Fox / Album
246 Everett Collection
247 Everett Collection
248 Album
249 20th Century Fox / Album
251 Everett Collection
252 Warner Independent Pictures / Lorey
     Sebastian / Album
253 Aramburu / Gamma / Eyedea
254 20th Century Fox / Everett Collection
255 Everett Collection
257 Columbia Pictures / Everett Collection
258 Keystone-France / Keystone
259 Picot / Gamma / Eyedea
260–61 MGM / Everett Collection
262 Everett Collection
263 Everett Collection
264 Pele coll. / Gamma / Eyedea
265 (*top left*) Everett Collection
265 (*top right*) Everett Collection
265 (*bottom left*) MGM / Everett
     Collection
265 (*bottom right*) Warner Bros. /
     Everett Collection
266 Columbia Pictures / Everett Collection
267 20th Century Fox / Everett Collection
268–69 Fabio Lovino / Contrasto
270–71 Sas Andre / Gamma / Eyedea
272 Philippe Achache / Gamma / Eyedea
273 Everett Collection
274 20th Century Fox / Everett Collection
275 Everett Collection
277 Keystone-France / Keystone
278 Inge Morath / The Inge Morath
     Foundation / Magnum Photos
279 Everett Collection
280 Warner Bros. / Roven-Cavallo / Album
281 Everett Collection
282 Warner Bros. / Everett Collection
283 Paramount / Everett Collection
285 Lionel Flusin / Gamma / Eyedea
286–87 Wayne Miller / Magnum Photos
288 Everett Collection
289 Everett Collection
290 Keystone-France / Keystone
291 Burt Glinn / Magnum Photos

292 Burt Glinn / Magnum Photos
293 (*top left*) Everett Collection
293 (*bottom left*) Everett Collection
293 (*right*) Everett Collection
295 Burt Glinn / Magnum Photos
296 Fair Film / Album
297 Everett Collection
298 Snowdon / Camera Press
299 Keystone-France / Keystone
300 Eve Arnold / Magnum Photos
301 Everett Collection
303 Everett Collection
304 Warner Bros. / Everett Collection
305 Darren Star Prod. / HBO Films / New
     Line Cinema / Craig Blankenhorn /
     Album
306 David Lee / Touchstone Television /
     Everett Collection
307 James Atoa / Everett Collection
308 Everett Collection
309 Aaron Spelling Prods / Everett
     Collection
310 New Line Cinema / Album
311 Everett Collection
312 Everett Collection
313 Everett Collection
314–15 20th Century Fox / Album
316 Philippe Halsman / Magnum Photos
317 Everett Collection
318–19 Francoise Huguier / Rapho
321 TriStar Pictures / Everett Collection
322 Everett Collection
323 Everett Collection
324 Everett Collection
325 (*top left*) Universal / Everett
     Collection
325 (*bottom left*) Everett Collection
325 (*top right*) A713 / Gamma /
     Eyedea
325 (*bottom right*) Warner Bros. /
     Everett Collection
327 Album
328–29 Bim Distribuzione / Canal+ /
     France 3 Cinema / Album
331 Everett Collection
332 Burt Glinn / Magnum Photos
333 Federico Garolla / Contrasto

334–35 Universal / Courtesy Everett Collection
336 Benainous-Duclos / Gamma / Eyedea
337 Everett Collection
338 TriStar Pictures / Everett Collection
339 Album
341 Universal Pictures / Album
342 Columbia Pictures / Courtesy Everett Collection
343 Everett Collection
344 Everett Collection
345 Everett Collection
346–47 Album
348 Everett Collection
349 Everett Collection
350 Everett Collection
351 (*left*) Everett Collection
351 (*centre*) Everett Collection
351 (*right*) Everett Collection
352–53 Fabio Lovino / Contrasto
354 Keystone-France / Keystone
355 Everett Collection
356 Tony Gentile / Reuters
357 20th Century Fox / Everett Collection
359 Bob Henriques / Magnum Photos
360 Everett Collection
361 Everett Collection
362 Miramax / Album
363 Lions Gate Films / Album
364–65 MGM / Everett Collection
366 Gamma / Eyedea
367 Everett Collection
368 Everett Collection
369 Everett Collection
371 Alain Benainous / Gamma / Eyedea
372 Everett Collection
373 Warner Bros. / Everett Collection
374 Everett Collection
375 Pele coll / Stills / Gamma / Eyedea
376 Alain Benainous / Gamma / Eyedea
377 Warner Bros. / Everett Collection
379 Everett Collection
380 Eligio Paoni / Contrasto
381 Everett Collection
382 Shunsuke Akatsuka / Reuters
383 (*top left*) 20th Century Fox / Album

383 (*bottom left*) Reuters
383 (*top right*) Everett Collection
383 (*bottom right*) Keystone / Eyedea Presse
384 (*left*) Everett Collection
384 (*right*) Everett Collection
385 Everett Collection
386 Everett Collection
387 Reuters
389 Everett Collection
390 Alain Benainous / Gamma / Eyedea
391 Kieran Doherty / Reuters
392 20th Century Fox / Everett Collection
393 Everett Collection
394 20th Century Fox / Everett Collection
395 IFC Films/Courtesy Everett Collection
396–97 David Hurn / Magnum Photos
398 Everett Collection
399 Virgil Apger / Album
400 Keystone-France / Keystone
401 20th Century Fox / Everett Collection
403 The Weinstein Co. / Handout / Reuters
404 Benainous-Legrand / Gamma / Eyedea
405 20th Century Fox / Everett Collection
406 Everett Collection
407 Carlos Duran / Reuters
409 New World Releasing / Everett Collection
410 Everett Collection
411 Everett Collection
412 Everett Collection
413 (*top left*) Miramax / Everett Collection
413 (*bottom left*) Everett Collection
413 (*top right*) Everett Collection
413 (*bottom right*) SAS Andre / Gamma / Eyedea
414 Album
415 Everett Collection
416 Botti / Gamma / Eyedea
417 Keystone-France / Keystone
419 Federico Garolla / Contrasto
420 Everett Collection
421 Everett Collection
423 Everett Collection
424 New Line Cinema / Everett Collection
425 Everett Collection

427 Nicolas Tikhomiroff / Magnum Photos

428 Album

429 Everett Collection

430 Album

431 Swann / Gamma / Eyedea

432 Everett Collection

433 Bruce Davidson / Magnum Photos

435 Everett Collection

436 Everett Collection

437 Everett Collection

438 Everett Collection

439 (*top*) Riama-Pathe-Gray / Astor-Aip / Album

439 (*bottom left*) Davide Lanzilao / Contrasto

439 (*bottom right*) Davide Lanzilao / Contrasto

440 Giancolombo / Contrasto

441 Everett Collection

442 Philippe Halsman / Magnum Photos

443 Universal Pictures / Ray Jones / Album

444–45 Pool / Martin Bureau / Reuters

446–47 Everett Collection

448 Everett Collection

449 20th Century Fox / Everett Collection

450 Everett Collection

451 Philippe Halsman / Magnum Photos

452 Max Moore / Reuters

453 Lucas Jackson / Reuters

454–55 Buena Vista Pictures / Everett Collection

456 Robert Doisneau / Rapho / Eyedea

457 Frank Albertson / Gamma / Eyedea

458 M.G.M. / Jay Maidment / Album

459 Columbia Pictures / Everett Collection

460–61 Davide Lanzilao / Contrasto

462 Tsuni / Gamma / Eyedea

463 Alain Benainous / Gamma / Eyedea

464 Everett Collection

465 Shaun Best / Reuters

466–67 Jason Reed / Reuters

468–69 20th Century Fox / Everett Collection

Filmography

À bout de souffle, Jean-Luc Godard, 1960
The Accidental Husband, Griffin Dunne, 2008
Æon Flux, Karyn Kusama, 2005
A Foreign Affair, Billy Wilder, 1948
The African Queen, John Huston, 1951
Aida, Clemente Fracassi, 1953
Amanti, Vittorio De Sica, 1968
Les amants, Louis Malle, 1958
And God Created Woman, Roger Vadim, 1956
Annie Hall, Woody Allen, 1977
Arch of Triumph, Lewis Milestone, 1948
A Streetcar Named Desire, Elia Kazan, 1951
A Summer Place, Delmer Daves, 1959
Austin Powers: International Man of Mystery, Jay Roach, 1997
A Very Private Affair, Louis Malle, 1962
A View to a Kill, John Glen, 1985
Babette Goes to War, Christian-Jaque, 1959
Baby Boom, Charles Shyer, 1987
The Back-Up Plan, Alan Poul, 2010
Barbarella, Roger Vadim, 1967
Basic Instinct, Paul Verhoeven, 1992
Basic Instinct 2, Michael Caton-Jones, 2006
Beach Party, William Asher, 1963
Bedazzled, Harold Ramis, 2000
Belle de jour, Luis Buñuel, 1967
The Birds, Alfred Hitchcock, 1963
The Black Dahlia, Brian De Palma, 2006
Black Snake Moan, Craig Brewer, 2006
Blow-up, Michelangelo Antonioni, 1966
Bitter Rice, Giuseppe De Santis, 1949
Boccaccio '70, Vittorio De Sica, Federico Fellini, Mario Monicelli, Luchino Visconti, 1964

Bonjour Tristesse, Otto Preminger, 1957
Bonnie and Clyde, Arthur Penn, 1967
Breakfast at Tiffany's, Blake Edwards, 1961
Bride Wars, Gary Winick, 2009
Brüno, Larry Charles, 2009
The Burning Plain, Guillermo Arringa, 2008
Cactus Flower, Gene Saks, 1969
Career, Joseph Anthony, 1959
Casablanca, Michael Curtiz, 1942
Casino Royale, Martin Campbell, 2006
The Cassandra Crossing, George P. Cosmatos, 1976
Cat on a Hot Tin Roof, Richard Brooks, 1958
La chamade, Alain Cavalier, 1968
Charlie's Angels: Full Throttle, McG, 2003
Cher, Art Fisher, 1975
Les choses de la vie, Claude Sautet, 1970
Christopher Strong, Dorothy Arzner, 1933
The Client, Joel Schumacher, 1994
Comes a Horseman, Alan J. Pakula, 1978
The Day the Fish Came Out, Mihalis Kakogiannis, 1967
Dead Ringer, Paul Henreid, 1964
Desperate Housewives, Marc Cherry, 2004
The Devil Wears Prada, David Frankel, 2006
Dick, Andrew Fleming, 1999
The Dick Van Dyke Show, Carl Reiner, 1961–66
Die Another Day, Lee Tamahori, 2002
Dr No, Terence Young, 1962
Doctor Zhivago, David Lean, 1965
La dolce vita, Federico Fellini, 1960
Domino, Tony Scott, 2005
Down with Love, Peyton Reed, 2003
The Drowning Pool, Stuart Rosenberg, 1975
The Dukes of Hazzard, Gy Waldron, 1979–85

Mr & Mrs Smith, Doug Liman, 2005
Modesty Blaise, Joseph Losey, 1966
Mona Lisa Smile, Mike Newell, 2003
Morocco, Josef von Sternberg, 1930
Moulin Rouge!, Baz Luhrmann, 2001
My Super Ex-Girlfriend, Ivan Reitman, 2006
National Treasure, Jon Turteltaub, 2004
Never Been Kissed, Raja Gosnell, 1999
Never on Sunday, Jules Dassin, 1960
Nine, Rob Marshall, 2009
9½ Weeks, Adrian Lyne, 1986
90210, Jeff Judah, Gabe Sachs, Rob Thomas, 2008
The Notorious Bettie Page, Mary Harron, 2005
Notting Hill, Roger Michell, 1999
One Million Years B.C., Don Chaffey, 1966
On the Beach, Stanley Kramer, 1959
Operation Crossbow, Michael Anderson, 1965
Orlando, Sally Potter, 1992
Otley, Dick Clement, 1968
Our Man Flint, Daniel Mann, 1966
Passengers, Rodrigo García, 2008
Peggy Sue Got Married, Francis Ford Coppola, 1986
The Pelican Brief, Alan J. Pakula, 1993
Personal Best, Robert Towne, 1982
Pleasantville, Gary Ross, 1998
Plucking the Daisy, Marc Allégret, 1956
Prêt-à-Porter, Robert Altman, 1994
The Prime of Miss Jean Brodie, Ronald Neame, 1969
Puccini for Beginners, Maria Muggenti, 2006
Pulp Fiction, Quentin Tarantino, 1994
The Pumpkin Eater, Jack Clayton, 1964
The Queen, Stephen Frears, 2006
Queen Christina, Rouben Mamoulian, 1933
The Rat Race, Robert Mulligan, 1960
Rear Window, Alfred Hitchcock, 1954
Rebel Without a Cause, Nicholas Ray, 1955
Reflections in a Golden Eye, John Huston, 1967
The Restless Years, Helmut Käutner, 1958
The River Girl, Mario Soldati, 1954
The Rocky Horror Picture Show, Jim Sharman, 1975

Roman Holiday, William Wyler, 1953
Rowan & Martin's Laugh-In, Mark Warren, Digby Wolfe, 1968–70
Sabrina, Billy Wilder, 1954
Sadie McKee, Clarence Brown, 1934
The Sailor from Gibraltar, Tony Richardson, 1967
Seven Sinners, Tay Garnett, 1940
Sex and the City, Darren Star, 1998–2004
Sex and the City: The Movie, Michael Patrick King, 2008
Sex and the City 2, Michael Patrick King, 2010
Silkwood, Mike Nichols, 1983
Sin City, Frank Miller, Robert Rodriguez, 2005
Singin' in the Rain, Stanley Donen, Gene Kelly, 1952
Slogan, Pierre Grimblat, 1969
Some Like It Hot, Billy Wilder, 1959
Something to Talk About, Lasse Hallström, 1995
Son of Paleface, Frank Tashlin, 1952
The Spirit, Frank Miller, 2008
The SpongeBob SquarePants Movie, Stephen Hillenburg, 2004
Suddenly, Last Summer, Joseph L. Mankiewicz, 1959
Summer Stock, Charles Walters, 1950
Sweet Home Alabama, Andy Tennant, 2002
Sylvia, Christine Jeffs, 2003
Taxi Driver, Martin Scorsese, 1976
Thelma & Louise, Ridley Scott, 1991
There's Something About Mary, Bobby Farrelly, Peter Farrelly, 1998
They Won't Forget, Mervyn LeRoy, 1937
Tilt, Rudy Durand, 1979
To Catch a Thief, Alfred Hitchcock, 1955
Tonight or Never, Mervyn LeRoy, 1931
Tootsie, Sydney Pollack, 1982
True Romance, Tony Scott, 1993
Two for the Road, Stanley Donen, 1967
The Unsinkable Molly Brown, Charles Walters, 1964
Valentine, Jamie Blanks, 2001
Vamp, Richard Wenk, 1986
V for Vendetta, James McTeigue, 2005